MUGHAL I
AND
CENTRAL AS.

MUGHAL INDIA
AND
CENTRAL ASIA

Richard C. Foltz

OXFORD

UNIVERSITY PRESS

CONTENTS

ACKNOWLEDGEMENTS

I would like to thank first and foremost those whose support and patience made the research and writing of this work possible: my wife Aphrodite Désirée Navab, and the Foltz and Navab families. Thanks also to Shahrzad for brightening all our lives.

This book was developed out of my Ph.D. dissertation, entitled 'Uzbek Central Asia and Mughal India: Asian Muslim Society in the 16th and 17th Centuries', submitted to the Committee on Middle Eastern Studies at Harvard University in May 1996. Versions or parts of various chapters of the dissertation were reworked into the form of articles and papers, as follows: 'Muslim Asia: A Re-Assessment of Boundaries', paper presented at the second University of Manchester Workshop on Central Asia and the Caucasus, Manchester, UK, May 1995 and 'One World, Not Three: Muslim Asia Before Colonial Historiography', paper presented at the Resources on Central Asian Studies Workshop, the Ohio State University, May 1996 (which evolved into the present Preface and Introduction); 'Central Asia in the Minds of the Mughals', paper presented at the fifth European Seminar on Central Asian Studies, Copenhagen, Denmark, August 1995 and published in the collection edited by Touraj Atabaki, *Post-Soviet Central Asia*, I.B. Tauris, London, 1997, and 'The Turko-Mongol Self-Identity of the Mughal Emperors of India', paper presented at the Fortieth Permanent International Altaistic Conference, Provo, Utah, June 1997 (a part of the present Chapter 2, incorporating a small portion of Chapter 1); 'The Mughal Occupation of Balkh: 1646-1647', *Journal of Islamic Studies* 7/1 (1996) (Chapter 7 and part of the Conclusion); 'The Central Asian Naqshbandi Connections of the Mughal Emperors', *Journal of Islamic Studies* 7/2 (1996) (Chapter 5); 'Two Seventeenth Century Central Asian Travelers to Mughal India', *Journal of the Royal Asiatic Society*, ser. 3, 6/3 (1996) (Chapter 6); 'Central Asians in the Administration of Mughal India', *Journal of Asian History* 32/1 (1998) (Chapter 3); and 'Cultural Contacts Between Central Asia and Mughal India', *Central Asiatic Journal* 42/1 (1998) (Chapter 4). I thank the editors of the above publications for permission to reproduce these materials here.

The following individuals have read various stages or drafts of this material either in part or in its entirety, and kindly offered their comments: Ali Asani, Yuri Bregel, Stephen Dale, Devin DeWeese, Riazul Islam, Robert McChesney, Roy Mottahedeh, and André Wink. The book in its present reassembled form owes its revisions largely to their comments and suggestions. I remain responsible for any errors.

My research during the academic years 1994-6 was greatly facilitated by a National Security Education Programme grant administered by the Academy for Educational Development. Additional support for research in Uzbekistan in 1994-5 was given by the International Research and Exchanges Board. For their help during my stay in Tashkent, I would like to thank William Dirks (then of IREX, now at Indiana University), and Ghulam Karimov, Oidin Imamkhojaeva, and Azamat Ziaev at the Institute of Oriental Studies, Uzbekistan Academy of Sciences, and in Samarqand, Shavkat Shukurov and the faculty of the Department of Tajik Philology at Samarqand State University. For their warm hospitality in Lahore and elsewhere in Pakistan we thank Nadim Hasan of Khanewal and Selim Basra of Gujranwala.

Finally I would like to thank Ahmad Mahdavi-Damghani for his help in working with three of the primary source manuscripts, the Research Institute for Inner Asian Studies at Indiana University for providing a photocopy of the

Berlin *Matlab al-talibin,* and Robert McChesney for kindly lending me his personal photocopy of the Dushanbe *Muzakkir-i-ashab* along with 125 pages of very helpful notes.

And last but certainly not least, my warmest heartfelt thanks go out to Ameena Saiyid, Zohrain Zafar, and all at OUP Karachi for their help in bringing this work to publication.

ABBREVIATIONS

AA	*A'in-i-Akbari*
AN	*Akbar-nama*
AS	*ʿAmal-i-Salih*
BA	*Bahr al-asrar*
BN	*Babur-nama* (Thackston trilingual edition, 1993)
HN	*Humayun-nama*
IOSUAS	Institute of Oriental Studies, Uzbekistan Academy of Sciences
JN	*Jahangir-nama*
KM	*Khatirat-i-Mutribi*
MA	*Ma'athir-i-ʿAlamgiri*
MatT	*Matlab al-talibin*
MT	*Muntakhab al-tawarikh*
MU	*Ma'athir al-'umara'*
MuzA	*Muzakkir-i-ashab*
PN	*Padshah-nama*
RA	*Ruq'at-i-ʿAlamgiri*
SJN	*Shah Jahan-nama*
SL	*Shamlu Letters*
SNS	*Sharaf-nama-yi shahi*
SS	*Silsilat al-salatin*
ST	*Shajara-yi türk*
TA	*Tabaqat-i-Akbari*
TJ	*Tuzuk-i-Jahangiri*
TMK	*Tazkira-yi-Muqim Khani*
TQK	*Tarikh-i -Qipchaq Khani*
TR	*Tarikh-i-Rashidi*

PREFACE

This book is about the Central Asian aspect of the great civilization which has come to be known in Western languages as Mughal India. The term 'Mughal' itself—a Persian corruption of the word 'Mongol'—bears witness to Central Asian origins, as does the more correct name of the dynasty which ruled much of South Asia from 1526 up to 1857 (albeit nominally for some of that period), the Timuriyya—the Timurids, or descendants of Amir Timur Gurgan (Tamerlane).

While this book is primarily about the pre-colonial history of South Asia, it must, like the Mughals themselves, approach the subcontinent from the direction of Central Asia. The history of Central Asia is at present one of the most poorly researched of any world region, and the bulk of its scholarship does not meet high standards. In the opinion of Yuri Bregel, who having worked for many years in both the Soviet and American academic worlds is uniquely qualified to judge, '...the history of no other world area is plagued by such rot.'[1] Unfortunately, without a proper understanding of Central Asian history and civilization, it is impossible to fully understand and appreciate the culture presided over and nourished by the Mughals of India.

The poor state of Central Asia scholarship can be blamed on two main factors. First, until quite recently the field was monopolized by scholars burdened by an ideological agenda, Marxism-Leninism in the case of the Soviets, and Kremlinology in that of Westerners. Neither approach offered an appropriate framework for the study of an Islamic society. The second problem has been one of sources. With the exception of Arabic theological and

scientific treatises, the vast majority of documents written
throughout Muslim Asia are in Persian. Few Central Asian
sources have been published, and many of the manuscripts
have until recently been nearly inaccessible in Soviet
archives. Translations and commentaries, when extant, have
been in Russian, a language few scholars not directly
concerned with Russian culture or Soviet-era politics have
had access to. Because of the ideological constraints which
hampered Soviet-era scholarship on both sides, most of the
work done under those conditions needs to be reassessed
and perhaps entirely rewritten now.

Unfortunately the former constraints are being
maintained in new forms in the newly independent
republics, which means that any objective 'internal'
rewriting of Central Asian history may still be some way off.
A new version of the official *Istoriia Uzbekistana*,[2] for
example, produced by the History Institute of the
Uzbekistan Academy of Sciences in 1993, shows that the
old approaches and ideas are still fully in force, as the
current Uzbek government relies on Soviet-style nationality
theory to maintain the legitimacy of its regime.

Contrary, however, to the ideology which has prevailed
throughout this century, the newly independent former
Soviet republics of Central Asia are not nation-states.
Rather, they consist of complex and diverse societies,
among which a strong though nowadays rarely stated
historical bond is the common Perso-Islamic layer of their
cultural heritage, which they share with Iran, Afghanistan,
and the Muslims of Western China and the Indian
subcontinent. This shared heritage was downplayed by the
colonial powers, and as often happens with nationalist
movements, it continues to be distorted today for political
ends. The current attempt of the Uzbek government to
claim Babur as a great 'Uzbek' historical figure, for
example, is hardly calculated to help Muslims in Asia better
understand their shared history.

Nor are such vain efforts likely to foster greater co-operative research between Central and South Asian scholars. During the Soviet period, following political trends, academics were occasionally encouraged to study cultural ties between Central Asia and the Indian subcontinent. During the 1960s, for example, Tajik SSR Communist Party Chairman Babajan Gafurov, himself something of a would-be historian, opened the door of scholarly co-operation with Pakistan by giving Pakistani scholars a copy of a valuable seventeenth century history work, the *Bahr al-asrar* of Mahmud b. Amir Wali.[3] To this day, however, scholarly exchange between Central Asia and the subcontinent is impeded by a language barrier. Where once Persian united their peoples, these countries have now been divided by the use of English and Russian.

The best Soviet work on Central and South Asian culture during the Uzbek period is that of A.A. Semënov in the 1940s and 1950s. Semënov had wide interests, however, and his attention to our particular subject is disappointingly brief.[4] The late Uzbek scholar Ilyas G. Nizamutdinov, on the other hand, devoted his entire career to the study of Central Asian-Indian relations. His work is valuable for its assembly of data; his analyses, however, are ideologically tainted and fairly superficial.[5] The work of other Soviet scholars is more topical, such as N.B. Baikova's studies on economic history[6] or the Tajik Abdul-Ghani Mirzoev's on literature.[7] More recently, academicians such as the Qazaq Timur Beisembiev and the Uzbek Buri Ahmedov have recycled the work of previous Soviet scholars and published it in new forms and configurations, with the virtue of at least keeping the subject alive.[8] Part of the aim of this book is to present and make available some of the substance of the Soviet historiography to readers who may be little familiar with it.

Research on the Mughal side is far more accessible and complete. During the British period many of the major primary sources on Indian history were published, often both in the original language and in English translation. Fortunately, such works are reprinted regularly in Pakistan and India.

Riazul Islam stands out as a Pakistani scholar who has helped familiarize the world with important Central Asian sources contemporary with the Mughals, such as the *Bahr al-asrar* and the *Silsilat as-salatin* (which he calls the *Tawarikh-i-badi'a*). He has also catalogued much of the diplomatic correspondence of the Mughal period. His contribution has been mainly one of organizing material, however; the interpretation of this material he has largely left to others. With older academics moving into retirement and leaving their work to a new generation, it has become apparent that interest in learning Persian is not what it once was on the subcontinent. And, as elsewhere, scholars who know both Persian and Russian are very rare indeed.

With the Central Asian republics' recent independence, one would expect the theme of Central and South Asian cultural relations to take on a renewed relevance and fresh interpretations, particularly in regard to the regional powers of Uzbekistan and Pakistan as neighbouring Muslim-majority states. Over the past five years this trend has been discernible, but perhaps not up to expectations. The Muslims of Central and South Asia, having lived under very different sorts of colonial rule, have grown apart in many ways. Pakistanis and Indians doing business in Uzbekistan today, for example, find the country terribly underdeveloped in terms of the infrastructure and economy they are used to at home. Uzbeks, meanwhile, when they visit Pakistan, often say they find it 'oppressively Islamic' in comparison with their own highly secularized culture.

Whatever direction future studies may take, it is important for scholars outside Central Asia to play a part in the historical reassessment that is beginning there. It is hoped that scholars in the West and Asia alike will participate actively in the rejuvenation and redirection of this international, cross-cultural dialogue concerning the shared legacy of Muslims and others in a vital yet often overlooked part of the Islamic world.

In fact there has been a recent upsurge of interest in Central Asia among Western academics, although for the most part this has been driven by geopolitical concerns which do not lend themselves to a careful treatment of cultural history. Over the past few years several dozen new 'scholarly' books on Central Asia have been published in English. Most of these, however, are quickly assembled collections of articles by political scientists, seemingly desperate to fill the void of informed predictions regarding the future importance of the region, but with little or no analysis of the pre-Soviet past.

None of this scholarship, Soviet, Indo-Pak, or Western, has ventured as far as the argument I am presenting in this book—that Muslim Asia (including Iran) of the sixteenth and seventeenth centuries was, in terms of the dominant elite culture, one world and not several. Even such work as has been done linking Central and South Asian history, be it from the Soviet or the Indo-Pak side, has been in the spirit of 'friendly nations'; the emphasis has been on citing historical bridges between societies, societies which remain implicitly distinct from each other as backward projections of modern-day states. I intend to go further than this, by indicating ways in which educated Muslims of Central Asia and those of the subcontinent, who defined themselves first and foremost as Muslims, shared a culture in common, one which facilitated the large-scale migration of talented individuals mainly from Iran and Central Asia to South Asia where opportunities were perceived as being better.

In recent years it has been popular to emphasize the 'locality' and diversity of Muslim communities throughout the world. While this trend has offered a welcome and necessary antidote to the traditional, monolithic view of Islam, I believe that one must be wary of taking the argument too far so that the various cultural ties which unite Muslims are lost sight of. Some scholars continue to depict South Asia as 'historically isolated' and insist on the uniqueness of Muslim society there. The logical conclusion of such an argument is to call for dismissing any discussion even of 'South Asian' Islam, since the diversity that exists within the subcontinent itself is not less than that which exists between India and Central or West Asia. It should be emphasized that these various Islamic societies, for all their diversity, were sufficiently integrated to foster constant cultural interchange and communication, mainly through the movement of individuals. By most accounts, these individuals found enough commonality from one region to another that they did not feel displaced as Muslims.

The primary aim of this book, therefore, is to suggest a unified, broad framework for viewing pre-colonial Asian Muslim history. I have drawn from both South and Central Asian primary sources, and likewise from both Western and Soviet-language secondary ones, in an attempt to begin to bridge the gap which has been created between the study of Central Asia and that of South Asia. This book is *not* intended to serve as an exhaustive treatment of the relationship between Central and South Asia even within the limits of the sixteenth and seventeenth centuries; rather, it is meant to serve as a *preliminary* argument for a new approach. The subject is too vast to be treated in a single volume, but offers much fertile ground for future scholarship.

For spellings and transliterations of foreign names and terms, I have attempted to follow the system of the International Journal of Middle East Studies, without diacritics, except in cases of direct quotation where I have left the citations intact.

A Note on the Definition of 'Central Asia'

Few geographical terms have been more variously (often opportunistically) employed than 'Central Asia', all the more now that the region has re-entered the world's spotlight to some extent. The term has been used to encompass areas as far west as Iran and as far east as Xinjiang; generally it is understood to refer at least to the region between the Caspian Sea and the T'ien Shan mountains, from the steppes below the Siberian taiga down to the Hindu Kush. Some scholars, particularly at Indiana University, have favoured the term 'Inner Asia', which seems to suggest a centre of gravity somewhat north and east of that implied by 'Central Asia'.[9] I will use 'Central Asia' roughly in the sense laid down by Robert McChesney, where it covers the lands referred to in Persian/Arabic as *Ma wara an-nahr* (Transoxiana) and *Balkh*,[10] since this region is the main provenance of most of the cultural phenomena I will be discussing. Likewise, I will use 'Inner Asia' to imply the sense of north-easterly 'pull' mentioned above.

NOTES

1. Yuri Bregel, 'Notes on the Study of Central Asia', Papers on Inner Asia, Indiana University Research Institute for Inner Asian Studies, Bloomington IN, 1996, p. 58.
2. *Istoriia Uzbekistana*, v. 3, Fan, Tashkent, 1993.
3. See the articles by Gafurov and Riazul Islam in *Journal of the Pakistan Historical Society* 14/2 (1966).
4. See for example 'K voprosu o kul'turno-politicheskikh sviaziakh Bukhary i "Velikomogol'skoi" Indii v XVII v.', in *Materialy vtorogo soveschaniia archeologov i etnografov Srednei Azii*, Moscow, 1959; and *Sredniaziatskii traktat po muzyke Dervisha Ali (XVIIv.)*, Tashkent, 1946.
5. I.G. Nizamutdinov, *Ocherki istorii kulturnykh sviazei Srednei Azii i Indii v XVI- nachalie XX vv.*, Tashkent, 1981, which is condensed from his doctoral thesis, Uzbekistan Academy of Sciences, Tashkent, 1978;

also the more general work *Iz istorii Sredneaziatsko-indiiskikh otnoshenii*,
Tashkent, 1969.

6. N.B. Baikova, *Rol' Srednei Azii v Russko-Indiiskikh torgovykh sviaziakh:
    pervaia polovina XVI- vtoraia polovina XVIII v.*, Tashkent, 1964.

7. Abdul-Ghani Mirzoev, ed., *Khatirat-i Mutribi Samarqandi*, Karachi,
    1977; 'Az torikh-i ravobit-i adabi-yi Movaronnahr va Hind', *Sadoyi
    sharq* 5 (1964), 35-39; 'Iz istorii literaturnykh sviaziei Maverannakhr
    i Indii', *Trudy XXVIogo mezhdunarodnyi kongress vostokovedov*, Moscow,
    1963.

8. A particularly useful catalogue of sources is B.A. Ahmedov, *Istoriko-
    geograficheskaia literatura Srednei Azii XVI-XVIII vv.*, Tashkent, 1985.

9. See Devin DeWeese, *Islamization and Native Religion in the Golden
    Horde*, University of Pennsylvania Press, State College PA, 1994, p. 7.

10. R.D. McChesney, *Waqf in Central Asia*, Princeton University Press,
    Princeton NJ, 1991, p. ix.

INTRODUCTION

Modern historiography has tended to treat the early
modern Islamic civilizations of Asia as discrete entities, in
terms of their respective colonial heritages and according
to European-style nation-state analysis. These civilizations
are conceptualized dynastically: the empire of the 'Great
Mughals' in India, the Safavid Empire in Iran, the Uzbek
khanates of 'feudal' Central Asia. But whereas the focus of
modern historiography has been on politics, activity in
other domains draws a very different map.

In fact, cultural contacts between Central Asia, Iran, and
India have always transcended political realities. The
subcontinent has been integrally connected to the 'world
system' since pre-historic times, primarily via the mountain
passes over the Hindu Kush to the north-west. From about
1500 BCE, Aryan-speakers entered the Gangetic plain in this
way from Central Asia.[1] The same may be true even of the
pre-existing Indus peoples, since the subsequent movement
of the Dravidians was a south-easterly one. Sea routes
connected the subcontinent with the Mediterranean world
at least as early as Roman times, and most probably much
earlier.

Both the Graeco-Bactrian Seleucid culture of ancient
times and its Kushan successors crossed over the Hindu
Kush from Central Asia, encountering Indian civilization
and thereby promoting the development of the great
Gandhara culture. Buddhism left India by the same route,
and made its long trip to China via the Central Asian silk
roads. While Muslim Arabs gained a foothold in Sindh in
the early eighth century, the first permanent Islamic
conquest of South Asian territory came from Mahmud of
Ghazna, a Persianized Turk of Central Asian origin.

Successive Muslim dynasties to rule over parts of the subcontinent all came from the north-west, and were mainly (with a few notable exceptions such as the Tajik Ghurids) either Persianized Central Asian Turks or Turkified Pukhtuns, all coming from the direction of what is now Afghanistan. These successive waves of Muslim conquerors all brought with them elements of Central Asian and Persianate culture which they added to the ever-evolving mix of South Asian society. It was under the Mughals that this steady process of cultural amalgamation between Central and South Asia reached its peak, and in many ways this was a happy synthesis indeed.

Never were the lines of cultural communication and interaction more open between Central and South Asia than they were under the Mughals. The same is true for channels leading from Iran and even the Mediterranean world of the Ottomans. As a result, the sources for the period of this study—the sixteenth and seventeenth centuries of the common era—strongly suggest that despite regional diversities there existed within certain levels of society an underlying, widespread sense of perceived unity in terms of Islamic and Persianate culture across the Uzbek, Safavid, Ottoman, and Mughal territories. Within the upper social strata, Muslim Asia at this time was in many ways one world, and not three, and the unifying effects of the dominant elite culture would naturally trickle down in varying degrees to influence consciously or unconsciously the outlooks, perceptions, and cultural vocabularies of the general population.

Just how much did these neighbouring Muslim societies have in common? How extensive was their mutual influence? And what was the mental geography of the Muslim inhabitants of these contiguous lands—did they see the boundaries of their world as we see them today? These are all important issues, which have been discussed very inadequately, if at all, up to now. A proper discussion, however, calls for the re-drawing of scholarly boundary lines concerning Muslim Asia. The historical evidence calls for applying a more integrated, multi-layered, and internally-referential approach to the study of Asian Muslim society than has been the rule.

This book will discuss factors which tied together culturally the people living under Uzbek and Mughal rule during the sixteenth and seventeenth centuries, emphasizing the commonalities rather than the differences which have long been used to justify separating them. These commonalities are illustrated to a large extent in the travel or migration of individuals from all walks of life, and the maintenance of cultural ties and ongoing influences which this activity ensured.

A major component of the psychological geography of this time is the legacy of the Timurid empire. This empire, based first in Samarqand and then Herat during the fifteenth century and ruled by the Turkic '*Chaghatay*' retinue of Timur-i-Lang,[2] encompassed the lands of Transoxiana (*Ma wara an-nahr*), Khurasan, and Balkh, as well as parts of northern India (*Hindustan*). The Shibanid[3] Uzbeks who ousted the Timurids from Central Asia and Khorasan by the beginning of the sixteenth century considered themselves the heirs to the political power and great cultural tradition which the Timurid dynasty had possessed.[4] The group we have come to call the Mughals, on the other hand, who represented the actual blood-line continuation of that dynasty, saw themselves as the victims of usurpation.

A sub-theme of this discussion is the particular example of the Mughal rulers and their notions of Central Asia as their 'true' homeland and hereditary domain. The first six Mughal emperors, whose collective reign spanned almost two centuries from 1526 to 1707, representing the most significant period of Muslim rule over the Indian subcontinent, each demonstrated strong emotional ties to the Central Asian homeland—a place which most of them had never even seen. Nostalgia for the homeland, expressed by the Arabic term *hanin 'ila al-awtan* ('longing for the homeland') or the Persian *mihan*, has a long history in Islamic tradition, dating back to the sayings of the Prophet (*hadith*) which approve of such longings as natural and good.[5] I believe that many of the actions and expressed preferences of the Mughal emperors were driven to some extent by this nostalgia for Central Asia.

This book will concentrate on the region encompassing the Uzbek-ruled lands of Transoxiana and Balkh and the Mughal-held areas of the Indian subcontinent. Of course, Safavid Iran constitutes the third crucial pole, if no longer the *axis mundi* itself, of eastern Islamic culture for this period. Iran, in fact, is historically the major source, generating and dominating the culture of Islam in Asia. This Persian influence, however primary for all the Muslim civilizations of Asia, is not the focus of the present book. I have chosen instead to concentrate on the effects of Central Asian elements in Mughal India, which rank in importance second only to Iranian ones.[6]

Central Asia, Iran, and India had strong economic and social links from pre-history,[7] as has been stated above. Beginning in the eleventh century with the Ghaznavid dynasty, the three regions began to share a common dominant Persian-Islamic culture which only began to break up with the advent of European colonialism. As a result of this shared dominant Persian-Islamic culture and not through political conquest, a vast number of poets, painters, craftsmen, philosophers, and musicians all found a marketplace for their skills throughout the common area of Iran, Central Asia, and India. In fact, it seems that Muslims with the means to travel could relocate almost at will, even during the periods of greatest political conflict between the three regions.

The Muslim religion and the Persian language and literary tradition united Turks, Iranians, Afghans, and others, as well as converted Christians, Jews, and Hindus, for nearly a millenium. To a large degree, non-converts were also able to participate in this international culture, especially in South Asia. An individual version of the Asian Muslim cultural map is drawn by the life and legacy of Shaykh ʿAli Hamadani, a fourteenth-century sufi from Iran who traveled to India and is credited with the conversion of Kashmir. He was buried in Central Asia, and his shrine in present-day Tajikistan has been attracting Indian pilgrims for centuries.[8]

Another striking individual example is that of ʿAbd al-Qadir Bidel, an Indian of apparently Uzbek ancestry who composed his work in Persian. As late as the nineteenth century, he was Central Asia's favourite poet.[9] Timur Beisembiev has discussed in a recent article how the nineteenth century rulers of Kokand attempted to tie their legitimacy to the Mughals of India.[10] And for the present century, M.N. Roy, an Indian member of the Comintern, describes how the connections between Central Asia and Muslim India were recognized by the Bolsheviks, who set up a school in Tashkent during the 1920s which was attended mainly by Indian Muslims.[11]

Clearly, certain aspects of cultural unity throughout Muslim Asia have been recognized by some scholars and politicians. Both the quantity and the quality of research conducted up to now, however, have been quite lacking. This is particularly the case in the field of cultural relations between Central Asia and the better-known Muslim empires of India and Iran during the sixteenth-eighteenth centuries.

No more vivid example can be found of the link bridging Central and South Asia in this period than that of the Mughal ruling house. As the last reigning Timurids, the Mughals were a Central Asian Turkic Muslim dynasty transplanted to the Indian subcontinent. This Central Asian influence, therefore, forms a major theme in the present work. On a larger scale, the importation to India of Central Asian (and Iranian) culture which occurred during the Mughal period tells us something about the way Muslims in Asia perceived their cultural landscape—that is, the inter-

relationship of Central Asia, India, and Iran as lands of
Perso-Islamic civilization.

The Mughals brought with them to India not only
Central Asian political, administrative, and military
influences (lasting ones, unlike Timur's), but also painting,
poetry, and architectural styles which were Persian in origin
and common to Iran, Central Asia, and elsewhere. The
most celebrated Mughal monument in India, the Taj
Mahal, was directly inspired by Timur's tomb in Samarqand,
the *Gur-i-Amir*. Shah Jahan, who commissioned the Taj, was
obsessed with the dream of reconquering the Central Asian
'homeland', and finally put the Mughal dream to the test
by invading Central Asia via the gateway province of Balkh
in 1646. This attempt proved a fiasco, however, and after a
humiliating withdrawal a year and a half later, the Emperor
redirected his attentions towards Safavid-held Qandahar to
the south, waging four increasingly desperate campaigns
which exhausted the empire's resources and were
instrumental in bringing about his downfall at the hands
of his ambitious son Aurangzeb.

In Mughal letters and other writings concerning Shah
Jahan's plans for Balkh, the standard epithet designating
Central Asia is 'the graveyard of our ancestors' (*gurkhana-
yi-ajdad*). Even Aurangzeb, who reversed so many of his
father's other policies, maintained this Mughal mindset
toward Central Asia during his reign. One seventeenth
century Central Asian source, the *Muzakkir-i-ashab*, mentions
the last of the 'Great Mughals' as having sent both money
and manpower to Samarqand for the restoration of the
Gur-i-Amir, just as his grandfather Jahangir had done; both
evidently perceived the tomb as a 'family' monument. In
fact, as will be seen, the most persistent common theme for
all the Great Mughal rulers was this aspect of their foreign
policy: their frustrated desire to regain control of their
ancestral lands despite phenomenal successes in other
directions.

The problem of Mughal identity is complex, reflecting the social complexity of the eastern Islamic world. Timurid rule, which tends to fall under the rubric of Central Asian history, is generally—and falsely—considered to have ended with the Uzbek conquest of Herat in 1507. Rarely, if ever, are the Indian Timurids, the Mughals, described as anything other than an Indian dynasty. The culture they promoted in South Asia was a composite of foreign and indigenous elements, though the magnificent cultural achievements of their reign took place entirely on Indian soil.

On the other hand, even after generations in India, the Mughal ruling class continued to refer to themselves as *Turanis* (Central Asians), and at times their Indian subjects referred to them in that way too. But in my opinion, the nostalgia expressed by the Mughal emperors for their Central Asian 'homeland' indicates not that they felt they were not a part of the 'Indian' world, but rather that they had lost the 'centre' of their world, Samarqand, which in Timur's time had been the glorious capital of an empire that included not only northern India but also Iran, Syria, Anatolia, and the steppe lands of Inner Asia. This was the world as the Mughals saw it, a world they felt was their just inheritance to rule over. It is the question of what comprised the social unity of this world that will concern us here.

NOTES

1. For a re-assessment of the 'Aryan invasions' see Jim G. Shaffer, 'Indo-Aryan Invasions', in *The People of South Asia*, ed. John R. Lukacs, New York and London, 1984, and Edmund Leach, 'Aryan Invasions over Four Millenia', in *Culture Through Time*, ed. E. Ohnuki-Tierney, Stanford, 1990.
2. Lit., 'Timur-the-lame', following an accident as a child which left him with a limp. For a discussion of the organization of Timur's supporters see Beatrice F. Manz, *The Rise and Rule of Tamerlane*, Cambridge University Press, Cambridge, 1989.

3. The spelling stems from the Mongol name 'Shiban'; the more commonly seen transliteration 'Shaibanid' (or 'Shaybanid') dates from early Persian sources.
4. This is not to say that they accorded superior status to the Timurids, who had a weaker claim to legitimacy from the Uzbek point of view. See Chapter Two below on issues of legitimacy.
5. M.M. Reyshahri, ed., *Mizan al-hikmat*, x, 522, no. 21627.
6. For the Iranian influence see Yar Muhammad Khan, *Iranian Influence in Mughul India*, Lahore, 1978. For a discussion of Safavid-Mughal political relations see Riazul Islam, *Indo-Persian Relations*, Tehran, 1970. The Safavid-Uzbek conflict in the sixteenth century is analyzed in Martin B. Dickson, Shah Tahmasp and the Uzbeks, Ph.D. thesis, Princeton University, 1959.
7. See for example S.P. Gupta, *Archaeology of Soviet Central Asia and the Indian Borderlands*, 2 vols., Delhi, 1979; A. Guha, ed., *Central Asia: Movement of Peoples and Ideas from Times Prehistoric to Modern*, Delhi, 1970; G.M. Bongard-Levin, *Studies in Ancient India and Central Asia*, Calcutta, 1971; B.A. Litvinskii, 'Archaeological Discoveries on the Eastern Pamirs and the Problem of Contacts Between Central Asia, China and India in Antiquity', in *International Congress of Orientalists* XXV, Moscow, 1960; B. Prabodha-Chandra, *India and Central Asia*, Calcutta, 1955.
8. Devin DeWeese, 'Sayyid ʿAli Hamadani and Kubrawi Hagiographical Traditions', in *The Legacy of Medieval Persian Sufism*, ed. L. Lewisohn, London, 1991.
9. Sadruddin Aini, *Mirzo Abdulkodir Bedil*, Stalinabad, 1954; Alessandro Bausani, 'Note su Mirza Bedil 1644-1721', *Annali Institute Università di Napoli*, nuova seria v. 6, (1954). Also see Chapter Four of the present work.
10. Timur Beisembiev, 'Ferghana's Contacts With India in the 18th and 19th Centuries', *Journal of Asian History* 28/2 (1994), pp. 130-2.
11. M.N. Roy, *M.N. Roy's Memoirs*, Ajanta, Delhi, 1984.

CHAPTER 1

PERSO-ISLAMIC SOCIETY

A very rough and fuzzy line can be drawn between the Western and Eastern realms of the Islamic world, with Arab culture dominating the former sphere and Persian culture dominating the latter. Ethnic Persians were significant in the development of Islamic institutions and thought, but in later centuries it was often Persianized individuals of other ethnic backgrounds who became the transmitters and champions of Persian culture.

The Iranian Sassanian Empire was one of the first great conquests of the Arab Muslim armies in the late seventh century. Soon, however, slightly transformed Persian administrative infrastructures came to serve as Islamic ones, old Persian families such as the Barmakids came to wield enormous political power. Within two centuries the Persian language had struggled from under Arabic hegemony to re-establish itself as a major literary language and was, by the fourteenth century, the principal lingua franca from Konya to Kashgar.

Of the great figures illuminating the period of Islamic civilization's greatest achievements, an astonishing number were Persians, from Avicenna and Khwarazmi to Saʿdi and Hafiz. European traders from Marco Polo to the adventurers of the English East India Company had to learn Persian in order to do business in Asia. The North African Ibn Khaldun, writing in the fourteenth century, states that,

> ...with few exceptions, most Muslim scholars both in the religious and intellectual sciences have been non-Arabs

(*ajam*)...Only the Persians engaged in the task of preserving knowledge and writing systematic scholarly works.[1]

Richard Frye, in a chapter entitled 'Iran's Conquest of Islam', likens the Persian role in the spread and development of Islamic culture to that of Greek civilization for Christianity.[2] Although Persian influence is most evident as elite culture memorialized in literature, art, and monuments, to a greater or lesser extent its effects permeated all levels of Muslim society in Asia, just as Graeco-Roman civilization remains the foundation stone of Western thought and culture today.

The Prestige of Perso-Islamic Elite Culture

The legacy of Timur provides an example of how solidly established the Persian type of Islamic civilization was in Asia by the fourteenth century. Although himself of Turko-Mongol stock, (like most great military figures of Muslim Asia) he founded a dynasty which has become synonymous with Persian painting, poetry, science, and architecture through such names as Bihzad, Jami, Ulugh Beg, and Sultan Husayn 'Bayqara'. One legend even has the conqueror of Asia seek out the poet Hafiz of Shiraz in Syria in order to question him about one of his Persian love poems.[3] The Mughal dynasty which ruled northern India from 1526 to 1857 was an extension of the Timurid line, and was so thoroughly Persianized that the corpus of Persian literature produced in India vastly outweighs that from Iran. Under Mughal patronage, Persian poetry and painting flourished and evolved to new heights.

The establishment of Shi'ism in Iran from 1501 led to a degree of estrangement between the lands under Safavid control and those of the Mughals and Uzbeks. Although the break was never complete, the centre of gravity for Persian culture felt an eastward pull towards India, carried by a severe 'brain-drain' of talented Iranians seeking greater success under the wealthier and more tolerant Mughals. A similar exodus occurred among Central Asians under the rarely stable and economically deteriorating Uzbek rule, although many travelled to India only temporarily. From the sixteenth century onwards Central Asia, which had always been an integral part of the Iranian world, tended instead to look southwards to India and north-west to Russia. The Uzbek-controlled lands became increasingly marginal, and Persian-speakers began to lose some of their historical pre-eminence (although the harshest blow was to be dealt by the Soviets four centuries later, by carving out 'national' republics and allocating the cities of Samarqand and Bukhara, traditional bastions of Persian culture, to Turkic Uzbekistan).[4]

The wide dissemination of Persian culture across the Asian continent over the centuries owes itself not to Persian hegemony, but rather to the willingness with which non-Persians embraced and supported Persian cultural traditions. Thus the following assertion by John Richards seems to go too far:

> The Mughals suffered from the long-standing Persian claim of cultural superiority over the colonial Islamic lands in India (or for that matter over Turan). The Timurids accepted this judgement, even as they chafed under it.[5]

The objectionable words here are 'suffered' and 'chafed'. In fact, the Mughals had themselves internalized a wide range of Persian practices and characteristics, which they would not necessarily have thought of as 'Iranian' as opposed to 'Turkish'—although a modern ethnologist might be tempted to classify the Mughals as a 'Turkic' dynasty. There is nothing to suggest that the Mughals considered the ancient Persian New Year (*No ruz*) traditions, for example, as anything other than their own, any more than do the Uzbeks of today. In fact, it appears that most Uzbeks (and Tajiks) today consider *No ruz* to be an 'Islamic' festival!

The most visible Persian heritage shared among non-Persians is literary. Amir Khusraw of Delhi is claimed by Indians on the basis of geography, and by Iranians on the basis of language. Mawlana Rumi has been proclaimed an Afghan by birth and a Turk by both residence and his attributed founding of the whirling dervish (*mevlevi*) order, but for students of literature he is simply a great Persian poet. The 'Indian Style' of Persian poetry (*sabk-i-hindi*), which began to develop during the sixteenth century, reached its apogee two centuries later in the person of the poet Bidel.[6] The Soviet academician A.A. Semënov has said it was knowledge of the Persian language that allowed Central Asians 'to feed on the milk of Indian Muslim culture'.[7]

The very late rise to predominance of Turkic language over Persian in the East—as recently as this century—indicates the strength of the unifying role Persian played across Asia for many centuries. The Ottomans in the West were the first of the Turkic Muslim dynasties to raise the Turkish language to a dominant level. In Central Asia this task was accomplished only by the Russians, and in India, English finally superseded Persian only a few decades before Indian independence.

This is not to say that Turkish had been without its champions outside the Ottoman world. The Timurid poet Nawa'i, who together with his rival Jami, adorned the court of Sultan Husayn Bayqara at Herat in the late fifteenth century, wrote in both Persian and Turki, but was more accomplished in the latter.[8] Shah Isma'il I is credited with composing a collection (*diwan*) of Turkish poems, many of which aided him effectively as political propaganda while he fought to establish the Safavid state. Babur, the founder of the Mughal Empire in India, wrote his celebrated memoirs in Turki, and his Turki poetry was considered by Haydar Dughlat as second only to Nawa'i's.[9] Babur also wrote a book on Hanafi law entitled *Mubayyan*, in Turki.[10] Abu'l-Ghazi, the seventeenth century Uzbek ruler of Khwarazm, claims his *Shajarah-i-turk* to be an improvement over Rashid al-din's fourteenth century history of the Mongols, the *Jami' al-tawarikh*, which he complains is half corrupted by (Persian) copyists who knew no Mongolian or Turkish.[11] Nevertheless, among the major non-theological works commissioned by the Turkic emperors of the Safavid, Mughal, and Uzbek empires, nearly all were written in the Persian language. The overwhelming prejudice to which Muslims across Asia subscribed was that to be taken seriously, one had to write in Persian. Those who wrote in local languages, such as Turki or 'Hindawi', did so primarily for their own amusement, and only in certain rare cases for reasons of asserting or maintaining identity.[12]

Persian prestige often did offer benefits to ethnic Persians in service outside Iran. For example, although the army and administration of the Mughal empire were made up of Persians, Central Asian Turks, Arabs, Indian Muslims, and even Hindus, the dominant group in terms of ranking (though not numbers) was always the 'Persians' (*Iranis*, more often Persianized Turkmen from Iran), with Central Asians running a close second.[13] It is my impression that the *irani-turani* rivalry in India somewhat reflected, though in reverse, the struggle for supremacy between ethnic Iranians and Turkmen *qizilbash* in Safavid Iran.[14] In the Indian case it was usually more of a rivalry than open conflict, and generally the two factions shared their pre-eminence over the remainder of society.[15]

A Three-Way Political Contest

Political relations between the Mughals, Safavids, and Uzbeks were complicated by several factors. From the mid-1500s the Mughals, Uzbeks, and Ottomans made occasional

overtures to each other to unite under the banner of
Sunnism against the Twelver Shiʿi Safavid 'heretics'.
However, this seemingly natural alliance was negated by
several factors. One was the Mughals' claim to be the
legitimate rulers of the Central Asian lands, which they
considered the Uzbeks to have usurped. Each of the first
six Mughal rulers had articulated plans to reconquer the
dynasty's ancestral lands in Central Asia. Another was the
fact that both Babur and Humayun had at various points
accepted the status of Safavid vassals (an issue glossed over
in the Mughal sources and finally dispensed with by Akbar
in 1579).[16] A third factor was the large number of
influential Iranian Shiʿis in Mughal service.

The enduring effects of Mughal deference to Persian
(or Safavid) prestige can be seen in an account by the mid-
seventeenth century French traveller Francois Bernier, who
states that only Persian ambassadors were allowed to salute
the Mughal emperor 'according to the custom of their own
country' or to deliver their letters to him 'without the
intervention of an *Omrah*' (an *amir*).[17]

In practice the ongoing Mughal-Safavid conflict was
primarily economic, and centred on the struggle for control
over the trade route passing through Qandahar. Safavid-
Uzbek discord likewise focused on the rich heartland of
Khorasan. Tensions between the Mughals and the Uzbeks
are more difficult to characterize. Central Asia held little
strategic importance for the Mughal Empire. Uzbek raids
on the frontier were an annoyance, but hardly posed a
serious threat to the stability of the realm. The Uzbek lands
had lost their centrality in global trade, and were poor in
resources. In strictly material terms the Mughals had little
to gain by reconquering the land of their forebears, yet it
remained an obsession. Simple nostalgia appears to have
been a major factor in determining the Mughals' foreign
policy, and may well provide historians with an example of
psychology overriding economics. (This argument will be
further developed in Chapter Seven).

Trade and Shared Economy

The economy of Muslim-controlled Asia in the sixteenth and seventeenth centuries was in some respects a single and integrated system. The rulers of the three empires had a mutual interest in stabilizing and preserving the trade routes. In addition to sea routes and the land route through Qandahar which connected India with Iran and points west, the *A'in-i-Akbari* lists seven different routes through the Hindu Kush employed by Turanis travelling between India and Central Asia.[18] The efforts of the Safavid, Mughal, and Uzbek rulers to facilitate trade bore fruit which was advantageous to all. As Stephen Dale has noted, 'The simultaneous pacification of trade routes and construction of roads and caravanserais throughout North India, Iran and Turan in the late sixteenth and seventeenth centuries established exceptionally favourable conditions for trade throughout the entire region'.[19] Moving goods became faster, less dangerous, and therefore cheaper.

The silver currency used in the three empires was originally based on the *tanga-i-shahrukhi*, established by the Timurid Shah Rukh in the fifteenth century.[20] This was replaced in Central Asia by *khani*s, in India by rupees, and in Iran by *tuman*s, but the Mughal chronicles very often quote costs in all three currencies.[21] In the *Tabaqat-i-Akbari*, the sums remitted to Akbar in taxes are said to represent amounts equal to the entire annual revenues of Iran and Turan.[22]

The Mental Geography of Asian Muslims

The repetitive, automatic three-way currency references just mentioned are one of many examples demonstrating the official Mughal world-view. This is even more obviously illustrated by the 'Iran-Turan-Hindustan' paradigm which comes up again and again in the Indian sources. It does

not appear, furthermore, that this tripartite conception of
the world was limited to the Mughal ruling class itself.
According to Abu'l Fazl, 'it was a common saying that
Turkistan is the head, Khurasan the breast, and Hindustan
the foot [of the world]'.[23] Babur describes the existing view
in India on his arrival as slightly less developed: 'Just as
Arabs call every place outside Arabia, ᶜAjam, so Hindustanis
call every place outside Hindustan, Khurasan.'[24]

In the sixteenth century the three principal regions of
Muslim Asia were conceptualized in terms of somewhat
vague but nevertheless significant borders. Central Asia,
including lands both north and south of the Oxus river
and known alternately as *Turan* or *Ma wara an-nahr*
(Transoxiana), extended westward to the Caspian Sea,
northward to the Qazaq steppe in the area of the town of
Turkestan, eastward to Turfan, and fluctuated about
Badakhshan in the south and Khurasan to the south-west.
Northern India, called *Hindustan* in the sources, extended
to Qandahar in the west, Badakhshan and Kashmir in the
north, Assam in the east, and to the Deccan in the south.
Iran, often not referred to as such, included mainly the
Shiᶜized areas of ᶜ*Iraq-i-ᶜajami*, Khurasan, Sistan, Fars,
Azerbayjan, and the border regions of the Caucasus.

Tracing the Interchange

The evidence attesting to movement within this broader
society of Asian Muslims is varied. Official records give a
good picture of who and what came and went, as do
individual written accounts. Numismatic research is another
avenue.[25]

Some manuscripts appear to have had rich and eventful
lives, turning up in unexpected places in ways that make
one wonder how they got there. Annette Beveridge writes
regarding a copy of the *Babur-nama* found in Central Asia:
'If the question arises of how writings that had had place in

Jahangir's library reached Bukhara, their open road is through the Padshah's correspondence'.[26] In exchange, Jahangir's collection included a mid-sixteenth century illustrated copy of Sa^cdi's *Bustan* commissioned by the Uzbek ruler ^cAbd al-^cAziz at Bukhara.[27]

Indeed, royal gifts account for many a transfer of treasures, but the movement of ideas is more subtle, complex, and ultimately conjectural. One thing which is clear is that copies of manuscripts were enthusiastically commissioned from one region to another, a practice which continued even into the twentieth century. For example, the Oriental Institute in Tashkent alone possesses at least a dozen Central Asian manuscript copies of Abu'l Fazl's *Akbar-nama*, dating from the early seventeenth to late nineteenth centuries, as well as works by ^cUrfi, Huzuri, Faizi, Mulla Naw'i Khabushani 'Hindustani', Zuhuri, Lahauri, Mulla Shah-i-Badakhshi, Muhammad Tahir Ghani Kashmiri, Binesh, Mir Mu^cizz al-Din Muhammad Musawi Khan, Nasir ^cAli Sirhindi, ^cAbd al-Haqq, and others.[28] The existence of large numbers of Indian books in Central Asian libraries demonstrates both an awareness and an interest which only in this century came to be diminished.

NOTES

1. Ibn Khaldun, *Al-Muqaddima*, tr. F. Rosenthal, New York, 1958, iii, p. 311.
2. Richard Frye, *The Heritage of Persia*, World Publishing House, Cleveland, 1963, p. 244. See also Idem., 'Iranian Contributions to Islamic Culture', *The Golden Age of Persia*, Wiedenfeld and Nicolson, London, 1977; Robert Canfield, *Turko-Persia in Historical Perspective*, Cambridge University Press, Cambridge, 1991; and S.K. Chatterji, *Iranianism*, Calcutta, 1972, for a discussion of the influence of Persian culture from Achaemenid to modern times.
3. Timur is said to have taken affront at Hafiz's couplet which says, 'If that Shirazi beauty would take my heart in hand/For the dark mole [on his/her cheek] I would give Samarqand and Bukhara'.

4. This process is documented in Rahim M. Masov, *Istoriia topornogo razdeleniia*, Irfon, Dushanbe, 1991.

5. John Richards, *The Mughal Empire*, The New Cambridge History of India, Cambridge University Press, Cambridge, 1993, p. 111.

6. Jiři Bečka, 'Tajik Literature from the 16th Century to the Present', in *History of Iranian Literature*, ed. Jan Rypka, Dordecht, 1968, p. 488.

7. See Semënov, 'Kul'turno-politicheskikh sviaziakh', p. 19.

8. *Babur-nama*, ed. and tr. W.M. Thackston, Jr., Cambridge MA, 1993, pp. 354-5. This recent edition presents the original Chaghatay Turkish text facing ʿAbd al-Rahim Khan-i-Khanan's sixteenth century Persian translation, with a new English translation beneath. An English-only version of Thackston's new translation has recently been published (Smithsonian Institution and Oxford University Press, Washington, New York and Oxford, 1996).

9. Dughlat, Mirza Muhammad Haydar, *The Tarikh-i-Rashidi of Mirza Muhammad Haydar Dughlat*, tr. Denison Ross, ed. N. Elias, London, 1895, p. 173.

10. Nizam al-din Ahmad, *Tabaqat-i-Akbari*, tr. B. De, 3 vols, Calcutta, 1911-41, ii, p. 40. For a study of Persian-Turki bilingualism in sixteenth century Indian literature, see R. Imomkhojaev, *Tiurko-persidskoe dvuiazychie v literaturnoi zhizni Indii XVI v.*, Tashkent, 1993.

11. Abu'l-Ghazi Khan, *Histoire des Mongols et des Tatares* (the *Shajara-yi Turk* of Abu'l Ghazi Khan), French tr. P.I. Desmaisons, St. Petersburg, 1874, p. 36.

12. Ali S. Asani, 'Amir Khusraw and Poetry in Indic Languages', *Islamic Culture* 62/2-3 (1988), p. 53.

13. See M. Athar Ali, *The Apparatus of Empire: Awards of Ranks, Offices and Titles to the Mughal Nobility (1574-1658)*, Oxford University Press, Delhi, 1985, p. xx.

14. *Qizilbash*, literally 'red-head' was a term, initially derogatory, applied to the tribal Turkmen supporters of Ismaʿil I, in reference to their disinctive headgear which later became a stylized mark of Safavid identity.

15. For example, during his crackdown on illegal land conferrals, Akbar initially exempted Irani and Turani women from the investigation, although they too were eventually among those convicted of fraud (Abu'l Fazl ʿAllami, *A'in-i-Akbari*, tr. H. Blochmann and H.S. Jarrett, 3 vols., Calcutta, 1877-96 (reprint New Delhi, 1977-8), i, p. 269).

16. See F.W. Buckler, 'A New Interpretation of Akbar's Infallibility Decree of 1579', in *Legitimacy and Symbols*, ed. Michael Pearson, Ann Arbor, 1985, pp. 131-48.

17. François Bernier, *Travels in the Mogul Empire A.D. 1656-1668*, tr. Irving Brock, rev. Arthur Constable and Vincent Smith, London, 1934 (reprint New Delhi, 1992), p. 120.

18. *AA*, ii, p. 405.
19. Stephen Dale, *Indian Merchants and Eurasian Trade,1600-1750*, Cambridge University Press, Cambridge, 1994, p. 41.
20. Ibid., 29.
21. Nur al-din Muhammad Jahangir, *Tuzuk-i-Jahangiri*, tr. Alexander Rogers, ed. Henry Beveridge, Calcutta, 1909-11; i, pp. 3, 96, 128, 152, 401; Inayat Khan, *Shah Jahan-nama*, tr. A.R. Fuller, ed. W.E. Begley and Z.A. Desai, Delhi, 1990, p. 147.
22. *TA*, ii, p. 527.
23. Abu'l Fazl ᶜAllami, *Akbar-nama*, ed. ᶜAbd al-Rahim, 3 vols., Calcutta, 1877-87, i, p. 335; tr. Henry Beveridge, London, 1902-39 (reprint New Delhi, 1993), i, pp. 612-13 (Persian text p. 335).
24. *BN*, 265.
25. See J.F. Richards, ed., *The Imperial Monetary System of Mughal India*, Delhi, 1987; N.M. Lowick, 'Shaybanid Silver Coins', *The Numismatic Chronicle*, 7th ser., VI (1966), pp. 251-339; and E.A. Davidovitch, *Istoriia denezhnogo obrascheniia srednovekovoi Srednei Azii*, Moscow, 1983.
26. Annette Beveridge, *The Babur-Nama in English*, London, 1921, p. xlvi.
27. Stuart Cary Welch, Jr., *India, Art and Culture 1300-1900*, New York, 1985, p. 210.
28. The Institute's holdings are being catalogued in the *Sobranie vostochnykh rukopisiei Akademii Nauk Uzbekskoi SSR*, 11 vols. to date, Tashkent, 1952-85.

CHAPTER 2

THE TIMURID LEGACY AND TURKO-MONGOL IDENTITY

The political and social systems of the Mughals in India, the Uzbeks in Central Asia, and the Safavids in Iran had common origins in the nomadic Turko-Mongol tradition, although by the mid-sixteenth century they had evolved divergently and each had developed its own distinctive characteristics. The Uzbeks more conservatively maintained the relatively egalitarian clan-oligarchy structure of the steppe nomads than did the Safavids, who adopted the Persian model of royal quasi-divine absolutism, or the Mughals, who also built a more centralized state and initiated considerable administrative reforms. Even so, traditional steppe ethos continued to be an underlying impulse force common to the three systems, particularly in military matters.

The inaccurate application of the term 'Mughal' (that is, 'Mongol') to the Timurids of India appears to have arisen from the common usage of the Indian subject population, who following the thirteenth century invasions tended to see all invaders from Inner Asia as 'Mongols', just as Europeans long persisted in applying the term 'Tatar' to all steppe peoples, and Middle Easterners that of 'Frank' to all Western Europeans. In order to clarify this ambiguity, modern Uzbek scholars refer to the Mughal dynasty of India as the 'Baburids', but this usage has not gained acceptance outside the former Soviet Union.

According to an Indian writer of the nineteenth century, 'most of the people in India' by his time were under the impression that the Mughals were actual descendants of Chingis Khan's son Chaghatai, and therefore ethnically Mongols.[1] The confusion arises from the term 'Chaghatai' itself, its eventual association with predominantly Turkic tribal groups being due to the fact that Central Asia had been Chaghatay Khan's inheritance following his father's death. At the turn of the fifteenth century, however, 'Mughal' in Persian-language sources referred specifically to the eastern branch of Chaghatay-Chingisids, those occupying Mughulistan or Jungaria (i.e., the family of Haydar Mirza Dughlat, author of the *Tarikh-i-Rashidi*, who was a friend, supporter, and cousin of Babur), as distinguished from the Chaghatays of Ma-wara-e-nahr and Ferghana. Babur, the founder of the Timurid dynasty which would rule northern India for nearly four centuries, belonged to this latter, western group. Annette Beveridge explains his genealogy thus:

> ...if Babur were to describe his mother in tribal terms, he would say she was half-Chaghatai, half-Moghul; and if he so described himself, he would say he was half-Timurid-Turk, half-Chaghatai. He might have called the dynasty he founded in India Turki, might have called it Timuriya; he would never have called it Moghul, after his maternal grandmother.[2]

Uzbek khanate sources refer to Babur and his successors as 'the Chaghatays'.[3] An eighteenth-century Central Asian historian, cAbd al-Rahman Tali, referring to the loss of Timurid lands to the Uzbeks, states that the conjunction of Jupiter and Saturn in 1501 signalled the end of the 'Chaghatay period',[4] but speaking of Shah Jahan's 1646 Balkh invasion says that Nazr Muhammad 'gave over Balkh to the Chaghatays'.[5] This suggests that the Uzbeks acknowledged the continuity from Timur to the Mughals of India.

The Mughals seem not to have resisted the application of the term 'Chaghatay' to their own line; even in 1725 the writer Muhammad Hadi Kamwarkhan called his history of the Indian Timurids the *Tazkirat al-salatin-i-Chaghata*.[6] However, according to the French traveller François Bernier, by the late seventeenth century the term 'Mughal' was applied by Indians to any light-skinned Muslim of foreign descent, including Persians, Turks, Arabs, and even Uzbeks.[7]

Zahiruddin Muhammad Babur was born in Andijan in the Ferghana valley in 1483. He was fifth in descent from Timur, and at age 11 he inherited the throne of Ferghana from which he would launch repeated attempts to recapture his ancestor's glorious capital, Samarqand. He succeeded twice briefly, but was unable to hold the city against Shibani Khan's Uzbek army. He reluctantly set up his small kingdom in Kabul to the south, which would be his stronghold for two decades before he finally turned his attentions toward India, but his dream of Samarqand he held to the end of his life. Indeed this obsession was to be the inheritance he bequeathed to his own descendants, which would haunt them mercilessly despite their successes and glories in India for two centuries to come.

Babur makes his appearance on the pages of Indian history as a great conqueror, from his crushing defeat of Ibrahim Lodi at the Battle of Panipat on 21 April 1526. But in the Central Asian sphere of which he never ceased to consider himself a part, at his death four years later Babur probably left this world feeling like a colossal failure. He disliked India, which for all its riches was small consolation in his mind for the loss of his hereditary lands. The nostalgic reminiscences which fill his memoirs are curiously echoed by subsequent Mughal emperors who never even laid eyes on Central Asia.

Babur's son and successor, Humayun, was as Central Asian as his father. In 1549, nine years after his disastrous loss of northern India to the Afghan Sher Shah Suri, he

came out of Iran at the head of a Safavid army lent him by
Shah Tahmasp, but showed more interest in attacking
Balkh, the gateway to Samarqand, than in recapturing his
father's Indian conquests. Humayun's efforts toward Balkh
were thwarted, then as always, by his unco-operative brother
Kamran, but had he succeeded in re-establishing himself
in Central Asia it is quite doubtful there ever would have
been a Mughal dynasty in India. Since in 1549 Humayun
failed in what was clearly his first choice, one can speculate
that it was a somewhat reluctant Mughal who finally
reconquered Delhi in 1555.

The first arguably 'Indian' Mughal ruler was Akbar, who
was born of an Iranian mother at Umarkot in Sindh in
1542 during his father's flight toward Iran. Akbar, who
succeeded to the throne at fourteen after Humayun's
accidental death, ruled on his own behalf after overcoming
the influence of his Iranian Turkmen regent, Bayram Khan,
in 1560 and that of his own harem in 1562, although some
historians have wondered whether the magnificence of his
long reign wasn't more the work of brilliant intimates, such
as his biographer and friend, Abu'l Fazl, and the Hindu
financial wizard Raja Todar Mal.

Akbar was Indian not only by birth but in outlook as
well. His rule was a meritocracy characterized by tolerance,
heterodoxy, and innovation; he incorporated Hindus into
his military and administration, welcomed religious debate,
and his fiscal reforms, the brainchild of Todar Mal, did not
differentiate between Hindu and Muslim. Under Akbar,
the Mughal Empire expanded to cover two-thirds of the
Indian subcontinent and became the richest land in the
world. Although (as will be discussed later) Abu'l Fazl
claims that Akbar never ceased to dream of reconquering
Central Asia, in reality this was neither consistent with
Akbar's efforts to consolidate his Indian empire, nor
feasible in light of Central Asia's uncharacteristic stability
at the time under ᶜAbdullah Khan.

Akbar's wayward son Salim, who may have poisoned his father and in any case hastened his death by ordering the assassination of Abu'l Fazl which left the Emperor irreparably distraught, succeeded to the throne as Jahangir in 1605. Though popularly known as an ineffectual lush ruled over by his Persian wife Nur Jahan, Jahangir was a complex man who could display both great refinement and unbridled savagery. He revived in his person the Mughal obsession with Central Asia, although his dreams remained dreams and were not put into action. This remained for his son Khurram, who on Jahangir's death in 1627 became the emperor Shah Jahan, best known to the world as the man who commissioned the building of the Taj Mahal as a memorial to his wife, but also, more important to this discussion, as the Mughal who tried to reconquer the ancestral Central Asian homeland.

On hearing news of Jahangir's passing, Nazr Muhammad Khan, the Uzbek ruler of Balkh, seized the opportunity to attack Mughal Kabul. Though unsuccessful, Nazr Muhammad's attempt provided Shah Jahan with one pretext for turning Mughal military attentions at last toward Central Asia. After false starts in 1639 and 1641, Shah Jahan finally put the century-old Mughal fantasy to work and launched an invasion of Central Asia in 1646. The Mughal army captured and held Balkh for a year and a half, but was unable to penetrate further and ultimately abandoned the effort, withdrawing under humiliating circumstances in 1647 and returning the region to Nazr Muhammad's control.

Yet even this disaster was not enough to put the Mughal dream to rest completely. Aurangzeb, Shah Jahan's diligent third son whose regnal name was ʿAlamgir, dethroned his father and locked him up in Agra fort within view of his masterpiece, the Taj, and went on to make a career of reversing the policies of his forefathers. Nevertheless, as will be demonstrated subsequently, he retained a sufficient sense of duty to pass on the obligation of reconquering

Central Asia to his own son, Muʿazzam, and felt bound enough to Timur's tomb in Samarqand to undertake its annual maintenance. In practice, however, Aurangzeb's overriding obsession was the reduction of the Deccan to the south, which absorbed him for the bulk of his forty-nine year reign. It seems to have been his genuine intention to finish the task Shah Jahan had started, but he never got around to it, and he left his successors an empire too exhausted for such a mission.[8]

The Uzbek Khans

The term 'Uzbek' is no less problematic than the appellation 'Mughal', and is even harder to trace. Abu'l-Ghazi links the designation to the Juchid Mongol Özbek Khan whom he credits with converting his subjects to Islam. Folk etymology offers the explanation, 'öz'+'beg', or 'self-ruler'. According to R.D. McChesney, the term 'was applied by medieval historians to all the Turko-Mongol tribes of the White Horde (i.e., the peoples given to the Orda after the death of Juchi in 1225)', but properly speaking should be used only in reference to non-Chingisid tribals.[9]

The system by which the Uzbek-held lands of Central Asia were governed differed from that of the Mughals most fundamentally by its decentralization. As McChesney describes it, '...political life was shaped by the neo-Chingizid appanage system of state and its internal dynamic... sovereignty was corporate, embodied in the ruling or royal clan and shared among its eligible members'.[10] (Appanages are indicated by the Mongol term *tiyul* and by the Arabic *mamlakat*, as opposed to the terms *iqta'at* and *hukumat* which refer to land grants.)[11] Thus a clan would elect its leader—usually the seniormost member—in a clan meeting (the Mongol *quriltay*), and divvy out territories to clan members to be ruled more or less independently. (Often a distinction was made between the *sultan suri*, or apparent ruler, who was generally the eldest clan member and often unsuited to rule, and the *sultan ma'nawi*, who actually exercised power.)[12] The first requirement for leadership was agnatic descent from Chingis Khan's eldest son, Juchi. The Shibanid dynasty which ruled Central Asia throughout the sixteenth century traced descent from Juchi's son Shiban, while the Ashtarkhanid dynasty which ruled throughout the seventeenth century traced theirs from another of Juchi's sons, Toqay-Timur. It is on this basis that McChesney argues for calling the dynasty the 'Toqay-Timurids'.[13] The dynasty is referred to in Persian sources as the Ashtarkhanids, from its origins around Astrakhan, and by some modern scholars (particularly Soviet) as the Janids, after its nominal founder Jani Muhammad.[14]

The traditional Central Asian-style appanage system of rule provided less stability than the more centralized Safavid or Mughal systems. In the absence of an exceptionally able and charismatic leader (such as Timur had been, and ʿAbdullah II proved to be in the second half of the sixteenth century), civil disorder was the usual result.[15] Multiple power bases did exist in Mughal India with regional governors, often members of the royal family, frequently attempting rebellions. But in the Uzbek territories the power bases were more evenly matched, and thus served more often than not to weaken each other. Appanage rulers were heavily dependent on the support of their *amir*s, who could bring about the sovereign's downfall merely by withdrawing their support. Interestingly, Babur complains of exactly this type of authority problem during his early campaigns into India[16], and Humayun was plagued by struggles of a similar nature. It is Akbar, in fact, who represents the Mughal break with the traditional Central Asian system in favour of a more effective central authority.

Muhammad Shibani Khan—known alternately as Shaybani Khan, Shibaq, Shahi Beg, Shah Bakht or Shaybak—was born in 1451. A grandson of Abu'l Khayr, he succeeded by 1507 in bringing most of Central Asia under his control, but within a year of his death in battle against the Safavids in 1510 the Abulkhayrids had once again lost every major Central Asian city to rival clans.[17] Most of the subsequent leaders of the Abulkhayrid clan were elected on the basis of seniority until the death of ʿAbd al-ʿAziz in 1550, when civil war broke out between the appanages of Bukhara, Samarqand, Tashkent, and Balkh.

By 1582, however, ʿAbdullah Khan had consolidated the four major appanages into a unified state, and in addition that capable ruler took Badakhshan from the Mughals in 1584 and Khurasan from the Safavids in 1588. He broke precedent by naming an heir, ʿAbd al-Mu'min, in a 1590 *quriltay*, but the latter on his accession in 1598 caused such alarm by killing off relatives that he was himself assassinated. At this time the Ashtarkhanids, led by Din Muhammad, whose participation in the conquest of Khorasan had given them increasing power, proclaimed a khanate in Khorasan and Sistan, but Din Muhammad was killed at Herat by the Safavids and the clan regravitated toward Central Asia.

In 1599, under the leadership of Din Muhammad's brother Baqi Muhammad, the Ashtarkhanid clan defeated Pir Muhammad and the Shibanids at Bukhara. The victors held a *quriltay* and elected as leader their senior member, Jani Muhammad, who gave control of Bukhara to his son Baqi Muhammad as his appanage.[18] The latter was succeeded in 1606 by his brother Wali Muhammad, who in turn stepped down in 1611 after losing the support of his *amir*s. This event led to a number of Uzbek officials seeking refuge in India.

A bipartite Uzbek state evolved from 1612, with the sons of Din Muhammad, Imam Quli Khan, and Nazr Muhammad Khan, ruling the appanages of Bukhara and Balkh respectively. This arrangement persisted until Imam Quli, old and nearly blind, called his brother to Bukhara and abdicated in his favour in late 1641.[19] The ongoing conflict between the two brothers has perhaps been

exaggerated, following in the steps of informants of Shah
Jahan, whose menacing manoeuvres at Kabul in 1639
brought Imam Quli rushing to his brother's assistance. The
two Uzbeks then mustered a force which persuaded the
Mughal ruler that the time for invasion was not yet ripe.

The younger brother's short reign at Bukhara was
troubled by the disaffection of a faction of amirs led by
one Yalangtosh Biy, who goaded Nazr Muhammad's son
ʿAbd al-ʿAziz into chasing him back to Balkh. Filial disloyalty
combined with incessant harassment by tribesmen
(*'almans'*) forced Nazr Muhammad to appeal to Shah Jahan
for help.[20] The Mughal emperor needed no more than
such an invitation to set his army in motion toward Central
Asia.

Following the one-and-a-half-year Mughal occupation of
Balkh province, from which the region suffered even
greater and more lasting hardship than did the Mughal
army itself, Nazr Muhammad returned at Shah Jahan's
request and regained his throne. Unable to cope with the
devastation the Mughals had wrought, in 1651 he abdicated
in favour of his younger son Subhan Quli Khan, who once
again presided over half of a bipartite state, in conjunction
with his elder brother ʿAbd al-ʿAziz at Bukhara.

The double khanate lasted for thirty years, until ʿAbd al-
ʿAziz, seventy years old and wearied by constant attacks by
Shibanid Uzbeks from Khwarazm, gave over his throne to
Subhan Quli, who reigned over the re-unified Uzbek lands
until his death in 1702. He was succeeded by his son
ʿUbaydallah at Bukhara and his grandson Muhammad
Muqim at Balkh, but the resurgence of decentralizing
amirid power paved the way for the ultimate decline of the
dynasty.

By the second half of the sixteenth century Mughal India
was a colossus; Central Asia, while having enjoyed a period
of stability under ʿAbdullah Khan, was becoming something
of a backwater. The Mughal population in 1598 has been
estimated at anywhere from sixty to ninety-eight million,

while in Uzbek Turan, including Balkh, Stephen Dale has put the figure at around five million people. Northern India had a diversified economy, was a net exporter of goods, and had a positive trade balance; it exported mainly bulky staples, and imported 'specialty crops and luxury manufactures, most of them destined for the Mughal elite'.[21]

From Central Asia the Mughals received melons and other regional fruits, and the so-called *turki* steppe horses which were known for their endurance. Yet Central Asian coins, which weighed less than half the Mughal rupee even in the sixteenth century, were rapidly debased following the death of ʿAbdullah Khan.[22] While India produced most of its own wealth, the golden age of Central Asia's economy had come from trade. For centuries Central Asia's crossroads location had ensured its prosperity, but for reasons which continue to be debated, by the sixteenth century the region's 'centrality' was declining.[23] Muzaffar Alam has recently argued that the increased European domination of the seas actually spurred overland trade during the seventeenth century, and that 'the land-route in the seventeenth and early eighteenth centuries not only competed successfully with the maritime route, but also seems to have posed a kind of threat to it'.[24] But as the example Alam cites involves British attempts to control the routes taken by Armenian merchants in particular, his argument illustrates only the persistence of overland trade, and not its dominance.

The Mughals' Timurid and Turko-Mongol Self-Identity

The legitimacy of the Mughals both in their own eyes and in the eyes of others rested on their lineal descent from Timur. At a remove of five generations, Babur was one of a number of Timur's descendants who were struggling to hold on to the splintering remnants of the Timurid empire in Central Asia at the end of the fifteenth century. He was the only one to establish a power base in the sixteenth century, but he did so in India, which two centuries earlier Timur had conquered briefly and then left, not within the Timurid heartland—and even this accomplishment didn't come until near the end of Babur's life.

Yet although Babur's wish was not to remain in India but rather to rule from Samarqand as Timur did, his legitimacy as an Indian ruler derived from his ancestor's conquest. Babur writes in his memoirs, 'Since we had always had in mind to take Hindustan, we regarded as our own territory the several areas of Bhera, Khushab, Chenab, and Chiniot, which had long been in the hands of the Turk [i.e., the Timurids]'. Accordingly, he forbids plunder when launching his first raid into India.[25]

Numerous paintings commissioned by the Mughal emperors give vivid visual testimony to this fact. One, near the beginning of an *Akbar-nama* done in 1596, gives a comparative portrayal of the festivities surrounding Timur's birth and those surrounding Akbar's.[26] A later painting, commissioned by Shah Jahan in around 1635, shows Timur presenting his crown to Babur.[27] A 1653 portrait depicts Timur sitting on an outdoor throne together with Babur to one side and Humayun to the other, and handing a turban pin (*sarpich*), symbolizing his authority, to Babur.[28] Another, the two-page frontispiece of the official chronicle of the first part of Shah Jahan's reign, the *Padshah-nama*, has facing portraits of Timur and Shah Jahan.[29]

This legitimacy became increasingly important for the Mughals after Babur's death, as Humayun and his successors came to accept, to some degree at least, their role as Indian monarchs. But in a world where lineage was nearly everything, the Mughal descendants of Timur could not, ideologically speaking, abandon their paramount claim to Central Asia no matter how firmly established in India they became.

Abu'l Fazl calls Akbar the 'glory of the Gurgan (Timur's) family' (*furugh-i-khandan-i-Gurgani*) and the 'lamp of the tribe of Timur' (*chiragh-i-dudman-i-Sahib-qirani*).[30] Timur himself, being unable to claim genuine Chingisid lineage, had sought to add to his legitimacy by marrying into a Chingisid family; hence the *nisba* of 'Gurgan', from the Mongolian *güregän*, meaning son-in-law.

Abu'l Fazl's elder brother, the poet Faizi, calls the emperor the 'lamp of the court of dominion of Timur's dynasty'.[31] Jahangir ordered the erection at Kabul, Babur's burial site, of a stone engraved with his own name and those of his lineal ancestors back to Timur.[32] He also had a stone throne put up next to the one over Babur's grave, and had it engraved with his own name and Timur's.[33]

Echoing Abu'l Fazl, the chronicler Lahauri calls Shah Jahan 'that pride of the Gurgan dynasty'.[34] Shah Jahan fancied himself practically a re-incarnation of Timur, having supposedly been born, like his ancestor, during the conjunction of Venus and Jupiter (Shah Jahan's horoscope, unfortunately, was off by several months). One of Timur's favoured titles was 'Lord of the Auspicious Conjunction' (*Sahib-i-qiran*), leading Shah Jahan to assume the title of 'Second Lord of the Auspicious Conjunction' (*Sahib-i-qiran-i thani*).[35] More than any other Mughal emperor, Shah Jahan embodied the desire for Central Asia as an obsession, and was the first since Humayun, a century earlier, to actually put the attempt at reconquest into action.

Timur was the prime role model and reference point for the achievements of the Mughal emperors. According to the *Humayun-nama*, the *Timur-nama* (i.e., the *Zafar-nama* of Sharaf al-Din ʿAli Yazdi, completed in 1424-5) and other such books were Humayun's 'real companions'.[36] During his exile among the Safavids Humayun drew an omen from a dervish's gift of a boot that the time was ripe for him to reconquer India, the 'foot' of the world, remembering how Timur had divined from the breast of a sheep that it was his time to take Khurasan, the 'breast' of the world.[37] Abu'l

Fazl copiously quotes from Yazdi's work,[38] and compares Akbar's horoscope favourably to that of his illustrious ancestor, whom he calls 'that brightener of the face of fortune'.[39] He even goes so far as to say that Timur's 'holy existence was the forerunner of the perpetual dominion of his Majesty, the King of Kings (Akbar)',[40] and later points out that while during his India campaign Timur had captured 120 elephants, Akbar captured 1,500 during his campaigns.[41] Bada'uni mentions that on one occasion Akbar revived traditional Chaghatay dining hall customs for the visit of Mirza Sulayman, although he adds that they were discontinued again after the prince's departure.[42]

Jahangir and Shah Jahan were both avid readers of Yazdi's *Zafar-nama*. One copy of this work made in 1467-8 for the Timurid prince Aqa Mulla and now in the Walters Gallery in Baltimore, bears marginal notes in the hand of Jahangir and the seals of Shah Jahan and Aurangzeb.[43] More than a century later Aurangzeb was sententiously quoting anecdotes about Timur to his father, Shah Jahan, whom he had imprisoned. In his high-handed way, the usurping son claimed humility before God just as Timur had done after defeating the Ottoman Sultan Bayazid,[44] and told his father, 'I should disgrace the blood of the great Timur, our honoured progenitor, if I did not seek to extend the bounds of my present territories'.[45] One assumes from this that Shah Jahan had been urging his son to renew the attempt to reconquer Central Asia, since Aurangzeb is defending here his campaigns in Bengal and the Deccan.

Apart from carrying on the torch of Timurid triumph, however, the Mughals were also subtle perpetuators of numerous Mongol traditions, demonstrating the additional layer of their character as products of the pre-Islamic steppe world. Babur's death is said to have resulted from his taking an illness of Humayun upon himself—an old Mongol conception.[46] Legend has Chingis Khan's son Tolui sacrifice himself in the same way in order to save his brother Ögödei.[47]

Speaking of Emperor Humayun's manner of receiving people, the *Humayun-nama* mentions that 'His Majesty enjoined certain regulations (*tura*) which are fixed for interviews with kings'.[48] Another passage, describing how after a hunt the emperor's younger brother Prince Hindal offered his game to Humayun, 'following the rules of Chinghis Khan', uses a Persian synonym, *dastur* ('*ba dastur-i-Chingiz Khan*').[49] Referring to an earlier event, when all the Timurid princes came to join Babur's mourning march on the death of Sultan Husayn in 1506, Gulbadan states that one prince, Badi' al-zaman, would not come since he was Babur's elder, until Qasim Beg persuaded him by saying, 'younger [Babur] is by years but by the *tura* he has precedence because he has more than once taken Samarqand by force'.[50] Abu'l Fazl mentions that in 1548 Humayun received his brother Kamran 'according to [Mongol] custom (*ba didan-i-tura*)'.[51]

According to Bada'uni, writing in Akbar's time, it was a Mongol *tura* that 'if the Emperor cast his eye with desire on any woman, the husband is bound to divorce her'.[52] Jahangir, in his memoirs, describes himself as having performed obeisance and prostration when greeting his mother 'according to the *tura* of Chinghis, the *qanun* of Timur, and common usage'.[53] And when Jahangir's rebel son Khusrau is brought before him, the captive is led up to the emperor's left side, 'after the manner (*rasm*) and custom (*tura*) of Chinghis Khan'.[54] Mansura Haider has discussed the significance of the term *tura* to the Mughals in a recent article.[55] However, like earlier British historians, she equates the term with *yasa*, which is Chingisid law, whereas *tura* is Mongol customary law (Mong. *türä*).

The late sixteenth century Portuguese traveller Montserrate describes how the Mughals maintained the Mongol arrangement of tents and pavilions in setting up the royal camp while on campaign.[56] Akbar's *mansab* ranking system was derived from a Mongol model (the evolution of the *mansab* system from its origins in the army of Chingis Khan is first traced by the British historian W.H. Moreland).[57] Akbar also introduced to India a Chingisid category of land grant, which unlike other types of grants, were not to be changed or terminated.[58] Jahangir describes this in his memoirs:

> ...I informed the *bakhshis* that whoever wished to have his birthplace made into his *jagir* should make a representation to that effect, so that in accordance with the Chinghiz canon (*tura*) the estate might be conveyed to him by *al tamgha* and become his property, and he might be secured from apprehension of change. Our ancestors and forefathers were in the habit of granting *jagirs* to everyone under proprietary title, and adorned the *farmans* for these with the *al tamgha* seal, which is an impressed seal made in vermilion (i.e., red ink). I ordered that they should cover the place for the seal with gold-leaf (*tila-push*) and impress the seal thereon, and I called this the *altun* (gold) *tamgha.*[59]

The Mongol title 'Tarkhan', which offered privileges such as excusing the holder from otherwise mandatory attendance at court, was bestowed infrequently by the Mughal emperors on favourites, such as the Chingisid Mirza Jani Beg, who was honoured thus by Akbar. Other Tarkhans mentioned in the *Ma'athir al-'umara,* an eighteenth century 'peerage' of the Mughal empire, include Mirza Ghazi Beg (i, p. 582), Mirza ʿIsa (i, p. 689), Muhammad Salih (ii, p. 205), and Nur al-din (ii, p. 483).[60] The title was originally a hereditary one.[61] Under Timur a Tarkhan had free access to the palace, and criminal immunity for himself and his children up to nine offenses.

The number 'nine' also held a special significance for the Mughals. For example, gifts made to the emperor had to be given nine at a time; so that the Turkish word for nine, *tüqqüz*, came to mean 'a gift'.[62] As Humayun's sister Gulbadan writes, 'Even the gifts were presented in the

Mongol *tura*, namely all sorts of stuffs in *tüqqüz*.'[63] An enduring example of the number nine's continuing significance is given by the Khwarazmian Uzbek Abu'l Ghazi, who divided his *Shajarah-i-türk* into nine chapters because 'wise men have said: "nothing must exceed the number nine"'.[64] To cite a Mongol precedent, young Chingis Khan, giving thanks to the mountain Burkhan Khaldun for sheltering him from his Merkit enemies, knelt nine times facing the sun.[65]

Yet however much the Mughals preserved vestiges of steppe tradition, the Uzbeks remained closer to those shared roots. A description in the *Bahr al-asrar* of the ceremonial seating arrangements at the court of Nazr Muhammad shows, in the words of the Russian orientalist V.V. Bartol'd, 'how much the Uzbek khans...even in the mid-seventeenth century, had to take into consideration the traditions of nomadic life and kinship systems'. (Bartol'd goes on to point out that this situation had changed greatly by the nineteenth century.)[66]

The Mughals' consciousness of their Timurid roots was perhaps most enduringly manifested in the architectural legacy they left. Anyone who has seen Timur's mausoleum, the *Gur-i-Amir*, at Samarqand, Humayun's tomb at Delhi and the Taj Mahal at Agra can see the connection. Lisa Golombek has called the latter two monuments 'variations on the theme of the imperial mausoleum in a garden setting', bearing the two main characteristics of 'monumentality and rationalism' which Mughal tombs share with Timurid architecture. The Timurid double-dome inspired the double-domes of Mughal architecture, and the perfection of the transverse vault was 'the key to all the major innovations of Timurid architecture'.[67] John Hoag, citing examples such as the *Ishrat-khana* and the Bibi Khanum mosque at Samarqand, states in regard to the Taj Mahal that 'the very building of such a lavish tomb to the memory of a woman is a Turkish, Central Asian custom rather than Indian'.[68]

Foreign Recognition of the Mughals' Timurid Legitimacy

It has been argued that Babur's inability to establish himself at home in Central Asia stemmed from his failure to gather a sufficient support base amongst either of the two groups which could have ensured his power, the more urbanized Timurids or the still semi-nomadic Moghuls.[69] Even so, Babur's Uzbek rival, Shibani Khan, sought to strengthen his own connections to Timurid legitimacy, by marrying Babur's maternal aunt, two daughters of maternal step-uncles, and Babur's own sister, and arranged to have other members of his own family enter into similar marriages.[70] Later, when Babur took Kabul from the Arghuni clan, whom he saw as usurpers since they had captured the territory from Ulugh Beg's son ʿAbd al-Razzaq, they ceded the province to Babur 'by pact and agreement', suggesting they found it expedient to recognize his Timurid credentials.[71]

Once the Mughals were firmly established as rulers of India, the rest of the world found it expedient to recognize their Timurid pedigree as well. Shah ʿAbbas of Iran addresses Jahangir in official correspondence as 'him who sits upon the Gurgani throne and is the heir of the crown of Timur',[72] and at one point allowed a Mughal ambassador, Khan ʿAlam, to take away from Isfahan as a gift for the emperor, a rare painting of Timur and his sons and favoured generals battling against Tuqtamish Khan.[73]

Shah ʿAbbas later sent Shah Jahan a ruby inscribed with the names Timur, Shah Rukh, Ulugh Beg, Shah ʿAbbas (!), Akbar, Jahangir, and Shah Jahan.[74] Around 1640 Hasan Khan Shamlu, the Safavid governor of Herat, flustered by the proximity of the Mughal armies assembling at Kabul, wrote to Shah Jahan addressing him as the 'descendant of the family of pure wisdom' (*nata'ij-i-dudman-i-ʿaql-i-fahim*), the 'augmenter of the prestige of the Gurgan throne' (*kamal-afza-yi-takht-i-gurgani*), and 'Great Lord of the Auspicious Conjunction (*sahib-qiran-i-ᶜalikhagani*)'.[75]

Timurid princes and pretenders often claimed authority in the border regions, and the nature of Timurid prestige was such that such claims often gained local support. One example was a false Prince Husayn, son of Prince Shah Rukh, who sent a request to Jahangir for an army to help him retake Badakhshan from the Uzbeks. Jahangir rebuffed the request, since the Badakhshanis had already produced a number of Timurid pretenders each of whom the Uzbeks had succeeded in killing off.[76] Another pretender mentioned in the Mughal sources is a false Baysunghur, son of Prince Daniyal, one of Jahangir's brothers. This individual went to Balkh and presented himself to Nazr Muhammad, who received him well at first, but appears not to have offered actual support. The pretender next tried his luck in Iran at the court of Shah Safi, before proceeding to Baghdad and finally to Turkey where he was exposed as an impostor by the Mughal ambassador Waqqas Hajji.[77]

Legitimacy and Prestige Accorded to Uzbek Rulers

As true Chingisids, the Uzbek rulers enjoyed a claim to legitimacy which held to some extent throughout Muslim Asia. Within Central Asia itself they were the major force to be reckoned with for three and a half centuries, and a constant concern to neighbours on all sides including the Mughals, the Safavids, the Russian tsars, and the Ming Chinese. The *Tazkira-yi-Muqim Khani* portrays the Uzbeks as patrons and protectors of the Timurids during the Uzbek ascendancy in the fifteenth century. Shibani Khan's grandfather, Abu'l Khayr Sultan, who had taken Khwarazm from Timur's son Shah Rukh before he was even twenty years of age, is said to have become so famous and powerful that 'the great rulers of the world' came to seek his

assistance, 'such that, at the time of the conquest of Qara
Yusuf Turkmen's offspring, the descendants of Amir
Gurgan, Prince Abu Saʿid, Prince Manuchehr, Prince
Muhammad Chuki, and Prince Sultan Husayn took refuge
at his court and returned to their own states only with his
(Abu'l Khayr's) help'.[78]

Shah Jahan, striving to instil trust in Nazr Muhammad
while advancing on the latter's territory, refers to him in
his letters as 'the noblest of the dynasty of Chinghis Khan'.
(He also refers to the Balkh ruler as 'the brightest gem in
the crown of royalty', and 'the star of the constellation of
propriety'.)[79] The official Mughal chronicle of the time
likewise refers to the Uzbek as 'that descendant of Chinghis
Khan'.[80]

Subhan Quli Khan was arguably the last effective Uzbek
ruler of Central Asia. The *Tazkira-yi-Muqim Khani* boasts
that the power and prestige attributed to him was such that
he received simultaneous embassies from Turkey, Kashgar,
and Crimea.[81] However, while Subhan Quli was a frequent
correspondent with Aurangzeb and still a military threat to
the Turkic lands to the east, by the end of the seventeenth
century the Uzbek khanates despite their Chingisid lineage
were ceasing to be at the forefront of the thoughts even of
the Mughals, and had receded into obscurity in the minds
of most of the rest of the Islamic world. They remained,
perhaps, Chingisid legends mainly in their own minds. In
support of this interpretation, the early nineteenth century
Polish-Russian scholar, Joszef Senkowski, believes a
purported letter from Ahmet II cited in the *Tazkira-yi-
Muqim Khani* as proof of an Ottoman embassy is a forgery,
since it was written in a Central Asian dialect of Turkish
which the Ottomans would have considered beneath their
dignity to write.[82]

Mutual Perceptions

The Muslim inhabitants of Central Asia and those of
northern India in the sixteenth and seventeenth centuries
appear not to have thought of each other mainly as
foreigners or as subjects of another king. Rather, they
considered each other foremost as Muslims and secondarily
in terms of family connections or other loyalties which, as
has been seen, were spread out across their adjoining
territories.

Official chronicles attempt to mirror such perceptions.
Abu'l Fazl writes that, 'the mutual affection of neighbouring
nations, such as Persians, Turanians, Ottomans, and Indians
is too well-known to be described'.[83] Similarly, after
abolishing transit taxes in Kabul, Jahangir writes that he
has 'greatly benefited the people of Iran and Turan'.[84]
Although his motives can hardly have been entirely
altruistic, the emperor's statement at least reflects a sort of
ideal about how non-Arab Muslim peoples in Asia viewed
their interdependence.

The overriding perception of Central Asians towards
India appears to have been of its fabulous wealth. The
greatest evidence for the prevalence of this view is in the
number of Central Asians who travelled to India, either
permanently or temporarily, in search of financial
betterment. Even those Central Asians who never travelled
to India would have heard about it from those who did,
either through gossip or perhaps by reading travelogues
(safar-namas) such as those of Mutribi Samarqandi or
Mahmud b. Amir Wali. They also would have been aware
of the magnificent gifts brought to the Balkh and Bukhara
courts by Mughal ambassadors, sent by Indian Muslims to
friends and family in Central Asia, or bestowed on Central
Asian travellers and brought back home by them. Finally,
there existed in all major Central Asian towns successful
communities of Indian merchants, both Hindu and Muslim,
and, in the words of Muzaffar Alam, 'the fabulous wealth

and unmatched trading skill of the Indians often seem to have excited enough jealousy on the part of the local people to land them into trouble'.[85] However successful these Indian merchants may have been, they are said to have repeated a proverb: 'The pleasure that can be had in one's own courtyard cannot be had even in Balkh or Bukhara'.[86]

The Muslims of Mughal India, for their part, respected Central Asia primarily for its centres of religious learning, especially the seminaries at Bukhara, where some Indian Muslims went to study.[87] Central Asia, and Bukhara in particular with its many *madrasa*s, had long enjoyed a prestigious reputation in the realm of Islamic education. This reputation rested substantially on Bukharan-produced orthodox texts such as those of Taftazani (fourteenth c.), which were included in curricula throughout the Islamic world.

Rulers' Views of Their Mutual Relationship

In general terms, the prevailing theme in diplomatic correspondence is friendship between the corresponding parties. In this the Mughal and Uzbek rulers were no exception. The theme was enriched by the special historical ties between the two Central Asian groups. Rulers on both sides didn't fail to make mention of this in their communications, and official chronicles generally paint a rosy picture of love, understanding, co-operation, and mutual support between the two entities. The alleged purpose of ᶜAbdullah Khan's letters to Akbar, for example, is 'to recall ancient relations and renew friendship'.[88] Actually ᶜAbdullah Khan was attempting to explain why he had invaded and taken Badakhshsan from the Mughals. The *Tabaqat-i-Akbari* states that ᶜAbdullah Khan was 'always shaking the chain of friendship and alliance', and quotes from a letter Akbar sent the Uzbek ruler which ends with the couplet, 'While we each with the other are in amity/ Both land and sea from tumult and disturbance are free'.[89]

The *Tazkira-yi-Muqim Khani* claims that Imam Quli Khan was 'always friendly' towards the Mughals, glossing over the fact that he had broken off relations with them for several years because of a perceived insult by Jahangir. Jahangir had been frivolous with Imam Quli's envoy, asking after the Uzbek ruler's love life, meaning young boys. When the envoy replied, 'Our khan is free from worldly attachments, and never are his thoughts engaged in worldly things', Jahangir quipped, 'And what has your khan seen of the world, that he holds no more inclinations towards it?'[90] Imam Quli, on hearing this, kept a Mughal delegation waiting in Bukhara for months without receiving them, and finally took their gifts and gave them away except for a sword of Akbar. In the *Silsilat al-salatin*, written thirty years after the *Tazkira-yi-Muqim Khani*, the above mentioned remarks are attributed instead to Shah Jahan and Muhammad Sadiq, son of Imam Quli's ambassador Khwaja ʿAbd al-Rahim,[91] but the earlier account is more plausible. In any event no one could afford to brush off the Mughals for long. Even the Shibanids of Urganj in Khwarazm sent an embassy to Jahangir in order to 'shake the chain of hereditary connections'.[92]

The Mughals' sense of superiority over their Uzbek rivals to the north-west is clear, however. The official illusion hinted at in the Mughal chronicles is that the Mughals were still somehow the true and legitimate masters of Central Asia but were content to let the Uzbeks 'housesit' for them there as long as order was maintained. The *Shah Jahan-nama* calls Nazr Muhammad's march on Kabul following Jahangir's death 'rebellious', a term which implies Mughal suzerainty. Thus the invasion of 1646 was portrayed by the Mughal sources simply as a 'peacekeeping mission'.[93] But it is not difficult to see a very different picture between the lines, and throughout the sources' fear of the Mughals comes through far more profoundly than any talk of friendship. Specifically, the Uzbeks never forgot that the Mughals had come from Central Asia and dreamed of returning there as conquerors. Referring to Humayun, Abu'l Fazl writes that 'the dread residence of His Majesty in Badakhshan wrought dismay in all Turan'.[94] Further on he claims that ʿAbdullah Khan's motives in soliciting Akbar's friendship were, in addition to securing help against internal rivals, 'that he might repose in peace and be without apprehension of the world-conquering armies'.[95]

The Uzbek sources confirm the insecurity felt towards the Mughals. The *Tazkira-yi-Muqim Khani*, for example, states matter-of-factly that, 'it was known in Bukhara that Jahangir intended to invade Badakhshan'.[96] This concern, which Jahangir cannot truly be said to have warranted, was multiplied on the accession of the more assiduous Shah Jahan. Once the succession was clearly established, Nazr Muhammad sent an embassy led by Waqqas Hajji 'to apologize for his improper conduct' in attacking Kabul after Jahangir's death.[97] When Shah Jahan arrived at Kabul in 1639, supposedly to subdue the restive Hazara hill tribes, a nervous Nazr Muhammad immediately dispatched an embassy to meet him.[98] Soon afterwards he sent another embassy from Balkh, as did his brother Imam Quli from Bukhara.[99]

The Safavid governor of Herat, Hasan Khan Shamlu, was also unsettled by the proximity of the Mughal army at Kabul and sent a number of letters to high-ranking Mughal officials, such as Asaf Khan, making 'anxious inquiries' regarding their plans. Hasan hopes the Mughal intentions are to recover their 'ancestral burial grounds' (*gurkhana-i-mawruthi*), and promises Safavid troop support from the Khorasan regiments under his command.[100] He appears to have received a reassuring response, that indeed Shah Jahan's presence in Kabul signalled only his intent to recover the 'burial grounds of the great ancestors' (*gurkhana-yi-ajdad-i-ʿizam*).[101]

It was during the invasion and occupation of Balkh that the Uzbeks first encountered and acquired respect for Shah Jahan's fourth son Aurangzeb, who was sent to replace his elder brother Murad Bakhsh as field commander after the initial success of the expedition. The *Ma'athir-i-ᶜAlamgiri*, an official chronicle of the early part of Aurangzeb's reign, describes how the devout prince astonished his Uzbek foes on the field of battle by stepping down from his horse in the midst of the fray in order to perform the *zuhr* (noon) prayer. This act is said to have made ᶜAbd al-ᶜAziz give up the fight, on the grounds that 'to quarrel with such a man is to ruin one's self'.[102] This impression, if not the incident itself, is independently confirmed by the French traveller Bernier, who learns of it from the ambassadors Subhan Quli sent to ᶜAlamgir's court in 1661-2, following the latter's victory in the 1659 war of succession.[103]

Turkishness

The fact that by ethnological criteria, both Mughals and Uzbeks can be considered as Turks, highlights the need for precision and specificity in defining and applying ethnic terms. For purposes of historical discussion it would be preferable to concentrate on the usage of the sources—if only the sources were precise and specific themselves. In actuality they use the term 'Turk' in two senses. In one, an ethnic sense, the word applies to a group which is neither Mughal nor Tajik (Persian-speaking). The second, social sense, distinguishes a group which are not city-dwellers.[104]

These distinctions are confused by related genealogies and complicated by intermarriages, as the case of Babur and Shibani Khan vividly illustrates; the two arch-rivals were actually bound by a number of marriage ties.[105] The early sixteenth century *Tarikh-i-Rashidi* distinguishes between the Uzbeks, the Chaghatays, and the Mughals in a political sense; that is, as tribes in conflict: '...of the four great tribes,

three—namely, the Uzbeg, the Chaghatai, and the
Moghuls—had always been at variance...'.[106] Babur's
definitions, meanwhile, appear to be more of the social
type. In his memoirs, he applies the term 'Turk' to
herdsmen and shepherds, in opposition to the term Sart
which he uses for settled peoples (*Eli, agarçi sart u dih-
nishin dür, vali atrak dek gala-u ramaligh ellär dür,* ʿAbd al-
Rahim Khan-i-khanan translates both *Sart* and *dih-nishin*
into his Persian text as *Tajik*).[107] Babur also uses the same
terms as linguistic designations, when he proposes at a
banquet that, 'anyone who sang a song in Persian (*sartça*)
would be allowed to drink a goblet of wine... . Then it was
proposed that anyone who sang a song in Turkish (*türkiça*)
would be allowed to drink a goblet'.[108]

As has been stated earlier, both Chaghatays and Uzbeks
served the Mughals, particularly in the traditional Turkic
domain of military service. Twenty-seven of the fifty-one
nobles accompanying Humayun on his return to India in
1555 were either Chaghatay or Uzbek Central Asians, and
by 1580 Central Asian nobles still slightly outnumbered
Persians at forty-eight to forty-seven. In Shah Jahan's time
(1647-8) the balance, though tipped, was still fairly close,
with 23.3 per cent of the officials ranking above 500 being
Central Asian as opposed to 28.4 per cent Iranian.[109] Quite
a few of the military men included in the *Ma'athir al-'umara'*
are classified as Uzbeks: Abd al-Rahim Beg (i, p. 48),
Abdullah Khan (i, p. 82), Allah Quli Khan (i, p. 208),
Bahadur Khan (i, p. 351), Iskandar Khan (i, p. 691), Qazaq
Khan Baqi Beg (ii, p. 523), Ibrahim Khan (ii, p. 659), Shadi
Khan (ii, p. 727), Shah Beg (ii, p. 743), and Shamshir
Khan Arslan Biy (ii, p. 798).

The sources include many references, both positive and
negative, to the Chaghatays and the Uzbeks as specific
groups. At Akbar's coronation the officers and grandees of
Chaghatay lineage received special marks of attention.[110]
Jahangir in his memoirs calls Mir ʿAli b. Feridun Khan
Barlas, 'one of the trusted *amirzadas*' of the Timurid clan.[111]

(*Amirzada* would refer to a descendent of Timur, who titled himself *amir*. 'Barlas' was the name of the tribe to which Timur belonged, and was therefore a prestigious surname to have in Mughal India.) In addition to Feridun Khan (i, p. 527), the *Ma'athir al-'umara'* has entries for several other commanders of the Barlas clan, including Muhammad Quli Khan (ii, p. 183) and Tarbiyat Khan (ii, p. 926).

Timur's legacy carried sufficient weight in India two centuries after his brief conquest that the inhabitants of Pakli claimed descent from the Qarlughs he left there, although Jahangir dismisses them as 'pure Lahauris'.[112] Even at the tail end of Aurangzeb's reign a century later, the term 'Chaghatay' was bestowed upon favourites of the Emperor as a designation of honour.[113] The *Ma'athir al-'umara'* has entries for Sacid Khan Chaghatai (ii, p. 679) and Sarfaraz Khan Chaghatay (ii, p. 714), among others.

Not surprisingly, the Central Asian sources do not always give the Chaghatay designation such positive associations. The *Shajarah-i-türk* attributes Burke Sultan's loss of Samarqand in the mid-fifteenth century to the defection of Chaghatays in his army to Abu Sacid, despite the fact that their leader, Muhammad Chuki Mirza, 'recognized the justice of Burka's opinion'. (The army had been made up of 'Chaghatays and Uzbeks'.)[114] Even the Eastern Mughal Haydar Mirza, a relative and supporter of Babur and Humayun, states that at the time of Babur's birth 'the Chaghatai were very rude and uncultured, and not refined as they are now'. He claims they couldn't pronounce the future emperor's proper Muslim name, and so called him 'Babur' ('the tiger') instead.[115] For Abu'l-Ghazi, the author of *Shajarah-i-türk*, the Mughals were too far removed to mention, except for one vague passing reference to a Persian who had gone 'to fight the Chaghatais'.[116]

Timur was not actually a blood descendant of Chingis Khan, which is why even despite his nearly equalling the Mongol's conquests he never dared to take for himself the supreme Mongolian title of *khagan*, but called himself

simply *amir*, or 'commander'.[117] The Uzbek rulers, however,
unlike the Mughals, were true Chingisids, and thus looked
down upon the ancestry of the Timurids.[118] Yet, according
to Timur Beisembiev:

> The rule of the Shaybanids and Ashtarkhanids in Central Asia
> were [sic] regarded in Moghul India as a crying injustice and
> abuse of the Chingizid tradition, since both Shaybanids and
> Ashtarkhanids, although Chingizids, were descended from
> Juchi, the elder son of Chingiz Khan, and therefore had not
> any right on the ulus of his middle son Chaghatay.[119]

Even so, Shibani Khan did not consider himself an
Uzbek, a fact which highlights the difference between
historical and modern usage of the term. His official
chronicle, the *Shibani-nama*, has him say, 'Let the Chaghatai
not call me an Uzbek', which suggests 'that he had already
risen above his nomadic counterparts'.[120] In fact he was
not an 'Uzbek' in the usage of the time; he was a Chingisid.
Furthermore, as the inheritor of the high court culture of
the Timurid Sultan Husain's Herat, Shibani Khan had
pretensions of being a highly cultivated man himself.[121]

On the positive side, by Islamic standards, Uzbeks were
known throughout the Muslim world for their piety and
orthodoxy. A modern 'Uzbek' apologist, Edward Allworth,
somewhat improbably cites this as a major cause in the
Safavid-Uzbek conflict, claiming (on the basis of no cited
source) that Shah Ismaᶜil's pederasty 'greatly angered the
pious Uzbek [Shibani] Khan'.[122] According to the *Tazkira-
yi-Muqim Khani* ᶜUbaydullah Khan arrived one day late for
the Battle of Marv in 1510 where his predecessor lost his
life, but dutifully recited prayers over Shibani's corpse. (If
so it would have been an incomplete corpse, since Shibani's
head had been sent off to Ismaᶜil who, following an ancient
Turko-Mongol custom, had it fashioned into a drinking
cup.) ᶜUbaydullah is said to have spent most of his time in
pious activities, to have loved conversing with theologians,

composed several treatises on Islam, and to have been just and brave into the bargain.[123] Haydar Dughlat agrees that ᶜUbaydullah was 'a true Musulman, religiously inclined, pious and abstinent', as well as a calligrapher and a musician.[124] ᶜAbdullah Khan wrote to Akbar reprimanding him for veering off the straight path of Islam,[125] and even the Uzbek nobles in Akbar's service are said to have been constantly infuriated by his heterodox practices.[126] Of the Ashtarkhanid ruler Imam Quli Khan, the *Tazkira-yi-Muqim Khani* says he was 'just, disinterested, active, pious, and divided the day between administrative affairs and domestic virtues'.[127]

The Uzbeks, with nomadic detachment, also prided themselves on the simplicity of their tastes. Receiving an embroidered tent and other expensive gifts from Jahangir, Imam Quli Khan, 'who hated luxury', gave it all away to an attendant while the Mughal ambassador looked on.[128] The Uzbek chronicle claims, moreover, that he treated all who came to him with generosity, while 'retaining the utmost simplicity in his own home, habits, and customs'. Imam Quli is said to have kept only two horses in his royal stables, although in wartime 'his subjects gladly provided any mount he needed'.[129] The explanation given for Nazr Muhammad's inability to hold Bukhara is that the local inhabitants, 'accustomed to Imam Quli's economic simplicity, were revolted by Nazr Muhammad's ruinous innovations'.[130]

As the inheritors of the Mongol tradition, Uzbeks thought of themselves as superior horsemen and archers. The Venetian Niccolao Manucci attests to the validity of this characterization, calling the Uzbeks 'active horsemen and dextrous archers, their bows and arrows being large and powerful'.[131] A delegation sent by Subhan Quli Khan to Aurangzeb even boasted to the Frenchman Bernier that their womenfolk were like Amazon warriors. They claimed that during the Mughal occupation of Balkh, an Uzbek girl had single-handedly decimated a Mughal contingent which had plundered her village. Bernier, like Manucci, notes that Uzbek bows and arrows were much larger than the Indian articles. The said delegation brought with them some of these Amazon women to sell as slaves in India.[132] Manucci praises these Uzbek women for their skill with arrow, lance, and sword, and says they were valued as guards when the king was within his harem.[133]

It has been noted that the steppe tradition of clan politics implied a more decentralized pattern of authority than was found in the Mughal imperial system. This led to problems between the Mughal rulers and their Central Asian, often Uzbek, military commanders, who also felt a certain amount of friction on religious grounds with the Persian Shi'as who vied for power at court and were more used to accepting an unchallenged emperor 'in the Persian imperial tradition'.[134] Akbar's attempt to recall a senior Uzbek officer in Oudh touched off a unified Uzbek rebellion in 1565.[135]

In fact it appears that while the Mughals valued transplanted Uzbeks for their military excellence, they never really trusted them, and in the final balance the portrayal of Uzbek character in the Mughal sources is overwhelmingly bad. The Mughal sympathizer Haydar Dughlat calls them 'that abominable race', saying they are tyrannical and cruel.[136] Babur, citing Shibani Khan's outrageous behaviour on taking Herat (robbing holy men, 'correcting' the paintings of the master Bihzad with his own hand, and so on), points out that showing ritual piety doesn't mean one isn't still a heathen.[137] Shah Nawaz Khan, writing in the eighteenth century, states that 'Turk-like ignorance' (shararat-i-turkana) is innate, and that such people 'call bigotry and obstinacy the defending of the Faith'.[138]

The Uzbeks' 'egalitarian' inclinations often translated into simple anarchy, as individual military leaders refused to submit to authority and attempted to set up their own independent mini-domains. In the words of Abu'l Fazl, 'the wicked spirits of Transoxiana (*jina'ith-i-Ma wara' an-nahr*) in the darkness of their heart have no respect for glory or majesty'.[139] According to the *Tazkira-i-Muqim Khani*, the efforts of Balkh governor Mahmud Biy Ataliq to ensure justice and public order within his jurisdiction 'displeased the Uzbeks, always turbulent and accustomed to impunity in their violations'.[140] Whether one sees in Uzbek politics an unmitigated lawlessness or a romantic individualism, the destabilizing effects on Central Asia are undeniable. During the one hundred and eighty year period from 1526 to 1707, six Mughal emperors ruled northern India (not counting the interlude of Afghan Suri control), while throughout the same period Central Asia was ruled by no less than nineteen khans, who were often at war either with one another or with their own generals.

The early eighteenth century Central Asian historian Qipchaq Khan complains of the corruption and instability of Uzbek rule, stating that because of looting and disorder in the Uzbek lands 'the Sayyids, the Turks, and the Tajiks are coming over to Hindustan in large numbers'. He goes on to quip that 'it will take a thousand years to recount all the misdeeds of the Uzbeks'.[141] Qipchaq Khan[142] refers to the Uzbeks as 'unenlightened', (f.116b), 'blood-drinking' (f.114b), and says it was 'in their nature' to destroy property (f.113b). Another early eighteenth century history by a Central Asian living in India, the *Silsilat al-salatin*, echoes the theme of endemic official corruption, and condemns Nazr Muhammad Khan for allowing irregularities in the collection of taxes and in the forging of documents.[143]

The Mughal sources, equally harsh, state the Uzbeks' nature to be 'essentially compounded of treachery'.[144] They are shameless[145] and cowardly, plundering and pillaging when they can and then running away,[146] so that 'even the wind cannot overtake the dust raised by an Uzbek in his headlong flight'.[147] During the Balkh invasion of 1646, Nazr Muhammad fled rather than meet the Mughal armies he had ostensibly called to his aid.[148] Following Aurangzeb's success in eliminating his brothers for succession to the Mughal throne in 1659, Bernier states that 'the Tatars of *Usbec* eagerly dispatched ambassadors, out of fear of punishment, or expectation of advantage', since 'with their inbred avarice and sordidness they had been guilty of treachery when Aurangzeb was on the point of capturing *Balk*'. (Bernier betrays here a somewhat muddled understanding of the Balkh expedition.)[149] The Venetian Niccolao Manucci, who spent much of his life in India and served Aurangzeb as a physician and military adviser, concurs with this assessment. As he puts the matter, the Uzbeks had been so impressed by Aurangzeb's bravery during the Balkh campaign, that Subhan Quli 'dreaded that, having now become king, with so much wealth and so many valiant and victorious soldiers, he might take the route of Balkh, and renew the former wars'.[150]

Mughals thought of the Uzbeks as 'simple-minded' *(sada-lawhi)*,[151] although not necessarily beyond hope of redemption. Babur writes to his son Prince Kamran, 'The people of Transoxiana are simple, but when they have brains they are worthy of trust and office'.[152] Jahangir calls Arslan Biy 'a simple Uzbek (*Uzbak-i-sada-yi-pur-karist*)...fit to be educated and honoured'.[153]

A verse quoted by prince Aurangzeb highlights another interesting aspect of 'turkishness', associating it with idle boasting. While the old Persian literary convention was for using the term *turk* as a metaphor for youth and beauty, Aurangzeb gives it a new twist in reference to a turncoat officer who had once said, 'if I were to be commissioned, people would see what turkishness (*turkiyyat*) can do', to which Aurangzeb replies that it is one thing to boast but another to make it good, and quotes the verse: *Digar ba khud manaz/ ki turki tamam shud* ('enough of praising yourself; your *turki* is at an end').[154] Perhaps what was implied in the original verse is that youth has a tendency toward boastfulness, but Aurangzeb seems to be making a play which associates the trait with Turks.

Although pederasty was known and often accepted throughout the Muslim world, there appears to have been a stereotype among some Mughals associating the practice with Uzbeks. Abu'l Fazl and Bada'uni show rare concord in condemning the Shibanid Khan Zaman (ᶜAli Quli Khan) for his affair with the son of a camel-driver, behaviour which Bada'uni refers to as 'following the manners of Transoxiana'.[155] Emperor Jahangir's penchant for baiting Central Asians about their homosexual affairs will be mentioned again in Chapter Six.

Two Europeans present at the Mughal court during the Uzbek embassy of 1662 have left very unflattering accounts of how the ambassadors' behaviour was perceived there. To the Frenchman François Bernier, one shared meal was sufficient to convince him that the Uzbeks were an unsalvageable race: 'I found them ignorant beyond all conception...not a word was uttered during dinner (the meal consisted only of horseflesh); my elegant hosts were fully employed in cramming their mouths with as much *pelau* as they could contain; for with the use of spoons these people were unacquainted.'[156] Manucci had occasion to dine with Subhan Quli's ambassadors as well, having been asked to treat one of the party who was ailing. 'It was disgusting to see how these Uzbak nobles ate,' he says, 'smearing their hands, lips and faces with grease while eating'. His conclusion was that among the Uzbeks, 'he is most lovely who is most greasy'. Manucci adds that the ambassadors complained continuously of the lack of fat in the Indian diet and that Indian pilaf didn't contain enough butter.[157]

Bernier felt the Uzbeks' worst fault was their lack of cleanliness. He mentions that during the embassy's four-month stay at Delhi most of the retinue sickened and some died, either from the heat 'or from the filthiness of their persons, and the insufficiency of their diet'.[158] Manucci, with his medical pretensions, is more precise. Citing the Uzbeks' avarice in pocketing the living stipends given them by Aurangzeb, he says they ate sick horses and camels to save money.[159] Bernier goes on to say that 'There are probably no people more narrow-minded, sordid, or uncleanly than the Usbec Tartars', citing their hoarding of their expense money and living 'in a style quite unsuitable to their station [as ambassadors]'.[160] Manucci states that on their departure from India, the Uzbek emissaries were offered a parting gift of *pan* by the Mughal *wazir* Ja‘far Khan. The Uzbeks, he says, helped themselves not only to the *pan* but to the gold box it was offered in as well, causing the remaining Mughal dignitaries to make their offerings in cheaper containers.[161]

One cannot easily dismiss the words of Bernier and Manucci regarding Uzbek behaviour as being Euro-centric, since they nowhere make such vituperous comments about the Mughal customs which would have been to them just as foreign. Manucci was adaptable enough to live for many years in India, yet when the Uzbeks invited him to return with them to Central Asia, his avowed desire to see that part of the world was quashed by his disgust at the Uzbek ambassadors' habits.[162]

Nevertheless, we have in all this derogatory talk a clear case of cultural bias, working in both directions. The Mughals considered themselves to have risen above their origins, and attained the heights of civilization. The Uzbeks, meanwhile, proudly continued to embody those very same origins. To an extent they can be said to have represented the survival of the steppe ethic which René Grousset romanticizes in *The Empire of the Steppes*, where he likens the nomadic peoples to hungry wolves on the prowl, raiding the oases as if they were chicken coops.[163] In the end, whether one sides with the wolf or with the chickens is no more than a matter of personal sympathies.

The contest for the inheritance of Timurid glory is a rare case in history, where both sides can be considered the winners. The Uzbeks could count themselves as the possessors of the former Timurid heartlands, including

Timur's capital, Samarqand. The Mughals of India, on the other hand, were by the end of the sixteenth century, ruling over the wealthiest empire in the world.

NOTES

1. Murtaza Bilgrami, *Hadiqat al-aqalim*, Lucknow, 1879, p. 450; cited in Timur Beisembiev, 'Chinghiz Khan's Law in Eurasia and its Impact on Sarmatism in the Commonwealth of Poland and Lithuania', *Labyrinth* 2/1 (1995), p. 36.

2. Beveridge, *Babur-nama*, p. 320.

3. Semënov, "Kul'turno-politicheskhikh sviaziakh", p. 8. See for example Hafiz Tanish, *Sharaf-nama-yi-shahi*, Russian tr. M.A. Salahetdinova, 2 vols., Moscow, 1981-89, ii, p. 133 (MS f.176b); and Muhammad Yusuf b. Khwaja Baqa, *Tarikh-yi-Muqim Khani* (*Mukimkhanskaya Istoriia*), Russian tr. A.A. Semënov, Tashkent, 1956, pp. 98-101.

4. ʿAbd al-Rahman Tali, *Istoriia Abulfeiz-khana*, tr. A.A. Semënov, Tashkent 1959, p. 44 (MS f.42a-b).

5. Ibid., p. 46 (f.95a-b).

6. Muhammad Hadi Kamwarkhan, *Tazkira al-salatin-i Chaghata*, ed. Muzaffar Alam, New Delhi, 1980.

7. Bernier, *Travels*, p. 48.

8. On the Mughal decline in the eighteenth century see Muzaffar Alam, *The Crisis of Empire in Mughal North India*, Oxford University Press, Oxford, 1986.

9. R.D. McChesney, *Waqf in Central Asia*, Princeton University Press, Princeton, 1991, pp. 49-50.

10. Idem, 'Central Asia in the 16th-18th Centuries', *Encyclopaedia Iranica*, v. 5, fasc. 2 (1991), p. 176.

11. Idem, 'The Amirs of Muslim Central Asia in the 17th Century', *Journal of the Economic and Social History of the Orient* 26/1 (1980), p. 51.

12. Audrey Burton, 'Who Were the First Ashtarkhanid Rulers of Bukhara?' *Bulletin of the School of Oriental and African Studies* 51 (1988), p. 482.

13. R.D. McChesney, 'The "Reforms" of Baqi Muhammad Khan', *Central Asiatic Journal* 24/1 (1980), p. 70.

14. For a detailed political history of the Shibanid/Abulkhayrid and Ashtarkhanid/Toqay-Timurid dynasties, see McChesney, *EIr*.

15. Timur's unique ability to maintain central authority, and its apparently inevitable dissolution following his demise, are discussed in Beatrice Forbes Manz's, *The Rise and Rule of Tamerlane,* Cambridge University Press, Cambridge, 1993.

16. *BN,* 477.

17. Shah Isma'il even set up Babur on the throne of Samarqand after extracting a reluctant conversion to Shi'ism which, though superficial and temporary, was enough to alienate the population against Babur and cause his expulsion after a few months.

18. For an analysis of the complexities surrounding the first three years of Ashtarkhanid rule, see Burton, 'Ashtarkhanid Rulers'.

19. For a response to accusations that Nazr Muhammad forced Imam Quli's abdication, see Audrey Burton, 'Nazir Muhammad Khan Ruler of Bukhara (1641-5) and Balkh (1645-51)' *Central Asiatic Journal* 23/1-2 (1988).

20. Muhammad Yusuf b. Khwaja Baqa, *Supplément à l'histoire générale des Huns, des Turks et des Mogols (Tazkira-i-Muqim Khani),* French tr. Joszef Senkowski, St. Petersburg, 1824, p. 44.

21. Dale, *Indian Merchants,* p. 21.

22. Ibid., p. 30.

23. See Morris Rossabi, 'The "Decline" of Central Asian Caravan Trade', in *The Rise of the Merchant Empires,* ed. J.D. Tracy, Cambridge, 1990. Jos J.L. Gommans outlines recent objections to the traditional view of 'crisis' in overland trade in *The Rise of the Indo-Afghan Empire,* E.J. Brill, Leiden, 1994, pp. 1-8.

24. Muzaffar Alam, 'Trade, State Policy and Regional Change: Aspects of Mughal-Uzbek Commercial Relations ca. 1550-1750', *Journal of the Economic and Social History of the Orient* 37 (1994), pp. 212, 214.

25. *BN,* pp. 475-6, and again on p. 480.

26. British Library MS. Or. 12988, ff.20b, 34b.

27. Minto album, Victoria and Albert Museum, London.

28. Reproduced in Anthony Welch, India, in *Treasures of Islam,* ed. Toby Falk, Secaucus NJ, 1985, p. 172.

29. *Padshah-nama,* Royal Library, Windsor Castle, ff. 2b and 3a; reproduced in Milo C. Beach and Ebba Koch, *King of the World: The Padshahnama, an Imperial Manuscript from the Royal Library, Windsor Castle,* Azimuth, London, 1997. The painting is discussed on pp. 159–60.

30. *AN,* i, p. 17 (text p. 6).

31. '*chiragh-i-bargah-i-daulat-i-timur-khani*', *AN,* ii, p. 452 (text p. 307).

32. *TJ,* i, p. 107.

33. Ibid., p. 109.

34. *SJN,* p. 2.

35. Akbar also is referred to as *Sahib-qiran*, in his funerary inscriptions (John Hoag, 'The Tomb of Ulugh Beg and Abdu Razzaq at Ghazni, a Model for the Taj Mahal', *Journal for the Society of Architectural Historians* 27/4 (1968), p. 246). In fact this title gained general currency in the post-Timurid period. Akbar's Shibanid rival, ʿAbdullah Khan, for example, is also called *Sahib-qiran* by his court historian Hafiz Tanish (*SNS*, ff.9a, 65a, 66a, 97a, 99a, 111a, 151a, 195a, 215a, and elsewhere).

36. '*musahiban-i-maʿnawi*', *AN*, i, pp. 309-10 (text p. 136).

37. Ibid., pp. 612-3 (text p. 335).

38. Ibid., pp. 79 (text p. 25).

39. '*an chahra afruz-i -iqbal*', *AN*, iii, p. 314 (text p. 223).

40. *AN*, i, p. 200 (text p. 75).

41. *AN*, ii, p. 69 (text p. 44).

42. ʿAbd al-Qadir Bada'uni, *Muntakhab al-Tawarikh*, ed. W.N. Lees and Ahmad cAli, 3 vols., Calcutta, 1865-8; tr. G.A. Ranking (v. 1), W.H. Lowe (v. 2), W. Haig (v. 3), Calcutta, 1884-1927 (reprint Delhi, 1986), ii, p. 220 (text p. 216).

43. Ebadollah Bahari, *Bihzad, Master of Persian Painting*, I.B. Tauris, London, 1996, p. 68.

44. Bernier, *Travels*, p. 167. Timur is purported to have told the defeated Ottoman, 'What can there be within the circle of a crown which ought to inspire kings with inordinate self-esteem, since Heaven bestows the bauble on such ill-fated mortals?'

45. Ibid., p. 168.

46. Gulbadan Begum, *Humayun-nama*, copied and translated by Annette Beveridge, Royal Asiatic Society, London, 1902, (reprint Lahore, 1987) p. 24.

47. J.A. Boyle, *The Successors of Genghis Khan*, Columbia University Press, New York, 1971, p. 167.

48. '*chand tura ki dar mulazimat-i-hazrat-i-padshah nishasta-and*' (*HN*, p. 187 (f. 72a)).

49. Ibid., p. 197 (f. 78b).

50. Ibid.

51. *AN*, i, p. 536 (text p. 281).

52. *MT*, ii, pp. 59-60 (text p. 61).

53. '*muwafiq-i-tura-yi-chingizi wa qanun-i-timuri*' (*Jahangir-nama* (*Tuzuk-i-Jahangiri*), ed. Muhammad Hashim, Tehran, 1980, p. 44; *TJ*, i, p. 76).

54. '*ba rasm wa tura-yi-Chingiz Khani*' (*TJ*, i, p. 68; *JN*, p. 40).

55. Mansura Haidar, 'The Yasi Changezi (Tura) in the Medieval Indian Sources', in *Mongolia—Culture, Economy and Politics*, eds. R.C. Verma et al., New Delhi, 1992, pp. 53-66.

56. Cited in Richards, *Mughal Empire*, p. 42.

57. *The Agrarian System of Moslem India*, Cambridge, 1929; M.T. Awan, *History of India and Pakistan*, v. 2, Great Mughals, Lahore, 1994, pp. 527-8.
58. Awan, *History*, p. 671; cf. Khwandamir, *Habib al-siyar*, tr. W.M. Thackston, Jr., 2 vols., Cambridge MA, 1994, i, p. 8.
59. *TJ*, i, p. 23.
60. Shah Nawaz Khan and ʿAbd al-Hayy, *Ma'athir al-'umara'*, 2 vols., tr. H. Beveridge, rev. Baini Prasad, Calcutta, 1941-52.
61. *AA*, i, p. 364. See Gerhard Doerfer, *Turkische und mongolische Elemente in Neupersischen*, 4 vols., Wiesbaden, 1963-75, ii, pp. 460-74 (no. 879).
62. See Doerfer, *TMEN*, no. 976.
63. *HN*, p. 95 (f.10b).
64. *ST*, p. 4.
65. F.W. Cleaves, tr., *The Secret History of the Mongols*, Cambridge MA, 1982, p. 37.
66. V.V. Bartol'd, 'Tseremonial pri dvore uzbetskikh khanov v XVII v.', in *Sochineniia*, v. 2, pt. 2, Moscow, 1964, p. 389.
67. Lisa Golombek, 'From Tamerlane to Taj Mahal', in, *Essays in Islamic Architecture*, ed. Abbas Daneshvari, Undena, Malibu, 1981, 43-5.
68. Hoag, 'Tomb', p. 246.
69. M.E. Subtelny, 'Babur's Rival Relations: A Study of Kinship and Conflict in 15th-16th Century Central Asia', *Der Islam* 66/1 (1989), p. 115.
70. Ibid., pp. 111-2.
71. *HN*, p. 86 (f.4a). Ulugh Beg was a grandson of Timur who ruled from Samarqand in the first half of the 15th century. He was known for his erudition in the arts and sciences, and constructed an astronomical observatory which is now one of Samarqand's major tourist attractions.
72. *TJ*, i, p. 195; *JN*, p. 112.
73. *TJ*, ii, p. 116; *JN*, p. 322.
74. *SJN*, p. 147.
75. Hasan Khan Shamlu, *The Shamlu Letters*, ed. Riazul Islam, Karachi, 1971, ff.76a, 77b, 80b.
76. *TJ*, i, pp. 118-20; *JN*, p. 68.
77. *SJN*, p. 191.
78. *TMK*, p. 48.
79. *SJN*, p. 347.
80. Ibid., p. 398.
81. *TMK*, p. 155.
82. Senkowski, *Supplément*, p. 57.
83. *AN*, iii, p. 419 (text p. 285).
84. *TJ*, i, p. 47; *JN*, p. 28.

85. Alam, 'Trade', p. 205.
86. S. Gopal, 'Indians in Central Asia in the 16th and 17th Centuries', *Proceedings of the 52nd Indian History Congress*, New Delhi, 1992, p. 229.
87. McChesney, *Waqf*, p. 110.
88. *AN*, ii, p. 534 (text p. 368).
89. *TA*, ii, pp. 522-3.
90. *TMK*, p. 90; Semënov, 'Kul'turno-politicheskikh sviaziakh, p. 10.
91. Mir Muhammad Salim, *Silsilat al-salatin*, MS Bodleian Or.269, f.193a.
92. *TJ*, ii, p. 165; *JN*, p. 352.
93. *SJN*, p. 23.
94. *AN*, i, p. 497 (text p. 255).
95. *AN*, ii, p. 534 (text p. 368).
96. *TMK*, p. 90; Semënov, 'Kul'turno-politicheskikh sviaziakh', p. 11.
97. *SJN*, p. 4.
98. Ibid., p. 257.
99. In 1640. Nazr Muhammad's ambassador was Salih Dastar Khwanchi, and Imam Quli's was Uzbek Khwaja (Ibid., p. 268).
100. Islam, *Shamlu Letters*, pp. 2, 25.
101. Ibid., p. 34.
102. *MA*, p. 317 (text p. 531).
103. Bernier, *Travels*, p. 116.
104. *TR*, p. 83. For a discussion of the Turk/Tajik relationship through history, see M.E. Subtelny, 'Turks and Tajiks', in *Central Asia in Historical Perspective*, ed. Beatrice Forbes Manz, Westview Press, Boulder CO, 1994, pp. 48-59.
105. See Subtelny, 'Rival Relations', pp. 102-18.
106. *TR*, p. 305.
107. *BN*, pp. 194-5.
108. *BN*, pp. 532-3.
109. Richards, *Mughal Empire*, pp. 19, 145.
110. *AN*, ii, p. 150 (text p. 99).
111. *TJ*, i, p. 350.
112. *TJ*, ii, p. 126.
113. *MA*, p. 308 (text p. 518).
114. *ST*, pp. 199-200.
115. *TR*, p. 173.
116. Ibid., p. 336.
117. In the seventeenth century the Mughals attempted to bring themselves closer to Chingis by claiming he shared an ancestor with Timur; this story was taken up again in the nineteenth century by the rulers of Kokand, who claimed descent from an 'abandoned' son of Babur (Beisembiev, 'Ferghana's Contacts', p. 130). Even

today claims are made that Timur was a Mongol, particularly by
Mongolians. Recently a Mongol diplomat in India, in a non-
scholarly piece of propaganda, suggested that the Mughal Empire
henceforth be referred to as 'the Mongol Empire' in India! (O.
Nyamdavaa, 'Who are the Mughuls?', in *Mongolia*, eds. R.C. Verma
et al., p. 88.

118. M.E. Subtelny, 'Art and Politics in Early 16th Century Central Asia',
     Central Asiatic Journal 27 (1983), p. 132.

119. Beisembiev, 'Chinghiz Khan's Laws', p. 36.

120. Subtelny, 'Art and Politics', p. 137.

121. See Annemarie Schimmel, 'Notes on the Cultural Activity of the
     First Uzbek Rulers', *Journal of the Pakistan Historical Society* 8/3,
     pp. 149-166.

122. Edward Allworth, *The Modern Uzbeks*, Hoover Union, Palo Alto, 1989,
     p. 69.

123. *TMK*, p. 54.

124. *TR*, p. 283.

125. Islam, *Calendar*, ii, p. 207.

126. Richards, *Mughal Empire*, p. 17.

127. *TMK*, p. 83.

128. Ibid., p. 89. It would also seem, however that this gesture was
     intended as a deliberate snub to the Mughals—Imam Quli was
     apparently still angry over Jahangir's remarks on his love life made
     years earlier.

129. Ibid., p. 83.

130. Ibid., p. 94.

131. Niccolao Manucci, *Storia do Mogor*, tr. William Erskine, 4 vols.,
     Calcutta, 1907 (reprint New Delhi, 1981), ii, p. 34.

132. Bernier, *Travels*, pp. 122-3.

133. Manucci, *Storia*, ii, p. 38.

134. Richards, *Mughal Empire*, p. 19.

135. Ibid., p. 17.

136. *TR*, p. 262. He appears to be referring to the Eastern 'Moghul'
     khans who rebelled against Babur; this only highlights the
     confusion surrounding group designations.

137. '*Agarçi saharxez edi, va besh vaqt namazini tark qilmas edi, qira'at cilmni
     tawri bilür edi, vala mundaq golana u ablahana u ustaxana u kafirana
     aqval u afcal andin bisyar sadir bolur edi*' (*BN*, p. 435).

138. *MU*, i, p. 566.

139. *AN*, ii, p. 105 (text p. 68).

140. Senkowski, *Supplément*, p. 58; cf. *TMK*, p. 158.

141. Islam, 'History of Central Asia', p. 16.

142. Qipchaq Khan, *Tarikh-i-Qipchaq-Khani*, MS Institute of Oriental
     Studies, Uzbekistan Academy of Sciences, no. 4468/II.

143. *SS*, f.211b.
144. *SJN*, p. 329, referring in this case to the Uzbeks attacking a retreating garrison.
145. *AN*, iii, p. 641 (text p. 429).
146. Ibid., pp. 668, 671 (text pp. 445, 447); also *SJN*, p. 24, which states that Nazr Muhammad killed and looted 'helpless people' near Kabul; he had very few salaried soldiers so that 'most of them were plunderers', but they gradually deserted him 'so he chose to flee instead'.
147. *SJN*, p. 328.
148. ʿAbd al-Hamid Lahawri, *Padshah-nama*, ed. Kabir al-din and ʿAbd al-Rahim, Calcutta, 1946, ii, pp. 573-6.
149. Bernier, *Travels*, pp. 116-7.
150. Manucci, *Storia*, ii, p. 32.
151. *AN*, ii, pp. 523, 568 (text pp. 360, 389); *TJ*, i, p. 27; *JN*, p. 16.
152. Islam, *Calendar*, i, p. 59.
153. *TJ*, i, p. 125; *JN*, p. 72.
154. *MA*, p. 213 (text p. 353).
155. '*ba rang-i-khabayith-i Ma wara an-nahr*' (*MT*, ii, p. 14 (text p. 21)).
156. Bernier, *Travels*, p. 121.
157. Manucci, *Storia*, ii, pp. 36-7.
158. Bernier, *Travels*, p. 120.
159. Manucci, *Storia*, ii, p. 35.
160. Bernier, *Travels*, p. 120.
161. Manucci, *Storia*, ii, p. 40.
162. Ibid., p. 37.
163. René Grousset, *The Empire of the Steppes*, Rutgers University Press, New Brunswick NJ, 1970, p. ix.

CHAPTER 3

DIPLOMATIC, MILITARY, AND COMMERCIAL CONNECTIONS

From the 1570s the Uzbek and Mughal-held lands were contiguous, following ʿAbdullah Khan's conquest of Balkh from his relatives and Akbar's of Badakhshan from his.[1] The following century produced many diplomatic exchanges between the two powers. For example, ʿAbdullah Khan sent embassies to India in 1572-3, 1577-8, and 1586.[2] An early eighteenth century Central Asian source, the *Silsilat al-salatin* (also known as the *Tawarikh-i-badiʿa*) describes embassies from Akbar to ʿAbdullah Khan in 1585-6 (ff. 128a-133b) and 1591-2 (ff.138b-143b), from Jahangir to Imam Quli Khan in 1611 (ff.189b-192b), from Shah Jahan to Imam Quli in 1628 (ff. 194a-196a) and to Nazr Muhammad in 1643 (ff.206a-209a), in 1645 (ff. 223b-224b), and in 1646 (ff. 259b-261a), from Nazr Muhammad to Shah Jahan in 1645 (f.223a), from Aurangzeb to Subhan Quli Khan in 1671 (f.305a), and from Subhan Quli to Aurangzeb in 1687 (ff.308a-312a). Meanwhile, a more or less continuous outflow of Central Asian manpower took up service in the Mughal Empire, where opportunites for advancement were seen as being greater.

The Mughal military was of course originally a Central Asian military, and from the start it included not only Chaghatays but also Uzbeks, even Shibanids.[3] One such figure is Khan-i-Zaman, whom the British historian H. Blochmann credits alongside Bayram Khan with restoring the Mughal Empire after Humayun's return to

India. Khan-i-Zaman's career in India was chequered; re-named ᶜAli Quli Khan by Akbar, he rebelled on three occasions, was disgraced for having an affair with the son of a camel-driver,[4] and was finally killed in battle by an elephant,[5] a scene depicted in an illustrated 1590 manuscript of the *Akbar-nama*.[6] Khan-i-Zaman's younger brother, Bahadur Khan Shibani, who had been the Uzbek governor of Mashhad, left for India after the death of ᶜAbd al-Amin and was appointed regent (*wakil*) in place of the disgraced Bayram Khan, although he is said by Abu'l Fazl to have been a figurehead controlled by Akbar's nurse Maham Anga, leading Abu'l Fazl to comment that 'Many a woman treads manfully wisdom's path'.[7] Bahadur Khan participated in his brother's rebellions and was eventually captured and killed on Akbar's orders.[8] Their uncle, Ibrahim Khan Shibani, served under both Humayun and Akbar.[9]

Despite the Uzbek-Chaghatay rivalry which had forced the latter into their Indian exile, being an Uzbek certainly did not preclude one from being entrusted by the Mughals with important tasks. Such was the case of Sikandar Beg who was sent by Akbar to put down a rebellion in Delhi.[10] In another example, ᶜAbdullah Khan Uzbek (not to be confused with the Turani ruler), who was an occasional rebel himself, was sent by Akbar to take over ᶜAli Quli Khan's Lucknow fief.[11] Abu'l Fazl once even says of the Uzbeks in Mughal service that 'their deeds and valour were such that the souls of [legendary Persian heroes] Rustam and Isfandiar sang their praises'.[12]

It is clear from this discussion that many Uzbeks would have had family or other connections already in place in India, which would have facilitated their transferral of allegiance. While there seems to have been much less movement in the other direction, towards Central Asia, defection to the Uzbeks was a common threat of Mughal rebels, especially around the border areas.

Diplomatic Exchanges

A recurrent theme in Uzbek-Mughal relations is the call of the Uzbeks, who were engaged in an ongoing struggle for Khurasan, for their powerful Mughal neighbours to unite with them against the Safavid 'heretics'. Occasionally the distant Ottomans even extended the same plea, as in a letter brought via the embassy of Salim Shah (a.k.a. Shah Salih) in 1590. Salim spent three years making the return journey via Central Asia. Attempting to return to Turkey via the Caspian route, he was attacked and robbed en route by the Khwarazmian Uzbeks, which prompted ᶜAbdullah Khan's second attack on Urganj in order to protect the northern caravan route circumventing Iran.[13]

The Safavids' obstruction of Sunni pilgrims on their way to Mecca from the Eastern Islamic lands was a major point of irritation with the Shiᶜa state. Sectarian arguments held little weight with the Mughals, however. Babur and Humayun had both succumbed to Shiᶜa 'apostasy' under Safavid coercion, however briefly, and either recognized their debt to the Safavids or were awed by their superiority. By Akbar's time the Mughals were no longer Iran's inferiors, yet that emperor rebuffed ᶜAbdullah Khan's invitations for a joint attack on Safavid lands, reprimanding the Uzbek for not respecting the Shah's purported connections to the family of the Prophet.[14] (From at least as early as the time of Ismaᶜil I, a bogus geneology made out the Safavids to be descended from Jaᶜfar, the sixth Shiᶜa Imam.)

Several decades later, in 1626, Imam Quli solicited the help of Jahangir, but negotiations with the Uzbek ambassador, ᶜAbd al-Rahim Juybari, were cut short by the Mughal emperor's death.[15] Shah Jahan, in his turn, felt it in his interests to keep Iran neutral while he planned his invasion of Central Asia. It was Aurangzeb who finally, in 1684, sent an embassy to Bukhara suggesting a united attack on the Shi^ca 'infidels', although the specific aim of this initiative was to regain Qandahar for the Mughals.[16]

In choosing ambassadors, the Uzbeks and the Mughals sought to impress each other each in their own way. It had long been a tradition in the Islamic world to employ religious figures as ambassadors, partly since this was thought to minimize the risk that royal recipients of bad news would be tempted to 'kill the messenger'. Central Asian rulers additionally played upon their region's reputation for orthodox scholarship and piety by sending religious figures, such as Naqshbandi shaykhs of the Juybari family which was very powerful in and around Bukhara.[17] The Mughals, for their part, tended to send emissaries of Central Asian origin, usually high-ranking officials who were sometimes promoted prior to their departure.[18] Mir Baraka of Bukhara, for example, was sent repeatedly to his native city as ambassador by both Jahangir and by Shah Jahan.[19] Waqqas Hajji, who had originally come to India as Nazr Muhammad's ambassador, was sent back to Central Asia as Mughal ambassador in 1633, in the company of another Central Asian, Tarbiyat Khan Fakhr al-din Ahmad Bakhshi, who had come to India in Jahangir's time.[20]

The job of these ambassadors often included conveying correspondence and gifts from important Mughals to religious leaders, friends and family members, or obtaining specific regional rarities. Some examples are Abu'l Fath Gilani's request that Hakim Humam obtain two copies of Sultan Husayn's book on pigeons for Akbar, one to be sent and the other to be brought personally,[21] and ^cAbd al-^cAziz Khan Naqshbandi's successful attempt to acquire for Jahangir tortoise-shell (*dandan-i-ablaq-i jawhar-dar*)[22] dagger hilts (supposedly containing an antidote to poison) by writing to Taj al-din Hasan and ^cAbd al-Rahim, two sons of Khwaja Kalan (Sa^cad) Juybari, whom Jahangir calls 'the leading holy men of the province of Transoxiana' (*muqtada-yi-wilayat-i Ma wara' an-nahr*). Taj al-din sent the Mughal emperor 'a perfect specimen'.[23] Jahangir's envoy, Mir

Baraka, likewise was given instructions 'to make every effort to procure mottled fish teeth, and to procure them from any possible quarter, and at any price'.[24]

This type of activity kept personal connections alive across the political boundary separating Mughal and Uzbek lands. It also helped to maintain a party in Central Asia sympathetic to the Mughals. Of course, this was in addition to the ambassadors' traditional task of obtaining intelligence, such as evidenced in a letter from Abu'l Fath Gilani to the Mughal envoy Hakim Humam at Bukhara in 1588, instructing him to spare no expense in entertaining friends of the Empire as more money was on the way. The same letter also states that Akbar's policy toward re-taking Badakhshan would be dependent on the envoy's reports.[25]

As late as Aurangzeb's reign, Central Asians in Mughal service were still being employed for diplomatic missions to the Uzbek rulers of Transoxiana and Balkh. Mulla Niyaz Kashgari, for example, who had served Subhan Quli in Balkh before moving to India, was sent by Aurangzeb as part of Zabardast Khan's embassy to Subhan Quli in 1687.[26]

Uzbeks Entering Mughal Service

The lure of India's proverbial riches and the Mughal reputation for generosity, together with the frequency of civil disorder within the appanage system, were the main factors enticing military and administrative personnel to give up their lives in Central Asia and relocate to the south. Of course the Mughal Empire was full of fortune-hunters and refugees of all origins, but the Mughals tended to receive defectors from their Uzbek and Safavid rivals with particularly open arms, and such figures often rose to great heights within the Mughal system.

Some of these Central Asians, unable to subordinate their traditional tribal notions of equality, developed inflated notions of their own power and rebelled, especially during the sixteenth century, while the empire was still in its building phase. But such rebels were usually forgiven, sometimes even after repeated offences.

One notable example is Tardi Beg Turkestani, Humayun's 'faithless companion' who, during the flight to Iran, refused the Emperor the loan of a horse and money and then defected to Humayun's brother Prince Askari. On the Mughal's return to power in India he came to beg forgiveness and was given charge of Mewat. Under Akbar he was made governor of Delhi and given a *mansab* (rank) of 5000 *zat* (infantry) before being murdered at the instigation of Bayram Khan.[27] The Shibanids Khan-i-Zaman (ʿAli Quli Khan) and his brother Bahadur Khan rebelled and were forgiven twice before finally losing their lives in a third attempt.[28] Nazr Biy, who had formerly been the Uzbek governor of Balkh, was given a *jagir* (land grant) in Handiah (located on the Narmada river, near or at present-day Nemawar), but soon rebelled in 1590 and was killed.[29] Nazr Biy came over to the Mughals with his three sons after a dispute with ʿAbdullah Khan.[30]

A number of individuals from powerful Central Asian sufi families took advantage of the Mughals' attachment to the Naqshbandi order, which dated from the late fifteenth century. Babur's father, ʿUmar Shaykh Mirza, was a disciple of Khwaja ʿUbaydullah Ahrar, several of whose descendants came to enter Mughal service in India. One was Sharaf al-din Samarqandi, who served Akbar but rebelled twice before losing his life in Bengal.[31] Another was ʿAbdullah Khan (not to be confused with his namesake who had come to India as part of Humayun's entourage, or with the Turani ruler), who had first gone to serve Sher Khwaja in the Deccan but later presented himself to Prince Salim (later Jahangir) at Lahore. In 1603 he came to Akbar's court and was given a *mansab* of 1,000 *zat* and the title Safdar Jang ('valiant in battle').[32] A later Ahrari immigrant, Sayf al-dawla (a.k.a. ʿAbd al-Samad), came to India in

Aurangzeb's time, and rose from a rank of 400 *zat* to 5000 *zat*/5000 *sawar* (cavalry) and became governor of Lahore.[33]

Despite the frequency of rebellions amongst Mughal administrators of Central Asian origin, double agents or re-defection to the Uzbeks were almost unheard of. The majority of Central Asian newcomers tended to become identified as 'Mughals' themselves, often enjoying benefits and lifestyles beyond their dreams.

Among those Central Asian immigrants who held high posts under the Mughals were ᶜAbd al-Baqi Turkestani, whom Akbar appointed *sadr* (prime minister).[34] Another was Abu'l-Biy, the former Uzbek governor of Mashhad under ᶜAbd al-Mu'min, who entered Akbar's service in 1603. Jahangir raised his rank to 1500 *zat* and sent him off to pursue the rebel prince Khusrau.[35] Arslan Biy, the Uzbek governor of Kahmard, handed over the province to the Mughals in 1608 and was made governor of Sihwan in Sindh. He was given the title Shamshir Khan, and eventually attained the rank of 3000 *zat*.[36] The inventor of Akbar's prostration ritual, the *sijda*, was a Central Asian by the name of Ghazi Khan Badakhshi, a former pupil of Shaykh Husayn of Khwarazm.[37]

Diplomats sent by the Uzbeks were occasionally enticed into Mughal service. Waqqas Hajji, who first came to India as ambassador of Nazr Muhammad in 1632, entered Shah Jahan's service and was given the *faujdari* (command of a regiment) of Kangra and the title Shah Quli Khan.[38] The *Ma'athir al-'umara'* states that, 'As he had seen the grandeur of India, and had become acquainted with the mode of administration there, his heart turned away from his native land.' He was eventually made governor of Kashmir, and attained a rank of 3000 *zat*/2000 *sawar*.[39]

The chronic unrest and instability which characterized Uzbek politics seems to have been a major reason for seeking employment in India. Following the 'disruptions' (*harj wa marj*) of 1611, for example, many Uzbek generals and soldiers, including such names as Husayn Biy, Pahlavan

Baba, Nawruz Biy Darman, and Bahram Biy, came to serve Jahangir and were rewarded with robes of honour, horses, cash, *mansabs*, and *jagirs*.[40] The Mughal invasion of Central Asia in 1646 triggered a number of important defections. One was that of ᶜAbdullah Beg Saray, grandson of Imam Quli's *ataliq* (tutor) Shakur Beg. He was sent along with his brother Muhammad Muhsin by his father Mansur Hajji, Nazr Muhammad's governor of Tirmiz, to pay tribute to Shah Jahan following the Mughal victory. ᶜAbdullah Beg later received the title Yakataz ('he who fights singly') Khan, and was killed during Prince Shuja's rebellion in 1658.[41]

In addition to such voluntary transfers of allegiance, according to the *Silsilat al-salatin*, during the Mughal occupation Shah Jahan sent 'a large group of scholars, theologians, and others' from Balkh to India where he granted them *soyurgals* (grants of land revenue—a Mongol tradition) in different parts of the empire.[42] The eighteenth century work also mentions the going over to the Mughals of two Ashtarkhanid tutors, Razzaqberdi Ataliq, who had served Nazr Muhammad,[43] and Hajji Bey Kushchi, who had been tutor to Wali Muhammad.[44]

Even Nazr Muhammad's sons Khusrau Sultan[45] and ᶜAbd al-Rahman[46] sought Mughal protection, as did Allah Quli, son of the powerful Uzbek commander and 'king-maker' Yalangtosh.[47] In Aurangzeb's time political refugees from Central Asia included Baltun Beg, who was given a rank of 600 *zat*,[48] and Mir Muhammad Amin, who was made a commander of 2000 *zat*.[49]

During the sixteenth and seventeenth centuries service under the Uzbek khans of Central Asia held considerably less promise than did a position in India, so it was a desperate Mughal indeed who threatened to join up with the enemy. Nevertheless, the occasion did arise. Disaffection generally resulted from resistance to Mughal absolutism, which Central Asian military men, with their more egalitarian traditions, often resented. The legacy of appanage politics lived on in fraternal rivalries, occasionally bitter, between Babur's descendants. Humayun lost his father's empire largely due to problems with his brothers, and Akbar had to put down a rebellion by his brother Muhammad Hakim during which the rebels boasted that the Turanis and Persians in Akbar's army would defect to them. Abu'l Fazl counters, however, 'that the fidelity of the Turanians and the Persians...is known to the whole world',[50] although he later mentions that some Badakhshis and Turanis became actively disloyal.[51] The rebel prince eventually fled Kabul and threatened to seek the protection of ʿAbdullah Khan at Bukhara, but Akbar pardoned his brother to prevent this occurrence.[52]

The mountainous border province of Badakhshan, which in Babur's and Akbar's times included lands north of the Oxus river, was a particularly volatile territory. This was the traditional domain of Timurid princes descended from Abu Saʿid who had killed the last Alexandrid ruler, and who remained at best only nominally subservient to their Mughal relatives.

A land of difficult terrain and access, Badakhshan was a perennial refuge of rebels from all corners. It was the last stronghold of Humayun's scourge of a brother, Kamran, who fled there from Kabul in 1547. Humayun followed with a successful siege, however, and after forcing Kamran's submission, sent him to take over the even more ungovernable region of Kulab.[53]

In the 1580s, bickering between the Badakhshan's rival Timurid rulers Sulayman and his grandson Shah Rukh enticed the Uzbek ʿAbdullah Khan to interfere, allowing him, according to Abu'l Fazl, to take the province without a battle.[54] Sulayman had earlier been dethroned and chased off by the disloyal Shah Rukh. He then set off on a wild ramble across Asia, first refusing Akbar's offer of the governorship of Bengal, then fleeing to Iran and unwisely enlisting the support of the unpopular and soon to be assassinated Ismaʿil II. Finally he returned via Qandahar and Kabul to Badakhshan, where he managed to raise an army and grab some land. At this point he sought ᶜAbdullah Khan's support against Shah Rukh, which brought on the Uzbek conquest of the province and caused both Sulayman and Shah Rukh to flee to India. Each found Akbar's forgiveness; Sulayman was made a commander of 6000 and Shah Rukh governor of Malwa.[55]

One of the most notable threats of Mughal defection came from Akbar's brother Hakim, governor of Kabul. When the tide began to turn against Hakim's rebellion, he thought of retiring to Turan 'like a [destitute] dervish'[56], but Akbar dissuaded his brother from this drastic course of action. A similar scenario played itself out during Jahangir's reign, when the emperor's eldest son, Khusrau, rebelled and fled to Badakhshan. Jahangir elected not to chase after him, since he feared that if he did then 'that wretch would certainly ally himself with the Uzbeks, and the disgrace would attach to this state'.[57]

Later in his memoirs, Jahangir mentions a certain Badiᶜ al-zaman, son of Khwaja Hasan Khaldar Naqshbandi, who 'after the death of [his patron] the Prince [Muhammad Hakim, Akbar's brother, governor of Kabul], ran away, and went to *Mawarannahr,* [and] in that exile, he died'.[58]

A later rebel, Karimdad, in the time of Shah Jahan, tried to foment an insurrection amongst the Nughaz hill tribes. According to Mughal sources, this occurred with the connivance of Nazr Muhammad. However, Karimdad and his brother were killed by the duplicitous tribesmen, who offered them as trophies to the Mughals as a 'propitiary offering'.[59]

Merchants

During the millenia throughout which Asia relied on overland trade, the India detour had been a southern spur off the silk route. The rise of a hostile Shiᶜi state in Iran in the sixteenth century made the Uzbek-controlled lands more dependent on the trade route running north-west toward the Caspian, and south-east along the mountainous path which the Mughals, like so many previous conquerors, had taken to India. Central Asia thus not only came to rely on India as its primary supplier for a great many types of items, but began as well to serve as a middleman connecting the Indian market with Russia.[60] The caravan traffic across the Hindu Kush was the conduit linking Central Asia with India for all manner of exchanges.[61]

During this period there were many Indian merchants and money-lenders (one profession facilitated the other) in Central Asia, as in Iran. Many were Hindus, particularly Multanis, although there were Muslims as well and cases of Hindu conversion.[62] For at least several centuries, numerous South Asians had also existed in Central Asia as slaves, and some of these slaves had apparently started out as merchants.[63]

Goods and Gifts

In real economic terms, neither Central Asia nor Russia could hope to offer anything remotely balancing the wealth of goods available in India in the sixteenth and seventeenth centuries. But the Mughals, being Central Asians, nostalgic for their lost roots, retained a particular love for Central Asian fruits, birds, and other items not really essential to their well-being in India. The *A'in-i-Akbari*, Abu'l Fazl's comprehensive gazetteer of the Mughal Empire under Akbar, begins its fruit section by listing Central Asian varieties, including their seasons and prices.[64] Akbar tried to have Turani melons and grapes cultivated in India,[65] but in Jahangir's time the demand for the real thing had only increased, and Samarqand apples were brought down every year by special runners, called *dakchuki*.[66] The French traveller Bernier, who was attached for some time to the court of Aurangzeb, mentions an Uzbek embassy which brought 'apples, pears, grapes, and melons; *Usbec* being the country which principally supplies Delhi with these fruits, which are eaten all the winter'. Among the other produce Bernier mentions are Bukhara prunes, apricots, and pitted raisins.[67] The Venetian Niccolao Manucci calls Bukhara plums 'the best in the world'.[68] Thus Stephen Dale may not be stretching things too much to suggest the politicization of fruit in the case of the Mughals, when he asserts that their 'nostalgic taste for melons, dried apricots and almonds echoed their political irredentism for Timurid homelands in Turan'.[69]

Another Central Asian preference the Mughals held was for falcons, hawks, and pigeons. The *A'in* states that Hajji ʿAli Samarqandi's pigeon stock was famous in India.[70] In 1638 Nazr Muhammad honoured Shah Jahan by sending his huntmaster along with an official embassy.[71] Indeed, among Uzbek missions to Mughal India in the sevententh century, which brought everything from Bactrian camels to lapis lazuli, the most common gift appears to have been birds.[72] According to Manucci, Subhan Quli's 1661-2 mission brought lapis boxes filled with musk, *zadwar* (an expensive medicinal root), skink (Ar. *saqanqur*—an aphrodisiac), eighty Bactrian camels, eighty Turki horses, and one special horse with amazing speed and endurance, in addition to the loads of fruit mentioned above.[73] The Mughals, in exchange, sent or bestowed gifts of money, textiles, gemstones such as diamonds, gold, and occasionally, elephants.[74]

The Mughals looked back along the trade route to Central Asia not only for reminders of the homeland they longed to regain, but more practically, as the source for so-called *turki* horses, the high-endurance mounts which had formed the backbone of many a successful Turko-Mongol cavalry.[75] This was, in fact, Central Asia's number one export item to Mughal India, amounting to as many as 100,000 horses per year.[76] The purchase of so many animals appears to have been covered by Indian imports such as cotton, indigo, and sugar rather than by cash, since very few Mughal coins have turned up in Central Asian hoards.[77] Thus India seems to have maintained a positive balance of trade with Central Asia during the Mughal period, and with the exception of goods travelling on to Russia, the Uzbek lands appear to have become less of a transit point for commerce and more of a terminus.

NOTES

1. Abdur Rahim, 'Mughal Relations with Central Asia', *Islamic Culture* 9 (1937), p. 82.
2. Ahmedov, *Istoriko-geograficheskaya literatura*, p. 53.
3. See *AN*, ii, p. 54 (text p. 33).
4. *AN*, ii, p. 104 (text p. 67).
5. *AA*, i, pp. 319-20.
6. Welch, *India*, p. 151.
7. *AN*, ii, pp. 150-1 (text p. 100).
8. *AA*, i, p. 328.
9. *AA*, i, p. 383.
10. *AN*, ii, p. 70 (text p. 44).
11. Ibid., p. 126 (text p. 82).
12. Ibid., p. 48 (text p. 29).
13. *ST*, p. 274.
14. *AN*, iii, p. 297 (text p. 211).
15. The ambassador was ʿAbd al-Rahim Khwaja of the Juybari family. His mission to India is described by Muhammad Talib b. Taj al-din in the *Matlab al-talibin*, MS Preussische Staatsbibliothek Or.1540, ff.172-176. See also M. Athar Ali, 'Jahangir and the Uzbeks', *Proceedings of the Indian History Congress*, 1964, p. 117.
16. Semĕnov, 'Kulʾturno-politicheskikh sviaziakh', p. 14; Senkowski, *Supplément*, p. 51.
17. Islam, *Indo-Persian Relations*, p. 227; Rahim, 'Mughal Relations, p. 194; Richards, *Mughal Empire*, p. 132.
18. Islam, *Indo-Persian Relations*, p. 226.
19. Rahim, 'Mughal Relations', pp. 92, 190.
20. *MU*, ii, p. 931. Tarbiyat Khan attained a rank of 2000 *zat*/1000 *sawar*, and was later appointed *Mir asp* ('Master of the horses').
21. Islam, *Calendar*, ii, p. 218.
22. Rogers translates this obscure term as 'walrus-tooth', but tortoise shell is perhaps more plausible.

23. *TJ*, ii, p. 166; *JN*, p. 352.

24. *TJ*, ii, p. 196; *JN*, p. 370. This would seem to be the same tortoise-shell dagger hilts mentioned above.

25. Islam, *Calendar*, ii, p. 216.

26. Muhammad Hadi 'Maliha' Samarqandi, *Muzakkir-i-ashab*, MS IOSUAS 4270, f.237a; hereafter *MuzA-T*. Also MS Tajikistan Academy of Sciences Or.610 (*MuzA-D*). See R.D. McChesney, 'The Anthology of Poets: Muzakkir al-ashab as a source for the history of 17th century Central Asia', in M. Mazzaoui and Moreen (eds.), *Intellectual Studies on Islam*, University of Utah Press, Salt Lake City, 1990, pp. 57-84.

27. *AA*, i, p. 318.

28. Ibid., pp. 319-20, 328.

29. Ibid., p. 519.

30. *MT*, ii, pp. 302-3 (text p. 294); *TA*, ii, p. 613.

31. *TA*, ii, p. 655.

32. *MU*, i, p. 97.

33. Ibid., pp. 71-2.

34. *AN*, iii, p. 351 (text p. 243).

35. *TJ*, i, p. 27; *JN*, p. 16, where he is called 'one of the distinguished inhabitants of Central Asia'. His name has also been read as Abu'l Wali or Abu'l Nabi. He is referred to in the *AN* as Abu'l Baqa (*AN*, iii, pp. 820, 839) and in the *Ma'athir al-'umara'* as Bahadur Khan Uzbeg. (*MU*, i, p. 351). The latter source describes how he fled Uzbek service by pretending to leave on a pilgrimage to Mecca.

36. *TJ*, i, p. 118; *JN*, p. 68; *MU*, ii, pp. 798-9.

37. *AA*, i, p. 440. He had first come to serve the Timurid prince Sulayman at Badakhshan, and following Sulayman's unsuccessful seige of Kabul went over to Akbar.

38. *SJN*, pp. 94, 205.

39. *MU*, ii, pp. 778-9.

40. *TJ*, i, p. 202; *JN*, p. 115-16. Mughal *mansab* rankings, expressed in terms of infantry (*zat*) and cavalry (*sawar*), represented the number of men an administrator was responsible for mustering in time of war. For an overview of the Mughal administrative system see Richards, *The Mughal Empire*, pp. 58-93; cf. Ali, *Apparatus of Empire*, pp. xxi-xxvi.

41. *SJN*, p. 395; *MU*, i, p. 510.

42. *SS*, f.240b.

43. Ibid., ff. 169a-b.

44. Ibid., f. 199a.

45. *SJN*, p. 341.

46. Ibid., p. 455.

47. Ibid., p. 272.

48. A Bukharan nephew of Qilich Khan (*MA*, p. 153 (text p. 250)).

49. He fled Turan after his father, Mir Baha'al-din, was killed on suspicion of plotting with the Urganj ruler Anusha Khan against ʿAbd al-ʿAziz (*MA*, p. 184 (text p. 303)).

50. *AN*, iii, pp. 537-8 (text p. 366).

51. Ibid., p. 609 (text p. 410).

52. *MT*, ii, pp. 302-3 (text p. 294); *TA*, ii, p. 551, which says that Akbar 'did not allow such a shameful proceeding'.

53. *HN*, p. 186 (ff.71b-72a).

54. *AN*, iii, pp. 652, 666 (text pp. 434-5, 443). In 1585 ʿAbdullah Khan wrote to Akbar in defence of his actions, that he had taken Badakhshan because Shah Rukh had been harbouring Central Asian rebels and had furthermore raided Balkh (Islam, *Calendar*, ii, p. 209). This Uzbek side of the affair is elaborated by Hafiz Tanish in *SNS*, f.101a. Akbar's return embassy led by Hakim Humam, which found ʿAbdullah Khan at Herat, is described in the *SS*, ff.128a-133b.

55. *AA*, i, pp. 311-2, *AN*, iii, p. 665 (text p. 443).

56. '*qalandar asa Turan zamin ghurbat guzinad*' (*AN*, iii, p. 539 (text p. 367).

57. *TJ*, i, p. 65; *JN*, p. 38.

58. '*wa dar an ghurbat, musafir-i-rah-i-ʿadam shud*' (*TJ*, ii, p. 91; *JN*, p. 308).

59. *SJN*, p. 228.

60. See S*bornik dokumentov*, 'Russko-indiiskie otnosheniia v XVII v.', Moscow, 1958; also Baikova, *Rol'*.

61. The trade relationship between the Mughal Empire and the Bukharan khanate is further detailed in Audrey Burton, 'Bukharan Trade, 1558-1718', Papers on Inner Asia, no. 23, Research Institute for Inner Asian Studies, Bloomington IN, 1993, pp. 25-30.

62. Alam, 'Trade', p. 219. See also Dale, *Indian Merchants*.

63. Alam, 'Trade', p. 207. Also see R.G. Mukminova, *Sotsial'naiia differentsiatsia naseleniia gorodov Uzbekistana*, Tashkent 1985. Hindu slaves are mentioned in Wasifi, *Badaʿi al-Waqaʿi*, MS IOSUAS B652, f.119a, which states that Kuchkunji Khan employed 95 of them in his irrigation works, and also in *MatT*, f.181, which notes that Khwaja Saʿad Juybari had 1000 Kalmuck, Russian and Hindu slaves.

64. *AA*, i, p. 65.

65. 'Skilled hands from Turkestan under His Majesty's patronage, sowed melons and planted vines, and traders began to introduce in security the fruits of those countries...' (*AA*, iii, p. 10).

66. *TJ*, ii, p. 101; *JN*, p. 314.

67. Bernier, *Travels*, p. 118.

68. Manucci, *Storia*, ii, p. 34. He mentions among the list of gifts brought by Subhan Quli Khan's mission of 1661-2 one hundred camel-loads of fresh fruit from Central Asia.

69. Dale, *Indian Merchants*, p. 22.
70. *AA*, i, p. 301.
71. *SJN*, p. 244.
72. *TJ*, ii, p. 10; *JN*, p. 270; *SJN*, pp. 148, 536.
73. Manucci, *Storia*, ii, pp. 33-4.
74. Arminius Vambéry, *History of Bukhara*, London, 1873, p. 315; *SJN*, p. 154; *MA*, p. 241 (text p. 397).
75. For an overview of the Central Asian horse trade see Gommans, *Indo-Afghan Empire*, pp. 68-104.
76. Bernier, *Travels*, p. 203; Manucci, *Storia*, ii, p. 391.
77. Dale, *Indian Merchants*, p. 26; see also Gommans, *Indo-Afghan Empire*.

CHAPTER 4

CULTURAL INTERCHANGE

Exchange of information and influences between Central Asia and India during the Mughal period was brought about mainly through individual contacts. The physical carriers were for the most part merchants, fortune hunters, religious figures and simple wanderers, although the distinction between them was often clouded. Central Asians in India, furthermore (and this included the Mughal emperors themselves), tended to remain in regular correspondence with family, friends, and religious advisers 'back home'.

The Mughal rulers, ever mindful of their Central Asian origins, maintained personal contacts with many individuals in Central Asia, especially sufi leaders of the Naqshbandi order. They also had a particular predisposition for lavishing gifts on Central Asians who honoured the court with a visit, and extended patronage to those who stayed on. Patronage, after all, served the political function of legitimizing the regime.[1] In the case of the Mughals, as Jahangir's conversations with a visitor from Samarqand suggest (see Chapter Six), their efforts to impress Central Asian visitors might to some degree have stemmed from insecurity about losing their original homeland to the Uzbeks and the desire to convey to Central Asians the fact of their having 'made good' in exile.

The most common motivation for Central Asians to relocate to India was the age-old prospect of improving their opportunities. The more individuals went and succeeded in attaining fame and fortune, the more others would be inspired to go. Other factors included disgrace or lack of recognition at home,[2] political difficulties, or simple curiosity, although frequently a combination of these was present. The result was a nearly two-hundred-year-long 'brain-drain', from which Iran also suffered with equal or greater severity. The Iranian scholar Ahmad Gulchin-Maʿani, who has catalogued the exodus of 745 Iranian poets to various parts of India during the Safavid period, explains the migration in terms which could apply almost equally to Central Asians:

> This group left [for India] not from the inattention of the Safavid kings, but for other reasons: the death of Shah Ismaʿil, the religious oppression of Shah Tahmasp, the intrigues of Ismail II's nobles and the massacre of the princes who had patronized poetry and poets, the inroads of the Uzbeks and Ottomans, invitations from the kings of India, accompanying Iranian embassies, personal difficulties or unhappiness, flight from suspicion of heresy, extirpation of their tribal leaders by Shah Abbas, harassment by family members or fellow townsmen, asceticism, attachment to acquaintances attaining positions [in India], business, relaxation, pleasure, lack of good fortune, the search for work, or to gain entry to the royal court.[3]

The Safavid writer Qazi Ahmad Qumi describes the situation in the following verse:

> I'm going to India, for there
> The affairs of clever people march nicely
> Whereas liberality and generosity run away
> From the men of [this] time, to the land of the Blacks.[4]

Saida Nasafi, whom the *Ubaydallah-nama* calls the greatest poet of the seventeenth century, complained that in Central Asia as well, the unfavourable political and economic situation enticed the region's most talented writers and artists to go abroad.[5] Mutribi Samarqandi, in Part Two of his anthology presented to Jahangir, also mentions a number of Central Asian poets who found success in India,[6] as does Muhammad Hadi 'Maliha' Samarqandi in his anthology, the *Muzakkir al-ashab.* But it appears that in certain cases it was the Uzbek rulers themselves who were responsible. A seventeenth century Central Asian tract on music tells of a number of poets, singers, and musicians who were sent to the Mughal court where they enjoyed great success.[7] It cannot have been pleasant for the Uzbek khans to realize how their fortunes had balanced out against those they once had conquered, but they seem to have accepted it. On the eve of his departure for India, Mir Shihab al-din of Balkh was reportedly told by Subhan Quli Khan, 'You are going to Hindustan where you will become a big man—don't forget about me'.[8]

Still other individuals travelled to India only temporarily for business, research, pilgrimage, or sightseeing. Often a prime reason was to visit the tombs of saints, as in the case of ᶜAbdullah Kabuli, who travelled through northern India during the 1590s. ᶜAbdullah travelled first to Ahmedabad where he spent two years, then to Lahore, Multan, Delhi, Agra, and Kashmir. He mentions the leading religious figures in each city, most of whom are Naqshbandi sufis from Central Asia, and also describes his visits to the tombs of literary, political, and religious figures, ranging from Amir Khusraw Dihlawi to Emperor Humayun.[9] The Tajik scholar S. Nurutdinov, in his recent book on ᶜAbdullah, suggests another reason for the journey was in order to do research for an anthology of poets.[10]

Prior to his visit to the court of Jahangir in 1627, Mutribi Samarqandi spent over a year in such 'research travel'. His travelogue and that of his contemporary Mahmud b. Amir Wali are some of the most fascinating and illuminating documents of seventeenth century Muslim Asia, and will be treated more fully in Chapter Six.

Literary Contacts

In sixteenth and seventeenth century Muslim society, a man of letters was by definition a poet. One of the major forms of correspondence between Central Asia and India was the traditional Persian practice of *mujavaba* which often included 'duelling verses', in which a person would write a line or two and send it to a friend, who would then write a response in the same rhyme and metre. The mailbags of caravans connecting the Uzbek and Mughal lands were filled with this type of back-and-forth one-upmanship.

Often these literary challenges accompanied letters and gifts, as with Akbar's poet laureate Fayzi who kept in constant touch with the sufi master Hasan Nisari at Bukhara. The *Tazkira al-shuʿara* anthology compiled by Mutribi Samarqandi for Wali Muhammad Khan lists Indian poets such as Fayzi, Sanaʿi Mashhadi, Zahir Kabuli, and Razmi, and includes odes of his own written to Razmi, a couplet of the ode *Karnama* which Sanaʿi sent to Central Asia and four lines of response, and a couplet which Nisari sent to India. On the other hand, the slightly earlier Mughal anthology of Ala' al-Daula, entitled *Nafa'is al-ma'athirat*,[11] includes Central Asian poets such as Manzari, Nadiri, Farughi Samarqandi, Mushfiqi, and Saka. Such evidence of abundant exchange shows clearly that the creative works of Indian poets were well known in Central Asia, and those of Central Asian poets in India.[12]

Even Emperor Babur, who was considered a talented poet, traded verses with the great court poet of Timurid Herat, ʿAli-shir Nawa'i.[13] This type of activity was not in any way unusual, since any self-respecting Muslim ruler considered himself a poet, and among the Uzbeks and the Mughals alike there were few exceptions to this royal prerequisite. Nearly a century later Khwaja Hashim Dihbidi, a leading member of one of Central Asia's major sufi families, sent Jahangir a couplet Babur had written for an earlier Dihbidi sheikh, along with a letter and gifts. Jahangir replied with a verse of his own, and sent Khwaja Hashim 1000 *muhr*s in tribute.[14] The longevity of such verses and the way they would pop up in diverse contexts, from private, familial collections to public anthologies, is typical of the Persian literary world, and says something about the importance that was attached to this type of correspondence.

In the Persian literary tradition, imitation was indeed considered the sincerest form of flattery. It was seen as perfectly good form to imitate the style of a better-known poet, and laudable in fact if one succeeded in doing so. The author of the *Tazkira-yi-Muqim Khani*, for example, praises Nazr Muhammad's nephew Qasim Sultan for his work in the style of the Mughal poet Sa'ib.[15]

The correspondence between Central Asian and Indian poets offers a significant insight into what they thought of as their world. Many literary men also travelled physically within the broader boundaries of that world. Jahi Yatman, a poet from Bukhara, made his reputation at Kabul in the early 1550s and attached himself to Humayun prior to the Mughal reconquest of Hindustan. His satirical skills brought him success, and illustrate the power of verse in court culture. After a falling out with the Mughal governor of Kabul, Shah Muhammad Salu, Jahi composed a lampoon which Humayun had him recite before an assembly of nobles which included the victim. The nobles were hysterical with laughter, Jahi earned a fortune from the Emperor, and Shah Muhammad and his family were utterly disgraced.[16]

Another Central Asian poet, Maulana Nadiri-yi Samarqandi, who came to serve at Akbar's court, is called by Bada'uni 'one of the wonders of the age' and 'a compendium of perfection'.[17] The orthodox historian was surely referrring to Nadiri's verse and not his character, as the poet is said to have been in love with a young boy named Nizam and Bada'uni elsewhere condemns the 'Transoxianian' sin of pederasty. He nevertheless quotes a typical love lyric. Nadiri's son Fahmi, also a poet, travelled to India as well but returned to Central Asia. Bada'uni calls the son 'jovial, expert at composing enigmas'.[18] On Nadiri's death in 1559, Mir Amani Kabuli composed the chronogram: 'one has gone from among the masters of speech'.[19] Nadiri's townsman, Sadiq Halwa'i, stopped for several years in India on his way home from Mecca, and for a time tutored Akbar's brother Muhammad Hakim at Kabul before returning to Samarqand.[20]

One of the sixteenth century poets best known in Central Asia, Mushfiqi, travelled at least twice to India. Darvish ʿAli, writing in the early seventeenth century, says of Mushfiqi that 'no poet of his era was more knowledgeable and talented than he'.[21] Other Central Asian poets whom Darvish ʿAli lists as having emigrated to India are Qasim Arslan, who served Sayyid Burhan Sultan at Bukhara until leaving for India in 1557; Wasili-i-Marwi, who served Sulayman Mirza in Badakhshan before coming over to Humayun; and Khwaja ʿAbd al-Karim Qazi, the son of Bukhara judge Mahmud Qazi, who went to India in Baqi Muhammad's time and became a panegyrist for Akbar.[22] Originally from Bukhara, Mushfiqi first left for Delhi in 1567-8 after failing to achieve his desired success at Samarqand.[23] He doesn't seem to have fared any better in India, however, at least initially, since he returned to Bukhara a year later. But before long he was named poet laureate by ʿAbdullah Khan[24] and sent back to India as part of an official delegation in 1585.[25] Abu'l Fazl implies that on this occasion Mushfiqi and a companion, Nasir of Balkh, stayed on in India, saying that 'they came to recognize the futility of their lives, and began their work anew'.[26] The *Tabaqat-i-Akbari* says that Mushfiqi was the 'recipient of great kindnesses' from Akbar, 'but afterwards returned to Bukhara'. This seems to refer to the poet's second trip to India.[27] A collection of Mushfiqi's *qasida*s in Tashkent[28] contains an ode to Akbar. Other Central Asian poets listed in the *Tabaqat-i-Akbari* are Mulla Sahmi Bukhari,

who was in the service of ʿAzam Khan, and Mulla Niyazi
Samarqandi, who served both Humayun and Akbar while
living in Sindh, where he died.[29]

On the other hand Bada'uni, an ethnic Indian, claims
that Mushfiqi's work was overrated, and that it suffered
'from the defects common to the poets of Transoxiana'.
Nevertheless, he concedes that Mushfiqi possessed 'a subtle
tongue in satire', and cites the following:

> The land of Hind is a sugar field
> Its parrots all sell sugar
> Its black Hindus are like flies
> In their turbans (*chira*) and long coats (*nagucha*).[30]

A Central Asian anthology of poets for the seventeenth
century, the *Muzakkir-i-ashab* of 'Maliha' Samarqandi, lists
some two hundred poets of whom over twenty were Central
Asians who had gone to India. Since such anthologies were
intended to be comprehensive, one can make the general
comment that, based on this account, at this time roughly
one in ten important men of letters appears to have had
this type of travel experience. Many of these individuals
attained ranks in Mughal service, such as ʿIbadullah
Tashkandi Imtihan (*MuzA-T*, f.37a), Dastur Nasafi
(ff. 67a-b), ʿAbd al-Rahman Munim (f.196b), and Mulla
Niyaz Kashgari (f.237a), to name a few. Others, such as
Amir Jalal Kitabdar (*MuzA-D*, p.69), Mulla Maniʿ
Samarqandi (*MuzA-T*, f.210b), and Mulla Lamiʿ Nasafi, were
not so successful. To the latter Aurangzeb remarked that
'even the offspring of slaves in Central Asia are so proud
that they think they can all come and get jobs here' (*ni az
mardan-i-khanazad-i-anja zahir mishawand badin sabab ru shuda
naukari girifta-and*). Mulla Maniʿ Samarqandi and Mulla
Lamiʿ Nasafi were supported by Qazi ʿAbd al-Rahman, who
received the title Qazi Khan in addition to a rank of 1000
zat.[31]

A sizeable contingent of the entourage accompanying ᶜAbd al-ᶜAziz Khan to Mecca in 1682, including Amir Jalal Kitabdar, Dastur Nasafi, Qazi ᶜAbd al-Rahman Munᶜim, Mulla Maniᶜ Samarqandi, Muhammad Salah Nasha, and Mulla Lamiᶜ Nasafi, went on from there to India following their patron's death in Mesopotamia. This was consistent with a long-established pattern of Uzbek subjects travelling to or from Mecca by the sea route via India, following the establishment of Shiᶜism in Iran which occasionally made for hostile transiting.

Certain individuals found degrees of success under both the Uzbek and Mughal patronage. Mutribi Samarqandi, recycling his own work, submitted an anthology of poets first to an Uzbek ruler, then twenty years later in a revised form to the Mughal Jahangir. He travelled to India at the advanced age of 70 in hopes of making a vast fortune, and from his memoirs it appears that Jahangir did not disappoint him. Jahangir had written an anthology of his own, including both immigrant and native Indian poets from the time of his father Akbar, and he paid Mutribi the honour of asking him to incorporate his anthology into Mutribi's.[32] A precedent for Mutribi's 'quick kill' venture may be found in Mulla Ghurbati Bukhari, who came in Akbar's time and, 'having been made happy by the Emperor's gifts, went back to Bukhara'.[33]

Another Central Asian who was in India at the same time as Mutribi was a young man from Balkh by the name of Mahmud b. Amir Wali. Mahmud, who left Balkh while he was in his twenties, spent over six years in India, the first three as little more than a wandering vagrant and the last three in the service of a provincial Mughal governor. His Persian-language travelogue contains numerous Hindi words, and he may have learned Indian music as well.[34]

Like the Mughal rulers themselves, Mahmud's family was originally from Andijan, which may partly account for the sympathetic treatment he later gives them when writing under the patronage of Nazr Muhammad.[35] While in India

Mahmud seems to have benefited from reading many history books, which later served him when writing his own monumental history, the *Bahr al-asrar*. This suggests that the libraries were better in India, and in any case, according to the Pakistani editors of Mahmud's first volume, the study of history as a discipline was 'more popular in the Mughal dominions than in his own land'.[36]

Other major Central Asian historians of the seventeenth century also lived or spent time in Mughal India, including Muhammad Yusuf Munshi, who was the author of the *Tazkira-yi Muqim Khani*, and Mir Muhammad Salim, author of the *Silsilat al-salatin*, written in 1730-1.[37] The latter historian was an Uzbek born and raised in India, his family having relocated there from Central Asia. In Islam's words the *Silsilat al-salatin* (which he calls the *Tawarikh-i-badi'a*) and the *Tarikh-i-Qipchaq Khani*, the two major Central Asian histories of the eighteenth century which were composed in India, 'are undoubtedly superior to those which were the work of Turani-based annalists',[38] and he joins the Uzbek scholar Nizamutdinov in praising the former work as the best history of seventeenth century Central Asia.[39] Although Islam and Nizamutdinov both state that its author is unknown, the text identifies him as Hajji Mir Muhammad Salim (f.3a, line 13), and while the title *Tawarikh-i-badi'a ra'y Shah Jahan imam* is written on the first page, an internal reference (f.3b, line 11) names the work *Silsilat al-salatin*, the name by which other scholars have referred to it.[40]

Another Central Asian history written in India is the *Tarikh-i-Qipchaq Khani*, whose author was born into a family that had stayed on in Balkh after taking part in Shah Jahan's 1646–7 occupation. The author's father had been governor of Daragez in Balkh province under Subhan Quli Khan, but returned the family to India in 1696 because of disagreements with the Balkh governor Mahmud Biy Ataliq.[41]

Perhaps the most significant literary figure among the Central Asian immigrant families in North India is the poet

ʿAbd al-Qadir Bidel, whose lifetime (1644-1721) spanned the long reign of Aurangzeb and saw the beginning of the decline of Mughal power. The popularity and influence of Bidel's work endures to the present day in Central Asia, and continues to be the subject of extensive study by contemporary Central Asian scholars. For example, a conference in honour of the poet's three hundred and fiftieth birthday was held in Samarqand, Uzbekistan in January 1995.[42]

Arts of the Book

One of the gifts of the pictorial arts of the Asian Muslim tradition, apart from their great inherent beauty, is that they fill in many gaps left by literary sources. Miniature paintings provide detailed historical records of architecture, textiles, jewellery and other handicrafts, tools and weapons, musical instruments, and so on,[43] in addition to visual information about lifestyles, work techniques, ceremonial protocol and such. The Mughals were some of history's most generous patrons, and their ateliers attracted many of Asia's most talented creative minds. Even Europeans were welcome in this syncretistic environment; Portuguese priests regularly participated in religious debates, Italian doctors tended to the health of the elite, and Madonnas and cherubim found their way into Indian paintings. Rarely has a political entity fostered such an open and receptive atmosphere toward influences from every possible provenance, and with such happy results.

The sixteenth century saw the rise and flowering of three great traditions in Islamic book arts, particularly miniature painting. The Safavid, Mughal, and Bukhara styles evolved as distinct but inter-related schools, sharing certain Timurid roots and influencing each other mutually in varying degrees. In particular, the Safavid school grew from the encounter of the Herat-based Timurid style, epitomized by the work of that most famous of all Persian painters, Bihzad, with the Tabriz-centred tradition which the conquering Safavids inherited from their Turkmen predecessors.[44] (It should be noted that the common practice among art historians is to name artistic traditions after the rulers who patronized them, rather than after the artists themselves with whom those patrons may have had little or no prior ethnic and social connections. Thus, when one refers to the 'Turkmen school', for example, it should not be understood that the style in question has any inherent association with the nomadic tribal organizations speaking the western Turkic dialect commonly referred to as 'Turkmen'. The painting styles associated with Tabriz, Shiraz, Herat, Bukhara, and elsewhere represent variants of an Iranian tradition of painting which dates to pre-Islamic times, although this is not to downplay the continuous influx of influences ranging from Byzantine to Chinese.)

During the first half of the sixteenth century Safavid masters trained under Bihzad such as Dust Muhammad, ᶜAbd al-Samad, Mir Musawwir and Mir Sayyid ᶜAli all went to work for Mughal patrons in India. ᶜAbd al-Samad and Mir Sayyid ᶜAli in particular are credited with founding the Mughal school of painting under Akbar. Another major figure in Safavid painting, Shaykh-zada (whom Bahari has recently identified with Mahmud Muzahhib of Herat), went instead to Bukhara and brought Safavid influence to the local Uzbek-sponsored tradition.

Beginning his career as an apprentice under Bihzad at Herat, before being captured and taken to Bukhara in 1530 by the Shibanid ᶜAbd al-ᶜAziz,[45] Shaykh-zada formed a living link between the Timurid, Safavid, and Bukharan painting traditions. His works do not appear in any Safavid manuscript after the 1527 Hafiz (now in the Fogg Museum), but are next seen in a 1537–8 Hatifi manuscript done at Bukhara for ᶜAbd al-ᶜAziz. The Herat style thus travelled to Uzbek Central Asia by two paths, via Iran and also directly.[46] Many Bukhara painters, in turn, later brought their techniques with them to India, thereby adding a Central Asian element to the Iranian-Rajput mixture already in place there.

Although Mughal miniature painting is commonly thought of as a synthesis between the formal delicacy of classical Persian painting with the more lively, nature-infused local traditions of northern India, a subtle Central Asian component is attested to by textual as well as visual evidence. ʿAbdullah Khan, for example, sent painters from Samarqand and Bukhara to work for Akbar.[47] A clearly Bukhara-style painting of a musician couple is attributed by the art historian Stuart Cary Welch to the atelier of Humayun, largely on the basis of the distinctive way the turbans are tied. A *Yusuf wa Zulaykha* manuscript commissioned by Humayun's brother, Prince Kamran, contains very similar illustrations, which may in fact be by the same hand, although the figures lack Mughal turbans.[48] (Again, Welch's use of the term 'Uzbek' to denote the painting style of the Bukhara court is misleading in that it refers to the patrons rather than the artists, since the populations of Bukhara and Samarqand were, as they remain today, largely Persian-speaking.) These examples would suggest a Bukhara-trained painter working for Humayun. The miniatures of an *Anwar-i-Suhayli* done for Akbar in 1571, though mainly in the Safavid style, include a few that Welch attributes to 'an artist trained at Bukhara who had not adjusted his style to the Akbari synthesis'.[49] An illustrated *Hamza-nama* from the same period also contains, according to Milo Beach, 'several scenes obviously painted by artists from Bukhara'.[50]

Beach considers the presence of Bukhara artists in India, 'a reference to Timur and to the Mughal inheritance of his artistic traditions'.[51] Yet the flat, heavily-stylized Bukhara paintings of the sixteenth century are greatly exceeded by Safavid and Mughal miniatures in sophistication and originality. In Beach's words, 'The Bukhara style can be

defined in part by, "Anushirvan Sends His Generals to
Battle the Turks,"... the composition is flat and broken into
clearly defined, self-contained, and often rectangular
compartments. Patterns are intricate but not vivid; rugs,
tile floors, and even pools of water (as here) are inevitably
seen from a bird's eye view to enhance their ornamental
strength. Unlike the Safavid style, the effect is usually
static'.[52] Therefore, the demand for Central Asian painters
at the Mughal court, where there was no lack of exceptional
talent, is best explained in terms of the rulers' nostalgic
desire for things Central Asian. This hunger is reflected in
the Mughal emperors' demand and appreciation for works
executed in Central Asia as well. It is interesting that a
copy of Saᶜdi's *Bustan* done at Bukhara in the 1540s, now at
the Fogg museum, bears an inscription in the hand of
Jahangir who had obtained it for his private library. The
manuscript contains three miniatures by Shaykh-zada,
although the typically characterless faces have been, in
Welch's observation, 'discreetly repainted in the Mughal
mode, probably by Bishn Das'.[53]

The sources mention a number of Central Asian painters
who wound up working in India, occasionally by quite
circuitous routes. Mir Musawwir, who was originally from
Termez on the banks of the Amu Darya (the Oxus river),[54]
is known as a Safavid painter who rose to fame under the
patronage of Shah Tahmasp. When first asked by Humayun
to come to India in 1544 he declined, leaving his son Mir
Sayyid ᶜAli to go instead. However, later in life, when
Tahmasp had begun to sour on painting, Mir Musawwir
followed his son to the Mughal court and lived out his life
there.[55] Dust Muhammad, a Safavid painter who travelled
to India and then returned to Iran and wrote a treatise on
painting and painters, describes Mir Musawwir's work as
'brilliant like ruby and lapis', metaphorically recalling the
latter's Badakhshani origins.[56] Aqa Riza may have come to
Agra from Bukhara at around the same time.[57]

Among those painters who moved directly from the Uzbek to the Mughal court was Muhammad Murad, a portrait painter born in Samarqand who worked in Bukhara before being sent to Akbar by ʿAbdullah Khan. To him are attributed no less than 115 of the Bukhara-style miniatures in a 1559 *Shah-nama* now in Tashkent. Nizamutdinov pushes his arrival in India up to the 1620s, thereby leading one to conclude that Muhammad Murad may have returned to Central Asia in Akbar's time and come again to India during Jahangir's.[58] Another is Muhammad Nadir Samarqandi.[59] The wayfaring careers of such a diverse group of Muslim painters, taken together, vividly illustrate the mobility of those exercising the profession within a very widely-flung geographical sphere, defined not by political boundaries but rather by social ones.

Religious Sciences

When the Mughals brought with them to India their Central Asian religious ties, they were merely adding their own connections to a network that had already long been in place. A number of Bukhara *sayyid*s (descendants of the Prophet), such as Shaykh Farid, had been in India for generations.[60] Throughout the Mughal period many sufi leaders in India retained followers in Central Asia, and vice versa.

More specifically, the Mughal emperors considered themselves devotees of Central Asian Naqshbandi sheikhs, following in the steps of Babur, whose Muslim name (Zahir al-din Muhammad) had been given him at birth by the politically powerful Khwaja ʿUbaydullah Ahrar.[61] (An exception to this preference was Akbar, whose first loyalty was to the Indian Chishti sect. Jahangir and Shah Jahan also occasionally extended patronage to the Chishtis, mainly perhaps because of the popular appeal of that order.) Babur himself states in his memoirs that

Transoxiana produced a greater number of 'leaders of Islam' than anywhere else in the world.[62] The connections which the Mughal emperors maintained with particular Naqshbandi shaykhs of Central Asia will be detailed in the following chapter.

It wasn't only Naqshbandis who sought and often attained Mughal favour, but also other religious figures who benefited from the inherited orthodox prestige of their part of the world, and from the Mughals' preference for things Central Asian. One such individual was Qazi Abu'l Maᶜali, an orthodox Hanafi theologian who was responsible for getting ᶜAbdullah Khan to ban the study of logic and dialectics at Bukhara. He came to India in 1560. Bada'uni refers to him as 'a master-builder in legal science, and a second glory of the Imams', and boasts enthusiastically of having had the opportunity to study briefly under him.[63] Whether or not Abu'l Maᶜali remained in India is unclear, but it is unlikely that his conservative religious slant would have found favour at Akbar's liberal court.

In addition to those religious figures coming to India in search of patronage, there were others who merely passed through on their way to Mecca. In one example, the *Tuzuk-i-Jahangiri* mentions an old mulla named Amiri, a former close servant of ᶜAbdullah Khan, who stopped to pay homage to Jahangir and received so many gifts he was 'unable to hold them'.[64] Another case is that of Mir Jalal al-Din, who visited Aurangzeb on his way back from performing the *hajj* and received gifts and cash from the emperor.[65]

In Akbar's time the Mughal reverence for men of religious learning was tempered by the heterodox mood of the court, which many Muslim theologians found distasteful. Thus while Akbar entertained proponents of every philosophical bent in his *Ibadat-khana* discussions, (*Ibadat-khana*, or 'House of Worship', was Akbar's official forum where he listened to and arbitrated debates between leading theologians of various religions, including Sunnism,

Shi'ism, Hinduism, Jainism, Zoroastrianism, and Roman Catholicism), he and his intimates (Abu'l Fazl in particular) had no patience for overly literal-minded and dogmatic individuals. The millenarian reformer Ahmad Sirhindi, the most prominent student of the Central Asian Khwaja Baqibillah who had formally established the Naqshbandi order in India in the late sixteenth century, was anathema to the court, and was finally imprisoned by Jahangir for insubordination. The orthodox-minded historian ʿAbd al-Qadir Bada'uni was disciplined for his 'narrow-mindedness' by being forced to translate the Hindu epic *Mahabharata* into Persian.[66]

Emperor Jahangir, despite apparently having made certain promises to Sirhindi and his associates early on, in the end proved no more dogmatic than his father. K.A. Nizami believes that Sirhindi had actually been instrumental in bringing Jahangir to power, in the hope that he would reverse Akbar's 'heretical' policies.[67] The tide against orthodoxy only began to turn after the first decade of the reign of Shah Jahan, and was reversed finally under Aurangzeb who has gone down in history as either the saviour of Muslim civilization in India or the destroyer of all hopes for ecumenical understanding, depending on one's point of view.

A major figure in implementing Aurangzeb's reactionary reform was Mulla ʿAwz Wajih, a native of Akhsikat in the province of Ferghana. While studying under Mir ʿAwz Tashkandi he is said to have surpassed all his classmates. He became a teacher at Balkh, then went to India during the thirteenth year of Shah Jahan's reign and became the *mufti* of the royal camp. Referred to in the *Ma'athir-i-ʿAlamgiri* as 'the leading theologian' (*aswa-yi-ʿulema*) Mulla ʿAwz served as Aurangzeb's *muhtasib* (chief of police) and 'exerted himself far beyond any other holder of the post in putting down vices' and was 'highly honoured by the nobility'.[68]

Astronomy, Mathematics, and Medicine

It comes as no surprise that the so-called 'Samarqand school' of astronomy flourished under Mughal patronage in India. The tradition had its roots in the work of Timur's grandson Ulugh Beg, known for having built the observatory at Samarqand and for his astronomical tables, the *Zij-i-Ulugh Beg*, many copies of which have been found in India. Babur describes Ulugh Beg's observatory in his memoirs.[69] A commentary on Ulugh Beg's tables, called the *Tahsil-i-zij-i-Ulugh Beg*, was prepared by Humayun's court astronomer Mulla Chand, who also calculated Akbar's birth horoscope. Mulla Chand is also known for his treatise on astronomy, *Maqala dar ʿilm-i-nujum*.

Shah Jahan commissioned his court astronomer, Farid al-din Dehlawi, to devise a new astronomical table in 1629, which was known as the *Zij-i-Shah Jahani*, based on Ulugh Beg's tables.[70] A number of Islamic works on astronomy were translated into Sanskrit during the seventeenth century as well, including Qushji's *Risala dar hay'at*.[71] Kamalakara's *Siddhantatattvaviveka*, furthermore, composed in 1658, shows clear influence from Ulugh Beg. Among the twenty cities for which it gives coordinates, only Samarqand and Kabul are located outside India, and for the seven which also figure in Ulugh Beg's work, the coordinates are identical. The Sanskrit author also refers to a sine table by 'Mirjolukabega' (Mirza Ulugh Beg).[72]

Greek (*yunani*) medicine made its way into the Mughal world from Central Asia just as Greek astronomy did, although less directly, through Iran. The tradition of the eleventh century Central Asian physician and philosopher Ibn Sina (Avicenna) took firm root in Iran through subsequent centuries, especially in Shiraz. Most of the important physicians in Mughal employ were from Shiraz or from northern Iran, but one notable exception is Khwaja Khawind Mahmud, a grandson of Khwaja ʿUbaydullah Ahrar from Samarqand. Khwaja Khawind had learned medicine at Shiraz, before coming to join Babur's court at Agra. A number of the descendants of Khwaja Khawind's brother Khwaja Yusuf, who came to be known in India as the Sharifi family, were noted practitioners of *yunani* medicine in the seventeenth and eighteenth centuries.[73]

Music

The Mughals, with their Central Asian tastes, retained their love for Central Asian music. How similar Central Asian music was to that of Iran at that time is a problematic issue; the terminology was the same, but that in itself is inconclusive. It does seem, however, that Central Asian and Iranian music differed considerably from north Indian music by that point, even though the latter was considered to have evolved from the Iranian tradition and through the thirteenth century poet and musician Amir Khusraw in particular.

That Central Asians were interested in Indian music is evidenced by a seventeenth century tract from Bukhara which compares the Central Asian *maqam* system with that of the Indian *raga*.[74] Likewise, Akbar commissioned a Central Asian, Qasim b. Dust Bukhari, to write a treatise called *Risala dar ʿilm-i-musiqi*, which must have dealt with Central Asian music.[75] A later treatise written at Bukhara for Imam Quli Khan by his court musician Darvish ʿAli, recounts the life of a celebrated sixteenth century Central Asian singer named Mawlana Qasim-i-Qahi Samarqandi, who was 'rewarded' with a trip to India, 'about whose climate he had heard so much'. On the way, Mawlana Qasim fell in love with Kabul, and stayed on there in the service of Humayun's brother Prince Kamran. Humayun, however, hearing of the singer's talents, sent for him, and overcoming Kamran's protestations, enticed him to come to Lahore. Darvish ʿAli also mentions a Central Asian *dutar* player, Yusuf Mawdudi, who went to serve Humayun.[76]

Sports

The Mughal elite enjoyed birds, particularly hawks and pigeons. Central Asia, which was known throughout the Islamic world for it birds and bird-trainers, often provided the wealthier classes of Hindustan with both. The *A'in-i-Akbari*, as was mentioned in Chapter Three, attests to the fame of Hajji ᶜAli Samarqandi's pigeon stock in India;[77] the same source names several Central Asian bird-keepers in Akbar's service, including ᶜAbd al-Latif and Quli ᶜAli from Bukhara and Maqsud and Masti from Samarqand.[78] Central Asians frequently sent pigeons and hawks as gifts to India. Nazr Muhammad's inclusion of his huntmaster in a 1638 embassy to Shah Jahan reflects his awareness of Mughal tastes.[79]

The Mughals also enjoyed watching wrestling matches, for which fighters were brought from Central Asia and elsewhere. Abu'l Fazl states that contests were held daily, and mentions the names of Turani wrestlers such as Sadiq Bukhari, Murad Turkestani, and Muhammad ᶜAli Turani.[80]

Architecture

Perhaps the most visible legacy the Mughals left in India of their Central Asian roots is their buildings. Although Mughal architecture, which has become known as one of the world's most remarkable and distinctive styles, appears from its marble and sandstone building materials and its temple-like tower structures to be above all Indian, many of the general plans, especially in mausoleums and gardens, are based on Central Asian precedents.

The tomb complex of Ulugh Beg and his son ᶜAbd al-Razzaq at Ghazni in present-day Afghanistan, modelled on such buildings as the *ᶜIshrat-khana* (festival hall) at Samarqand, forms a link between the Timurid architecture of Central Asia and that of India. (ᶜAbd al-Razzaq's

dethronement soon after inheriting his father's lands
formed the pretext for his first cousin Babur's invasion of
Kabul in 1504. Babur didn't re-instate ʿAbd al-Razzaq as
ruler, but made him governor of Ghazni. Work was never
completed on the tomb, which seems to have been begun
only shortly before Ulugh Beg's death.)[81] The vaulting
system of both buildings is derived from that developed by
an Iranian architect, Qawam al-din Shirazi, who worked for
Timur's son, Shah Rukh, at Herat during the first half of
the fifteenth century. Humayun's tomb at Delhi, the first
major Timurid monument to be built in India, also reflects
the layout of the ʿIshrat-khana as well as the tomb of Khwaja
Abu Nasr at Balkh.[82]

Nothing illustrates our discussion of professional mobility
better than the career of Mirak-i-Sayyid Ghiyath, a noted
landscape architect who gained renown under the
Shibanids at Bukhara where he designed a garden for
Muhammad Shah and possibly the Mir-i-ʿarab madrasa
(seminary).[83] Born in Herat, Mirak served first the Timurids
there, then the Uzbeks, then the Safavids, then the Uzbeks
again, then the Mughals, and finally the Uzbeks once more.
His contributions to Mughal India included work at Agra
and at Dholpur.[84]

Mirak's son Muhammad, who was born in Bukhara
during the 1540s, also came to India where he appears to
have been commissioned by Akbar to design Humayun's
tomb. M.E. Subtelny provides evidence from Hasan Nisari's
Muzakkir al-ahbab to show that it was Muhammad, and not
his father, who designed Humayun's tomb.[85] The diagonal
passageways of Humayun's tomb are like those of the Mir-i-
ʿarab, leading Lisa Golombek to comment that 'only a
Bukharan architect of the sixteenth century could have
built a "Timurid" mausoleum for the Mughals'.[86]

According to A.H. Dani, the buland darwaza (high gate)
at Akbar's Fatehpur Sikri was modelled on the entry gate
of Timur's Aq Saray (White Palace) at Shahr-i-sabz.[87] The
stylistic eclecticism of Akbar's tomb further represents that

ruler's attempts to blend Timurid with local influences, yet this demonstrates, as the architectural historian John Hoag puts it, a break 'more apparent than real' with the Central Asian tradition of Humayun.[88] In fact, half a century later this evolution would come full circle, and be brought to its greatest heights with the building at Agra of the Taj Mahal. Although the Taj's architect was an Ottoman, Muhammad ᶜIsa Effendi, the chief draftsman, Muhammad Sharif, was from Samarqand, and the head sculptor, Ata Muhammad, from Bukhara.[89]

The cultural achievements which took place under Mughal rule in the sixteenth and seventeenth centuries were not an exclusively 'Indian' phenomenon; rather, they were the result of a happy synthesis of elements from throughout the Asian lands where Persian-Islamic culture was dominant. The careers of emigrant poets, artists and musicians, the correspondence between literary men, the spread and influence of Naqshbandism, and physical evidence such as the development of Mughal architecture, all illustrate a remarkable mobility of individuals, styles, and ideas within a very widely-flung geographical sphere. The boundaries of this world were defined not politically, but socially, and thus covered a much larger terrain than any one empire could lay claim to.

NOTES

1. 'Through lavish expenditure and ostentatious consumption of the arts, which implied control over vast sums of money— itself a symbol of power—his court attained cultural prestige' (Subtelny, 'Art and Politics', p. 130).
2. Such as the court poet who made joking reference to ᶜAbd al-ᶜAziz's corpulence, was 'disgraced with magnanimity' by that ruler and so left for India, where he does not appear to have made anything of himself (Vambéry, *Bukhara*, p. 328); or Mufid Balkhi, who 'failed to please Subhan Quli Khan', and went to India where he received a stipend from Aurangzeb (*MuzA-T*, f.194b).

3. Ahmad Gulchin Ma'ani, *Karwan-i Hind*, 2 vols., Mashhad, 1370 (1990-1), i, p. v.

4. Qazi Ahmad b. Mirza Munshi al-Husayni Qumi, *Gulistan-i-hunar*, tr. Vladimir Minorsky, *Calligraphers and Painters: A Treatise by Qazi Ahmad c.1596-1606*, Smithsonian, Washington, 1959, 185. Minorsky translates the last phrase, '*ba zamin-i-siyah furu raftand*', as 'run away... to black earth'. This translation makes little sense; 'the land of the Blacks', on the other hand, is an image consistent both with the long-standing convention of referring to India as such and with that of contrasting black 'ugliness' with white 'beauty'.

5. Bečka, 'Tajik Literature', p. 510; see also A.G. Mirzoev, *Saido Nasafi i ego mesto v istorii tadzhikskoi literatury*, Stalinabad, 1954; and Mirobid Saido Nasafi, *Asarhoi muntakhab*, Dushanbe, 1977.

6. Mutribi al-Asamm Samarqandi, *Nuskha-yi-ziba-yi-Jahangiri*, ed. A.G. Mirzoev, Karachi, 1976.

7. Semënov, 'Kul'turno-politicheskikh sviaziakh', p. 8.

8. *MA*, p. 57 (text p. 91).

9. 'Abdullah Kabuli, *Tazkira al-tawarikh*, IOSUAS MS 2093.

10. S. Nurutdinov, *Tazkira al-tawarikh-i-'Abdullah Kabuli*, Kabul 1365 (1986), p. 62.

11. Ala' al-daula, *Nafa'is al-ma'athirat*, IOSUAS MS 848.

12. Nizamutdinov, *Ocherki*, pp. 24-5.

13. *BN*, p. 175.

14. *TJ*, i, pp. 303-4; *JN*, pp. 172-3. A Jahangiri *muhr* was a gold coin bearing on one side a portrait of the Emperor drinking a cup of wine and on the other the sun in Leo. It weighed a *tola* and was worth 14 rupees (Awan, *History*, p. 678).

15. Quoted in Semënov, 'Kul'turno-politicheskikh sviaziakh', p. 13.

16. *MT*, i, p. 618 (text p. 477).

17. Ibid., p. 611 (text p. 472).

18. *MT*, iii, p. 405 (text p. 294).

19. *MT*, i, p. 616 (text p. 475).

20. *MT*, iii, pp. 354-5 (text p. 255); *TA*, ii, p. 686.

21. Semënov, *Traktat*, p. 63.

22. Ibid., pp. 64, 68.

23. Bečka, 'Tajik Literature', p. 503. Bada'uni says Mushfiqi was from Marv, but Haig suggests this was perhaps only his family origin (*MT*, iii, p. 452 (text p. 328)). For a discussion of Mushfiqi and his work see Z. Ahrari, *Mushfiqi, hayat va ijadiyat*, Dushanbe, 1978.

24. Daghistani, quoted by Blochmann in *AA*, i, p. 583.

25. Semënov, 'Kul'turno-politicheskikh sviaziakh', p. 9.

26. *AN*, iii, p. 335 (text p. 236).

27. *TA*, ii, p. 726.

28. IOSUAS MS 1053/II.

29. *TA*, ii, p. 737.
30. *MT*, iii, pp. 452-3 (text pp. 328-9). In Abu'l Fazl's version, his pet phrase for mullas (*niku'an-i-diyar*) is substituted for 'Hindus' (*Hindu'an-i-siyah*) (*AA*, i, p. 653 (text p. 583)).
31. *MuzA-T*, f.282a.
32. Mutribi al-Asamm Samarqandi, *Khatirat-i Mutribi*, ed. A.G. Mirzoev, Karachi, 1977, p. 26.
33. *TA*, ii, pp. 750-1.
34. Riazul Islam, ed., *Bahr al-asrar* (*travelogue portion*), Karachi, 1980, p. 10.
35. H.M. Said, S.M. Haq, and A.Z. Khan, eds., *Bahr al-asrar*, v. 1, pt. 1, Karachi, 1984, p. 16.
36. Ibid., p. 21.
37. Islam, *Indo-Persian Relations*, p. 250.
38. Riazul Islam, 'A History of Central Asia', *Journal of Central Asia* 13/2 (1990), pp. 13-14.
39. Nizamutdinov, *Ocherki*, p. 18.
40. Ziaev, Silsilat al-salatin, Ahmedov, *Politiko-geograficheskaya literatura*, McChesney, *Waqf.*
41. *TQK-T*, ff. 123a-124a. This particular copy is mistitled *Tarikh-i-Shibani Khan wa mu'amalat ba awlad-i-Amir Timur*. See also *Sobranie*, ix, p. 17; Bregel, *Persidskaya literatura*, i, p. 447; Ahmedov, *Politiko-geograficheskaya literatura*; and Ph.D. dissertation by Enver Khurshid, IOSUAS, 1991.
42. 'Ba munosibati 350-solagii Mirzo Bedil' *Ovozi Samarkand*, 25 January 1995. See also Shavkat Shukurov, 'Pairavon va ikhlosmandoni Bedil dar Osioi Miona', *Ba'zi mas'alahoi an'ana va navovari dar adabioti tojik*, Samarqand, 1993, pp. 9-21; Idem, 'Ustod S. Aini dar tadkiki osori Bedil', *Mas'alahoi filologiia va robitai adabi*, Samarqand, 1978, pp. 19-40; M. Shukurov and J. Baqozoda, 'Avvalin fikru mulohizahoi ustod dar borai Bedil', *Jashnomai Aini*, v. 3, Dushanbe, 1966, pp. 151-158; Sadruddin Aini, *Mirzo Abdulqodir Bedil*, Stalinabad, 1954; and O. Idrisii, 'Mirzo Bedil hakida' *Shuro* 2 (1912), pp. 42-3.
43. M. Ashrafi, 'K izuchenyu material'noi kultury po dannym miniatury Maverannahr XV-XVI vv.', in *Borbad and Cultural Traditions of Central Asiatic Peoples: the History and the Present*, Dushanbe, 1990, pp. 86-8, 91.
44. See M.B. Dickson and S.C. Welch, Jr., *The Houghton Shahnameh*, Cambridge MA, 1981, Chapter One.
45. Welch, *India*, p. 210.
46. According to M. Ashrafi, the Herat style first began to penetrate Transoxiana under ʿUbaydallah Khan, leading to the evolution of a distinct Bukhara style in the 1540s (Ashrafi, 'Material'noi kultury', p. 260).

47. Semënov, 'Kul'turno-politicheskikh sviaziakh', p. 8.
48. Welch, *India*, p. 146.
49. Ibid., p. 155.
50. Milo C. Beach, *Early Mughal Painting*, Harvard University Press, Cambridge MA, 1987, p. 66.
51. Ibid., p. 72.
52. Ibid., p. 66. For a discussion of later Central Asian painting see O.F. Akimushkin and A.A. Ivanov, 'O Maverannahrskoi shkole miniatiurnoi zhivopisi XVII v.', *Narody Azii i Afriki* (1966).
53. Welch, *India*, p. 210.
54. *Nafa'is al-ma'athirat*, ff.60b-61a.
55. Dickson and Welch, *Houghton Shahnameh*, p. 39.
56. Ibid., p. 87.
57. Nizamutdinov, *Ocherki*. The *Tuzuk* edition of Rogers and Beveridge says he was originally from Marv (*TJ*, ii, p. 20), while a manuscript version says he was from Herat.
58. Semënov, 'Kul'turno-politicheskikh sviaziakh', p. 8; Nizamutdinov, *Ocherki*, p. 32. See also V.G. Dolinskaya, 'Khudozhnik-miniatiurist Mukhammed Murad Samarkandi', *Izvestiia Akademii Nauk UzSSR* 9, (1955), p. 54.
59. A.C. Castman, 'Four Mughal Emperor Portraits in the City Art Museum of St. Louis', *Journal of Near Eastern Studies* 15/2 (1966); T.V. Grek, 'Indiiskie miniatiury XVI-XVIII vv.', in *Al'bom indiiskikh i persidskikh miniatiurii XVI-XVIII vv.*, ed. L.T. Gyuzal'ian, Moscow, 1962, pp. 18-19.
60. *AA*, i, p. 413.
61. Beveridge, *Babur-nama*, p. xxviii.
62. Ibid., p. 75.
63. *MT*, ii, p. 45 (text p. 49).
64. *TJ*, ii, pp. 30-1; *JN*, p. 273.
65. *MA*, p. 167 (text p. 272).
66. *MT*, ii, pp. 329-30 (text p. 320). The Persian title is *Razm-nama*, or 'Book of Battles'.
67. K.A. Nizami, 'Naqshbandi Influence on Mughal Rulers and Politics', *Islamic Culture* 39 (1965), p. 47.
68. *MA*, p. 96 (text p. 156); Richards, *Mughal Empire*, p. 175.
69. *BN*, p.5.
70. *PN*, i, pp. 97-8, 286; *AS*, i, p. 361.
71. David Pingree, 'Indian Reception of Muslim Versions of Ptolemaic Astronomy', in F. Jamil Ragep and Sally P. Ragep, eds., *Tradition, Transmission, Transformation*, E.J. Brill, Leiden, 1996, p. 475.
72. Idem., 'Islamic Astronomy in Sanskrit', *Journal for the History of Arabic Science* 2/2 (1978), p. 322.

73. Hakeem Abdul Hameed, *Exchanges Between India and Central Asia in the Field of Medicine*, New Delhi, 1986, pp. 39-41. With the exception of Khwaja Khawind, all the physicians mentioned in this study are from Iran, and not Central Asia as the title suggests.

74. B. Na'ini, *Zamzama-yi-wahdat*, IOSUAS MS 10226/II; see also A.B. Djumaev, 'Unikal'nyi istochnik po istorii Sredniaziatsko-indiskikh muzikal'nykh sviaziei (*Zamzame-yi Vahdat* Naini) XVII v.', *Iz istorii kulturnykh sviaziei narodov Srednei Azii i Indii*, Fan, Tashkent, 1986, pp. 115-124.

75. Spector, 'Musical Tradition', p. 439.

76. Semënov, *Traktat*, p. 63. The *dutar* is a two-stringed Central Asian lute.

77. *AA*, i, p. 301.

78. *AA*, i, p. 315.

79. *SJN*, p. 244.

80. *AA*, i, p. 253.

81. Hoag, 'Tomb', p. 236.

82. Ibid., p. 241.

83. Golombek, 'Tamerlane to Taj Mahal', p. 48.

84. M.E. Subtelny, 'Mirak-i-Sayyid Ghiyas and the Timurid Tradition of Landscape Architecture', *Studia Iranica*, 24/1 (1995), p. 34.

85. Ibid., p. 31.

86. Golombek, 'Tamerlane to Taj Mahal', p. 49.

87. A.H. Dani, *New Light on Central Asia*, Sang-e-Meel, Lahore, 1994, p. 40.

88. Hoag, 'Tomb', p. 243.

89. Nizamutdinov, *Ocherki*, p. 14.

CHAPTER 5

THE NAQSHBANDIYYA AND THE MUGHALS

As was seen in the preceding chapter, one of the most striking examples of the ongoing link with Central Asia which the Mughals maintained can be seen in their attachment to religious figures of Bukhara and other Uzbek-controlled lands. A significant element of the Mughals' inheritance as Timurids was an attachment to the Naqshbandi sufi order. In particular, this connection was personified in the figure of Khwaja ʿUbaydullah Ahrar, who was intrumental in ensuring the political position of the Timurid, Abu Saʿid. While the latter was the nominal ruler of Transoxiana during the mid-1400s, it is generally considered that Khwaja Ahrar held the reins of actual power.[1]

Before his death, Khwaja Ahrar is said to have selected the Muslim name for the infant Babur.[2] A highlight of Babur's Central Asian career in his youth was when he was called to Samarqand by Khwaja Ahrar's son, Khwaja Yahya, to defend the city against Shibani Khan's Uzbeks.[3] Though he failed to hold Samarqand on this and other occasions, Babur later demonstrated his enduring attachment to the memory of Khwaja Ahrar by setting his work *Risala-yi-walidiyya* to verse.[4]

Another of Ahrar's sons, Muhammad Amin, was part of Babur's entourage at Kabul and in India.[5] Thus, while credit for establishing the Naqshbandiyya in India is usually given to Khwaja Baqi bi'llah, who emigrated from Central

Asia later in the sixteenth century, Babur's personal
connection to Khwaja Ahrar and his descendants represents
at least an element of Naqshbandi influence arriving in
Hindustan at the outset of the Mughal period.

This is not to say that the Timurids, or Chaghatays, as
they were known in the tribal context of the times, were
unique in their attachment to the Naqshbandi order. In
fact Babur's arch-rival, the Uzbek Shibani Khan, was, in the
words of Annemarie Schimmel, 'deeply bound to the
Naqshbandi order, and often sought help at the tomb of
Hazrat Naqshband'.[6] This apparent irony can be explained
by the fact that by the end of the fifteenth century, in
Central Asia it had become imperative for anyone with
political aspirations to have Naqshbandi support since it
was by patronizing the order that political figures built ties
to the general population.[7]

The universally recognized stature of certain Naqshbandi
sheikhs not only helped ensure their survival through
decades of political turmoil in Central Asia, but also
enabled them to benefit from the respect and tribute of a
broad base of often mutually antagonistic political figures.
Often, as in the case of Mughal-Uzbek diplomacy, it was
this position which led Naqshbandi shaykhs to be chosen
as ambassadors.

The Naqshbandiyya are unusual among sufi orders in
their historical proclivity toward political involvement. The
order has its origins in the twelfth century, but became
associated with the figure of Khwaja Baha' al-din
Naqshband (d.1389) two centuries later. Under Baha' al-
din's influence, the order focused on the practice of silent
repetition (*dhikr*), and became known as a sober sufi order,
repudiating common mystical practices such as music and
dance (*sama͑a*), miracle-working (*karamat*), and wearing
distinctive forms of dress, and by favouring fellowship
(*suhbat*) over seclusion (*khalwat*).[8] It was under Khwaja
͑Ubaydullah Ahrar that the order adopted the doctrine of
social participation (*khalwat dar anjuman*), which asserted

that sufi leaders should attempt to influence political
figures since the latter held so much influence over the
lives and well-being of Muslims.[9] By the end of the sixteenth
century, the Naqshbandiyya alone of the sufi orders in India
'considered it not only permissible but imperative to
establish contact with rulers, and to attempt to influence
their thoughts and policies'.[10]

In Central Asia, where through application of this policy,
Khwaja Ahrar became the most politically powerful
individual of the second half of the fifteenth century, a
number of Naqshbandi shaykhs acquired great economic
power and personal wealth as well, not only through tribute
from their disciples but also as the administrators
(*mutawallis*) of untaxable pious endowmments (*waqfs*),
reaping large profits and wielding influence through their
control of land, shrines, and other property. Their
acceptance as spiritual guides by members of the ruling
class ensured their continuing political influence, and
sometimes they even led troops in battle. By passing on
their positions to their sons, certain shaykhs established
virtual dynasties of wealth and local power.

The descendants of Khwaja Ahrar, based in Samarqand,
formed one such 'dynastic' group. In addition to their
stature as spiritual guides, the Ahraris had many important
financial interests, including control over several important
local shrines. Nevertheless, a number of them chose to go
to India and enter the service of the Mughals. Perhaps the
first of these was Khwaja Yusuf, a grandson of Khwaja Ahrar,
who accompanied Babur to India in 1526. One of Khwaja
Yusuf's brothers, Khwaja Khawind Mahmud, joined Babur's
court at Agra after travelling to Iran and Kashgar; according
to the *Akbar-nama*, Babur 'gave him the chief seat at
meetings'.[11] Khwaja Khawind's son, Khwaja Mu'in, was in
the service of Akbar. Khwaja Mu'in's son, Sharaf al-din
Husayn, rebelled twice and was eventually killed.[12] Khwaja
Khawind himself eventually returned to Central Asia, after

the Emperor Humayun began to seek the spiritual guidance of the Shattari shaykh ʿAbdullah Khan.[13]

Another brother of Khwaja Yusuf, Khwaja ʿAbd al-Shahid, spent twenty years in Mughal service before returning to Samarqand where he died in 1575.[14] The *Tabaqat–Akbari* states that ʿAbd al-Shahid held a *jagir* in the *pargana* of Jamari and used the revenues to support 2000 *faqirs*.[15] Akbar's court chronicler, Abu'l Fazl, lists ʿAbd al-Shahid among the scholars of the second class.[16] He says of his status at court:

> As the righteousness and seeking after God of this Khwaja was conjectured by some, and was known to others, the Khedive of the world in this worship [Akbar] paid attention to him, and having regard to the holy man he took him out of the lower ranks [of spectators] and gave him a place near himself.[17]

ʿAbd al-Shahid's influence with the Emperor was not without limits, however; his attempts to obtain a royal pardon for his relative, the rebel Sharaf al-din, were in vain.[18]

Two of Ahrar's great-grandsons, ʿAbd al-Kafi and Khwaja Qasim, held posts in Humayun's administration.[19] Another great-grandson of Khwaja Ahrar, Khwaja Yahya, was appointed by Akbar as Leader of the Holy Pilgrimage (*Mir hajj*) in 1578, and accompanied the Emperor's aunt, Gulbadan Begum, and other ladies of the royal house on their return from Mecca in 1580.[20]

In 1590, three Ahrari brothers came to seek their fortunes in India: ʿAbdullah Khan (not to be confused with the Uzbek ruler or the Shattari shaykh), Yadgar Khwaja, and Barkhurdar Khwaja. They first came to work for a relative, Shir Khwaja, in the Deccan, but soon relocated to Lahore in the service of Akbar's son and heir-apparent, Prince Salim (later Jahangir). ʿAbdullah Khan acquired a reputation as a successful military leader, which earned him the title of *Safdar jang* ('valiant in battle'), but his support of Akbar during Salim's revolt led to his disgrace upon the latter's accession and he was condemned to be blinded.[21]

Yet another of Ahrar's progeny in Akbar's service, Khwaja Zakariyya, is mentioned in Jahangir's memoirs (the *Tuzuk-i-Jahangiri*) as having fallen from favour, but was pardoned on Jahangir's accession in 1605.[22]

A second important clan of Samarqand Naqshbandis was the Dihbidi family, the descendants of Khwaja Kasani, a.k.a. Makhdum-i-ʿazam, who was spiritual preceptor (*pir* or *murshid*) to several Shibanid Uzbek rulers during the first half of the sixteenth century. Like the Ahraris, the Dihbidi sheikhs maintained connections with the Mughals in India. Emperor Jahangir's engaging in *mujawaba* with Khwaja Hashim Dihbidi has been mentioned in the preceding chapter. His memoirs mention a gift of five falcons which the shaykh sent 'by way of supplication' (*ba rasm-i-niaz*). Jahangir responded with 5000 rupees to be spent on 'whatever would be agreeable' to the Khwaja.[23] The *Tuzuk* also records that in 1620 the Emperor sent 10,000 rupees to Samarqand with an embassy led by Mir Baraka; half of this sum was to go to 'the custodians attached to the tomb of Timur' (*ba mansuban wa mujawiran-i-rawza-yi-muqaddasa-yi-hazrat-i-Sahib-qirani*) and the other half to Khwaja Salih Dihbidi, 'who from his fathers was one of the well-wishers of this state'.[24] Some years later, when Mutribi, visiting from Samarqand, mentions that Khwaja Hashim is his spiritual advisor, Jahangir excitedly interjects that he himself is one of the Khwaja's followers.[25]

A third group of Naqshbandi shaykhs, the Juybari family, was based in Bukhara. Soviet historiography has treated the Juybaris and their like as 'feudal landlords', finding in them equivalents to mediaeval European and Russian petty despots. The dynamics of *waqf* economics in Muslim society cannot be so neatly equated to that of European feudalism, but unfortunately the Soviet Marxist interpretation of Central Asian economic history has yet to be reworked. For

the present, the most extensive study on the subject is still
P.P. Ivanov's 1954 commentary on a collection of sale
documents from the Juybari family archives edited in the
original Persian by Ye.E. Bertel's in 1938.[26]

Ivanov's study concentrates on demonstrating the wealth
and power of the Juybari shaykhs, whose 'worldly despotism'
is seen as analogous to that of mediaeval European abbots
and feudal princes. Many of the documents studied are
bills of sale, showing property passing from various
members of the nobility into the shaykhs' possession. Ivanov
calculates, for example, that Khwaja Ahrar himself
controlled 35,000 hectares of agricultural land in the
Samarqand region.[27] He goes on to describe how the
Juybari shaykhs controlled not only productive lands but
the canals used to irrigate them,[28] in addition to other
interests such as shops and inns (*karwansarais*).[29]

For his biographical information Ivanov relies mainly on
a mid-seventeenth century family history, the *Matlab al-
talibin*, compiled by Muhammad Talib b. Taj al-din Juybari
by around 1665.[30] This chronicle traces the family origins
along the paternal line back to Imam Husayn, grandson of
the Prophet, and on the maternal side to Chinghis Khan
through Juchi and (rather implausibly) through the Edigü
to the first Muslim Caliph, Abu Bakr.[31] Thus, not unusually
for such family histories, the *Matlab* legitimizes the Juybaris
both as descendants of the Prophet (*sayyids*) and, like the
Uzbek ruling class of the time, as heirs to the Mongols.

The first major figure described in the *Matlab* is Khwaja
Muhammad Islam, a.k.a. Khwaja Juybari (1493-1563). Of
his father, Khwaja Ahmad, little is said apart from that he
was very rich and that he was murdered in a crowd.[32] At
age twelve, Khwaja Islam became a disciple of Khwaja
Kasani of the Dihbidi family. Years later, Khwaja Islam was
elevated to the position of spiritual head of the community
(*shaykh-al-islam*) by ʿAbdullah Khan following the latter's
emergence in 1557 as victor in the Shibanids' internecine

struggles for control of Bukhara, and is said to have 'advised the young ruler in all important matters of state'.[33]

At his death in 1563, Khwaja Islam passed on to his eldest son Sa{c}ad not only his personal property and assets, but his students and disciples as well.[34] Khwaja Sa{c}ad (a.k.a. Khwaja Kalan, 1531-89) increased the family's wealth through land purchases and other means, and played an important role in local administration. The *Matlab* gives him credit for helping elevate {c}Abdullah Khan to the unified throne of Transoxiana in 1583.[35] It states as well that Khwaja Sa{c}ad was 'constantly receiving gifts and letters' from rulers and administrators in India, Turkey, and elsewhere.[36] Poets are said to have dedicated over 10,000 lines to him,[37] and on his excursions out of the city, he is said to have taken no less than seventy to eighty tents.[38] Ivanov comments that, 'from his lifestyle Khwaja Sa{c}ad appears more as a typical feudal landlord of his time, than as the honourable sufi his biographer and contemporaries describe'.[39] He goes on to suggest that 'the khwaja's popularity among his contemporaries was connected not so much with his spiritual qualities, as with his wealth and his influence at the court'.[40]

Carrying on the tradition of primogeniture, Khwaja Sa{c}ad bequeathed the lion's share of his legacy to his eldest son, Taj al-din Hasan (1547?-1646). Of an 18,000 *ashrafi* cash inheritance, Taj al-Din received 14,000, and Sa{c}ad's second son {c}Abd al-Rahim (b.1575) a mere 4000, while the third son, {c}Abd al-Karim (a.k.a. {c}Abdi or {c}Abidin, b.1577), and two daughters received nothing.[41] The two younger brothers remained quite well off, however. {c}Abd al-Rahim had from six to eight hundred plots of land bearing a total average income of 40,000 *khanis*,[42] owned a number of houses and 400 slaves,[43] while {c}Abd al-Karim also controlled land, irrigation systems, and mercantile interests.[44] Yet both brothers eventually had political problems and emigrated to Mughal India.

First to go was ᶜAbd al-Karim, who fell foul of his 'disciple' Baqi Muhammad, leader of the new Ashtarkhanid dynasty, whose sister he had married.[45] On arriving in India c.1603-4, he entered Akbar's service, and at Jahangir's accession had his rank raised to commander of 1000.[46] ᶜAbd al-Karim died in India in 1606-7 before the age of 30.

ᶜAbd al-Rahim, meanwhile, had married his younger brother's royal ex-wife. But following the accession of Imam Quli to the throne of Bukhara in 1611, for reasons unknown the new ruler forced ᶜAbd al-Rahim to go on a pilgrimage to Mecca (a standard means for getting rid of disgraced individuals) and requisitioned his property.[47] ᶜAbd al-Rahim broke off his journey near Isfahan due to illness and returned to Bukhara to recuperate. After some time, in 1625, he was sufficiently restored to favour to be sent as Imam Quli's ambassador to the Mughal court.

According to the *Matlab al-talibin*, the trip was ᶜAbd al-Rahim's idea. He is said to have long wished to visit India (*hich waqt hawa-yi-ziyarat az khatir-i-Khwaja namiraft*) and to have voiced his concern to Imam Quli over the struggle between Jahangir and his son Prince Khurram (later Shah Jahan), who was in revolt. Imam Quli is quoted as replying that the Juybaris had proven their effectiveness in such reconciliations. Imam Quli's ministers, meanwhile, are said to have protested against sending such an important person as ᶜAbd al-Rahim to India, whereupon Imam Quli replied that it was the Khwaja who wished to go, and that he was powerless to stop him.[48]

Despite this version of the story, it is clear from other sources that Imam Quli eagerly wished a letter to be conveyed to Jahangir in which he called for a joint attack on the Safavids, whereby Qandahar would revert to the Mughals and Khorasan to the Uzbeks.[49] The *Matlab* plays up the extraordinary importance and significance given to ᶜAbd al-Rahim's trip, describing in detail how 'all the best examples of every type [of Central Asian specialty] which had never been seen or heard of [in India]' were gathered as gifts for the Mughal emperor, including horses, mules, furs, camels, expensive books, and calligraphies, in addition to 300,000 *tanga*s in cash from ᶜAbd al-Rahim and 100,000 from Imam Quli.[50]

ᶜAbd al-Rahim's reception by Jahangir, described in both Central Asian and Indian sources, provides what may be the most vivid illustration of the respect and esteem which the Mughals accorded to the Naqshbandi sheikhs of Central Asia. Jahangir ordered all his nobles and ministers to go out and receive ᶜAbd al-Rahim since, according to the *Iqbal-nama-yi-Jahangiri*, 'up to now no one as exalted and holy as the Khwaja had come to India'.[51] The Central Asian visitor, Mutribi, attests to Jahangir's anticipation of ᶜAbd al-Rahim's arrival, stating that the Emperor's annual excursion to Kashmir had been delayed for the occasion.[52]

The *Matlab* asserts that the Mughal subjects were so amazed by the hospitality lavished upon ᶜAbd al-Rahim and his entourage throughout their approach to Lahore that 'their fingers were in their teeth'. Upon his arrival at the capital, ᶜAbd al-Rahim refused to rest before obtaining an audience with Jahangir, news of which left the Emperor 'greatly pleased'. The Khwaja was greeted first by the Empress Nur Jahan and her brother Asaf Khan, then the Emperor himself descended from the throne to welcome him with a hug.[53] ᶜAbd al-Rahim rebuffed Jahangir's attempts to have him entertained by all the nobles of the court, saying that his purpose in coming was to offer advice and not to socialize. One piece of advice which the Emperor appears to have accepted was to pardon the disgraced Ahrari shaykh ᶜAbdullah Khan (before the sentence of blinding was carried out) and restore him to his former rank.[54]

As stated by Mutribi, Jahangir, whose health was failing, had delayed his trip to the healing climate of Kashmir in anticipation of ᶜAbd al-Rahim's arrival. The Emperor enticed the Khwaja to accompany the royal party on their journey north, and they spent the summer of 1627 there.

On the way back to Lahore Jahangir, his condition no
doubt exacerbated by overindulgence in the feasts he is
described as having thrown for ᶜAbd al-Rahim, finally passed
away on 27 Safar 1037 (28 October 1627) after a hunting
expedition.

After spending some time at Lahore following the
Emperor's death, ᶜAbd al-Rahim proceeded to Agra to
present himself to Shah Jahan. The new Emperor gave him
a gold-embroidered robe of honour and 50,000 rupees,
and seated him by the throne along with his sons, the royal
princes.[55]

ᶜAbd al-Rahim did not return to Bukhara, but died in
India like his brother, ᶜAbd al-Karim, during the month of
Sha'ban 1038 (March 1629), 'of a disease of long
standing'.[56] His son, Muhammad Sadiq, is said in the *Matlab*
to have accompanied the body back to Bukhara where it
was buried with full honours under the supervision of Imam
Quli Khan.[57] Taj al-Din divided his brother ᶜAbd al-Rahim's
property among his two surviving sons and six daughters.[58]

Following the Mughal conquest of Balkh province in
1646, which proved temporary, yet another Juybari sheikh,
Taj al-din's second son Tayyib, chose to come to India.[59]
He was richly rewarded by Shah Jahan, and soon his
children came from Central Asia and joined him at the
Mughal court.[60] When his elder brother Yusuf died, Tayyib
returned to Samarqand to become head of the Juybari
family.[61]

The Mughal attachment to the Naqshbandi order in
India persisted throughout the active life of the dynasty. A
letter written in the late seventeenth century by Shah
Kalimullah of Delhi, a shaykh of the Chishti order, to a
disciple who had been trying unsuccessfully to influence
the Emperor Aurangzeb, contains the following
admonition:

> The Emperor of Hindustan is a descendant of Amir Timur
> and Amir Timur was spiritually attached to Shah-i-Naqshband.

These Turanians, all and every one of them, are connected with the Naqshbandi order and they do not attach value to any other *silsilah*.[62]

This passage suggests that even after nearly two centuries of rule by the Mughals, at least some Indians still thought of them as Central Asians.

NOTES

1. See Jo-Ann Gross, Khoja Ahrar: 'A Study of the Perceptions of Religious Power and Prestige in the Late Timurid Period', Ph.D. thesis, New York University, 1982.
2. Beveridge, *Babur-nama*, p. xxviii.
3. Ibid., p. 124; Muhammad Salih, *Shibani-nama*, ed. P.M. Melioranskii, St. Petersburg, 1908, p. 31.
4. *AN*, i, p. 278 (text p. 118). Babur did this so that he might better be able to memorize it. See A.J.E. Bodrogligeti, 'Babur Shah's Chaghatai Version of the Risala-i-Validiya: A Central Asian Turkic Treatise on How to Emulate the Prophet Muhammad', *Ural-Altaic Yearbook* 56 (1984), pp. 1-61.
5. Muhammad Hashim Kishmi Badakhshani, *Nisamat al-quds*, Sialkot, 1990, cited in Arthur Buehler, 'The Naqshbandiyya in India', *Journal of Islamic Studies* 7/2 (1996), p. 212.
6. Annemarie Schimmel, 'Some Notes on the Cultural Activity of the First Uzbek Rulers', *Journal of the Pakistan Historical Society* 8/3 (1960), p. 153.
7. Gross, Khoja Ahrar, p. 13.
8. Hamid Algar, 'Naḳhsband', *Encyclopedia of Islam$_2$*.
9. Hamid Algar, 'The Naqshbandi Order: A Preliminary Survey of its History and Significance', *Studia Islamica* 44 (1976), pp. 137-8. See also Gross, Khoja Ahrar.
10. Nizami, 'Naqshbandi Influence', p. 41.
11. *AN*, ii, pp. 301-2 (text p. 194).
12. *TA*, ii, p. 655.
13. *MU*, i, p. 87. On leaving Humayun and India, Khwaja Khawind recited as a parting shot: 'Say, O Huma, ne'er cast thy shadow/ In a land where the parrot is less accounted than the kite.'
14. *AN*, ii, p. 195 (text p. 127); *AA*, i, p. 539; *MT*, iii, pp. 65-6 (text p. 40). Bada'uni states that ʿAbd al-Shahid's time in India was only seventeen years.

15. *TA*, ii, pp. 700-1; *AA*, i, p. 608.
16. *AA*, i, p. 608.
17. *AN*, iii, p. 109.
18. *MT*, ii, p. 174 (p. 171). Bada'uni says that 'Although the Emperor did not neglect any marks of due honour and respect... still his reverence felt much grief at the refusal'.
19. Buehler, 'Naqshbandiyya', p. 214.
20. *AN*, iii, pp. 569-70 (text p. 385). The royal entourage suffered considerable discourtesies at the hands of Mecca's Ottoman administration. See N.R. Farooqi, 'Six Ottoman Documents on Mughal-Ottoman Relations During the Reign of Akbar', *Journal of Islamic Studies* 7/1 (1996), pp. 32-48. Khwaja Yahya is not to be confused with his great uncle, mentioned above.
21. *MU*, i, pp. 97-102.
22. *TJ*, i, p. 31; *JN*, p. 18.
23. '*har qism-i-muta^c ki marzi-yi Khwaja danad*' (*TJ*, ii, p. 10; *JN*, p. 358).
24. *TJ*, ii, p. 196; *JN*, p. 370.
25. *KM*, p. 33-4.
26. Ivanov, *Khoziaistvo Dzhuibarskikh sheikhov*, Ye.E. Bertel's, *Iz arkhiva sheikhov Dzhuibari*, Moscow, 1938. Ivanov's work includes a Russian translation of the documents collected by Bertel's.
27. Ivanov, *Khoziaistvo Dzhuibarskikh sheikhov*, p. 13.
28. The word *juybar* itself means 'canal-master'. The Juybari family was so known because they came from the Juybar quarter of Bukhara.
29. Ivanov, *Khoziaistvo Dzhuibarskikh sheikhov*, p. 43.
30. Ivanov uses MS 60, Oriental Institute of the Russian Academy of Sciences. Three more copies exist at the Institute of Oriental Studies in Tashkent, nos.80, 1461/I, and 3757. I have consulted a copy from the Preussische Staatsbibliothek, Berlin, MS Or.1540 (*MatT*). An earlier work, the *Rawzat al-rizwan fi hadikat al-ghilman* of Badr al-din Kashmiri, details the Juybari family fortunes up to the end of the sixteenth century (IOSUAS MS 2094).
31. Ivanov, *Khoziaistvo Dzhuibarskikh sheikhov*, p. 48.
32. Ibid., p. 49. Ivanov assumes this must have been part of a 'peasant uprising'.
33. Ibid., pp. 50-1.
34. Ibid., p. 55.
35. Ibid., p. 66.
36. Ibid.
37. Ibid.
38. Ibid.
39. Ibid.
40. Ibid., p. 67.
41. Ibid.

42. The Central Asian *khani*, which as another term for the *tanga*, was worth 1/3 of a rupee from 1605-27, devalued to 1/5 of a rupee by 1633. In the mid-seventeenth century a *tanga* was equal to 1/9 of a French *écu* (Burton, 'Bukharan Trade', p. 87).
43. Ibid., p. 75.
44. Ibid.
45. Ibid., p. 77.
46. *TJ*, i, p. 60; *JN*, p. 35.
47. Ivanov, *Khoziaistvo Dzhuibarskikh sheikhov*, p. 7.
48. *MatT*, f.172.
49. *MU*, i, p. 605.
50. *MatT*, f.173.
51. Mu'tamad Khan, *Iqbal-nama-i Jahangiri*, Calcutta, 1895, p. 612; cited in Rahim, 'Mughal Relations', p. 93. The *Matlab al-talibin* devotes several pages to describing ʿAbd al-Rahim's reception in India (*MatT*, ff.173-176).
52. *KM*, p. 45.
53. *MatT*, f.174.
54. *MatT*, f.175.
55. *PN*, i, p. 194. In Lahauri's version, it is Shah Jahan, and not Jahangir, who grants ʿAbd al-Rahim's request to pardon ʿAbdullah Khan Ahrari. The *Ma'athir al-'umara'* follows Lahauri's account (i, p. 605). In this matter I am inclined to feel the *Matlab* account has less cause to be biased.
56. *MU*, i, p. 605.
57. *MatT*, f.177. According to the *Silsilat as-salatin*, an early eighteenth century source, Muhammad Sadiq stayed on in India after his father died (*SS*, f.193a).
58. *MatT*, f.177.
59. *PN*, ii, p. 611; *MU*, ii, p. 964-5.
60. Ibid., pp. 627, 632, 678-9; *AS*, iii, p. 22.
61. *AS*, iii, p. 153.
62. *Maktubat-i-Kalimi*, p. 75; cited in Nizami, 'Naqshbandi Influence', p. 42.

CHAPTER 6

TRAVELOGUES

The Mediterranean world viewed India as a land of miracles, wonders, and freaks from at least as early as Classical Greek times.[1] From the tenth century onwards, Muslim travellers fed this tall-tale tradition with their own accounts. Early examples of this type are included in the *Kitab ʿajaʾib al-hind*, written around 956 CE, attributed (probably falsely) to an Iranian sea captain by the name of Buzurg son of Shahryar, whose account is one of several in that collection. In this book it is stated that 'God...divided the marvels of His creation into ten parts...[of which] eight belong to India and China...'.[2] The first such major work by a Central Asian Muslim is, of course, the *Kitab fi tahqiq ma liʾl-Hind* of Abu Rayhan Muhammad Biruni, written in the early eleventh century.[3] Biruni comments, among other observations, that:

> ...the Hindus entirely differ from us in every respect, many a subject appearing intricate and obscure which would be perfectly clear if there were more connection between us... First, they differ from us in everything which other nations have in common...Secondly, they totally differ from us in religion, as we believe in nothing in which they believe, and vice versa...In the third place, in all manners and usages they differ from us to such a degree as to frighten their children with us, with our dress, and our ways and customs, and as to declare us to be devil's breed, and our doings as the very opposite of all that is good and proper.[4]

A near contemporary of Biruni, Abu Sa'id ibn Mahmud
Gardizi, while agreeing that 'In [the Hindus'] religion there
are differences, as well as in their customs', points out that:

> The people of India are skilful, clever, and shrewd. They make
> good and subtle things. From their midst come many sages,
> especially in the province of Kashmir. Their arts are very
> prodigious.[5]

Centuries later Babur, who came to India only as a last
resort when all attempts to re-establish himself in
Samarqand had failed, had fairly negative first impressions:

> Hindustan is a place of little charm. There is no beauty in its
> people, no graceful social intercourse, no poetic talent or
> understanding, no etiquette, no nobility or manliness. In the
> arts and crafts there is no harmony or symmetry, there are no
> good horses, no good meat, no good grapes, melons, or fruit.
> There is no ice, no cold water, no good food, or bread in the
> markets. There are no baths and no *madrasas*. There are no
> candles, torches, or candlesticks.[6]

Babur also complains frequently of the lack of running
water, so revered in his native part of the world. In fact the
only good things Babur has to say about India are that it is
a big place, has an abundance of gold and silver, and offers
a large work force. But it is for the Hindustani Muslims
that he saves his worst rhetoric. In his eyes they are
'unworthy, disgusting and importunate, most of them being
showy, superficial, and disagreeable'.[7] Yet he and his
entourage stayed, and two generations later the Mughals
had become the leading sponsors of Central Asian
immigration to the subcontinent.

From the early seventeenth century two very interesting
Central Asian accounts of Mughal India have come down
to us: the Indian memoirs of Mutribi al-Asamm Samarqandi,
and the travelogue of Mahmud b. Amir Wali. Written in
stylistically different but distinctly personal voices untypical

for their time, these accounts offer valuable first-person insights into the minds and outlooks of their authors and shed light on the nature of how Muslims in Asia thought about their world and its boundaries.

The first account is a chatty, personal memoir of the author's short tenure as a guest at the court of Emperor Jahangir.[8] The second is Mahmud b. Amir Wali's travelogue of India and Ceylon, published in an edition by Riazul Islam. It was originally appended as a *khatima* (appendix) to volume six of Mahmud's vast work, the *Bahr al-asrar fi manaqib al-akhyar*,[9] a monumental history of the world written at the behest of Nazr Muhammad Khan.

The two works under discussion differ enormously in style and content, reflecting the very different profiles of their authors. Mutribi's memoirs are written in a clear, simple, anecdotal style, while Mahmud's writing is deliberately difficult and abstruse, in the most convoluted tradition of Persian prose. Mutribi, who was well advanced in years when he set off for India, wrote as an intimate of the wealthiest emperor in the world, describing the numerous favours bestowed upon him during his stay at Lahore which lasted only a few months. Mahmud, on the other hand, spent the first several years of his six-and-a-half year sojourn in India as little more than a wandering mendicant, often grumpy, irritable, and hungry. As early as Kabul, Mahmud complains of despair and loneliness, until a friendly stranger offers to feed him out of pity.[10] Later, on his first visit to the famed former capital of Agra, he and a temporary travel companion become so exasperated at the lack of instant charity that they decide to leave the town immediately, without having seen anything.[11] Mahmud was a considerably younger man than Mutribi— he was probably under thirty—and with no resources, contacts, or reputation to rely upon; indeed, Mahmud appears to us like something of a seventeenth century predecessor to the rucksack-toting overlanders of the 1970s.

But age was only one of numerous differences between the two authors, though their backgrounds in Central Asia had some elements in common. Mutribi was born in Samarqand in 1559. Apparently something of a child prodigy as a musician (*Mutribi* is a sobriquet, meaning 'minstrel', or 'hired musician'), he went to Bukhara after completing his initial religious education. There he became a disciple of the illustrious Naqshbandi shaykh, Khwaja Hasan Nisari, in whose presence he developed his appreciation for poetry and literature. Mahmud was born in Balkh. His birth date is uncertain, but from subsequent events of his career it would appear to have been somewhere around 1595–8. He received his education at Bukhara, and composed a *mathnawi* (epic poem) entitled *Mahabbat-nama* and a divan known as *Najm-i-saqib* while still young.[12] He became a disciple of Shaykh Sayyid Mirakshah Husayni and spent ten years in a sufi hermitage. During that time he composed the *Rawa'ih-i-tayyiba*, and dedicated it to his sheikh.

Mutribi, meanwhile, had been enjoying the patronage of the Ashtarkhanid ruler, Wali Muhammad, for whom he composed an anthology of poets in 1604.[13] It was after the death of his patron in 1612 that Mutribi decided to travel, as many of his countrymen had done, to Mughal India in search of increased fame and fortune. Unfortunately, the responsibility of supporting twenty family members in Samarqand delayed him until their collective financial situation, at last in 1620, permitted him to begin preparations for his journey. It seems to have occurred to Mutribi about this time to revise his earlier anthology as a gift by which to ingratiate himself to Emperor Jahangir. With this aim in mind, he spent two years in Balkh and Badakhshan gathering additional information on Central Asian poets, and after spending a further year revising his work, he left for Lahore, arriving there in 1626 at the ripe old age of 70.

One can surmise that Mutribi's motivations in travelling to India at such an advanced age were to a great degree financial. From the intensity with which he prepared his 'offering' for Jahangir and the brevity of his stay once received at court, it appears he hoped to make a quick killing. In his first audience with the Emperor, Mutribi is told he will be given four things: spending money, clothing, a horse, and a slave boy. When Jahangir asks which his guest would like first, Mutribi unabashedly says he'll take the money.[14] In a later session, when Jahangir asks whether he would prefer to be given a *Turani* (Central Asian) or an *ʿIraqi* (Western Iranian) horse, Mutribi says, 'whichever is more expensive'. To this Jahangir somewhat mockingly replies that while *ʿIraqi* horses are more expensive, they are also harder to handle, implying that such a horse might be too much for his venerable guest.[15]

The suspicion that Mutribi's interest in India centred on material gain is further supported by the fact that once he sufficiently attained his desires—Jahangir seems to have been more than generous in heaping gifts upon him—he was impatient to return to Samarqand, fervently begging the Emperor's leave after only two months in Lahore, and then stubbornly insisting despite the initial refusal of his royal host, who urged him to come on a trip to Kashmir instead.[16]

Mutribi may still have felt the burden of family obligations, since he gave these responsibilities as his excuse for leaving India so hastily. However, since Jahangir's offer to send money to Samarqand for Mutribi's family to come join him in India doesn't seem to have influenced him, it might be more accurate to surmise that Mutribi simply didn't care for India or have any interest in staying there once his personal mission had been fulfilled. His only positive observation about India seems to be that it has very tasty ducks, a fact which previous Central Asian travellers had also noted.[17] In the end Jahangir released his elderly visitor, after extracting a promise that Mutribi would return to Lahore the following year. But as the Emperor himself died only a few months later, it is unlikely that Mutribi, who was 71 when he returned home to Samarqand in 1627, could or did ever make a second trip to India.

Mahmud's ambitions seem to have been both more modest and less materialistic, at least initially. He is generally far more observant and interested in what he sees than is Mutribi. His restless travels across India, which lasted from 1624–31, appear to have been motivated mainly by curiosity and traveller's itch. It is clear from Mahmud's introductory remarks to his *safar-nama* that the land of India continued to possess an awesome reputation in the minds of Central Asians of the seventeenth century. He writes:

> Since the immensity of India is full of seemly people, garnished with numerous rarities and symbols which witness the perfect force [of God], and landscapes illuminated by refinements and abundant grace, and the traces of Creation and the secrets of invention are to be found there, the bird of my intention took off in flight in that direction.[18]

It is interesting to compare Mahmud's preconceptions of the grandeur of India with those of Central Asian Muslims from other periods. The ninth century Central Asian poet Rudaki, considered to be the first great poet of the modern Persian language, wrote:

> The thorn that will prick me when I go to India
> Is better than staying home with a bunch of fragrant flowers in my hand.[19]

In his memoirs Babur, no great lover of India, after listing the many defects of the country concedes that it is indeed vast and full of resources, both mineral and human, and that its air during the monsoon season is delightful.[20]

But Mahmud seems, moreover, to have been drawn by a personal fascination for Hindu women. Riazul Islam goes so far as to say that 'certain passages suggest that this was one of his chief aims in wandering about'.[21] Indeed, he may have begun to cultivate a taste for them before ever leaving home, as many Hindu merchant families were living in Central Asian cities at that time,[22] but once in India his senses are overwhelmed. One of Mahmud's most emotional passages is his description of ritual bathing in the Jumna beside Raja Man Singh's temple at Mathura:

> ...then the Hindus, man and woman, great and small, rich and poor, go to the banks of the river and without shame, cloak, or modesty mix together and rejoice in the sound of the bell and perform their useless ceremonies, while thousands of vagabonds and capricious persons stand on the bank with hopeful, enthusiastic hearts and watch them. Many are Muslims, who are attracted by the ceremony and mix with them.[23]

It takes little imagination to visualize the narrator himself as part of the latter group, particularly when he adds apologetically, 'Really it's not surprising that in this nice landscape with so many beautiful women, the feet of Muslims slip and their purity is broken by the stones of their beauty'.[24] Mahmud recounts other such examples of his own wet-sari voyeurism. At Benares, having barely survived the journey from Patna on which he saw three Hindu travellers die of fatigue and was himself carried into town on the back of another, Mahmud sleeps for a day and on regathering his strength is told encouragingly by his Hindu hosts that such near brushes with death can trigger enlightenment. Hoping to assist in his salvation, they promptly take him to the bank of the Ganges where instead, once again, the young Central Asian is overcome by the beauty of the Hindu bathers, who appear to him as 'a hundred rose petals in every corner'. [25]

Mutribi, for his part, while also proving vulnerable to Indian beauty, seems to have preferred young boys. Jahangir almost seems to be taunting him when one evening, after asking the mulla which type of skin colour is most attractive, he calls for two slave boys, one white and one black, to be brought to stand at each side of his venerable guest.

> ...on my right a black-coloured child stood, but what a heart-breaker! Just seeing him took away my heart... by my left side stood a white-skinned boy, the ultimate in goodness and delicateness, to amaze the eye.[26]

Poor Mutribi's gaze keeps flitting back and forth between the two, until he can't tell which is white and which is black, and the two boys meld together in his eyes into a sort of 'candy-green' colour. Jahangir, obviously amused, agrees; yes, indeed, green must be the best colour of all for a slave boy!

Later on, Jahangir sells Mutribi's son Muhammad ᶜAli a slave boy who turns out to be deaf. The following day when Mutribi comes to pay for the slave, the Emperor mischievously asks Mutribi about it, and in the end gives the slave for free along with 1000 rupees for good measure. Mutribi, saving his own face perhaps, goes on to say that the slave served him excellently, and cites a story about a famously pious deaf slave in the Samarqand bazaar.[27] If the elderly mulla from Samarqand proved a great source of entertainment for the Mughal Emperor, however, this is not to say that Mutribi's appeal for Jahangir was merely that of a buffoon, at least any more than with anyone who came into the royal presence. The tone of his own royal memoirs, like the image in Mutribi's account, suggests a condescending sort of personality. He also seems to have been intoxicated on wine and opium much of the time, which could account in part for his bantering nature.[28] On the other hand what is certainly clear, even filtering out

the self-important bias of Mutribi's narrative, is that
Jahangir valued him as an important source of news and
information from Central Asia.

Moreover, the tone of the Emperor's frequent questions
to Mutribi about Central Asian people and places is
distinctly compatriotic: he inquires about the Juybari
shaykhs of Samarqand as of mutual acquaintances, and of
local affairs in the manner of a longtime expatriate plying
a more recent one for the latest from home. Given that no
Mughal monarch since Jahangir's grandfather had ever
even set foot on Central Asian soil, this attitude provides a
curious testimony to the dynasty's nostalgic mentality, which
persisted unsatisfied for at least three further generations.

In his first interviews with Jahangir, Mutribi asks
anxiously about the anthology he has offered the Emperor.
Jahangir, who clearly hasn't bothered to look at the gift
yet, keeps changing the subject to Samarqand. The first
thing he wants to know is, what is the state of repair of
Timur's tomb, *Gur-i-Amir*?[29] Mutribi coyly replies that he
has detailed this in his book. In a session several weeks
later, Jahangir wants to know the annual maintenance of
the mausoleum, which Mutribi estimates 'informally' at
10,000 rupees. The Emperor then states that, in accordance
with his guest's information, he will send that amount to
Samarqand, thereby assuming responsibility for the upkeep
of this Timurid family monument.[30]

No doubt mindful that Mutribi's impressions will be
reported in Central Asia, Jahangir seems consistently
concerned with impressing him. Among the seemingly
nonchalant Emperor's tactics are showing the visitor a huge
chunk of black gold and casually asking if it is the same
material Timur's sepulchre is made of (it is actually of
black jade),[31] demonstrating a novelty mechanical
contraption of great complexity,[32] inviting him to witness
the lunar weighing ceremony,[33] bringing out the world's
biggest sugar block,[34] and taking him to a nocturnal oryx
fight,[35] on each occasion repeating the question, 'Have

you ever seen anything like this in Turan?' to which a
suitably awestruck Mutribi each time replies that indeed he
hasn't. These exchanges suggest a peculiar Mughal
characteristic, something like a subtle longing for
acknowledgement from home that the banished son has
done surprisingly well for himself in his exile.

Jahangir's 'news from home' queries often concern
people assumed to be common acquaintances. One is Mirza
Baqi Anjomani, who had come to serve Akbar.[36] Another is
Abu'l Biy Uzbek, who was in Jahangir's service. Jahangir
tries here to trick Mutribi, showing him two men, neither
of whom is Abu'l Biy, as Mutribi correctly responds.
Jahangir then shows his guest a portrait, which Mutribi
recognizes as the true personage.[37] While the Emperor
gives only token deference to Mutribi's own religious
qualifications (addressing him frequently as 'Preacher') he
speaks admiringly of several shaykhs of the Dihbidi and
Juybari families, maintaining the notion that the Mughal
rulers considered themselves disciples of Central Asian
Naqshbandi shaykhs.[38] In turn, Mutribi says the only person
in Central Asia worthy of receiving Jahangir's giant sugar
block, other than Imam Quli Khan, would be Khwaja
Hashim Muhammad Dihbidi. Jahangir replies that he
himself is one of Dihbidi's followers. Later on, Jahangir
says he will delay his departure for Kashmir until the arrival
of ʿAbd al-Rahim Khwaja Juybari at court.[39]

On another occasion, Jahangir expresses a desire to hear
Mutribi sing a Central Asian tune—not a traditional one,
though, like the ones he used to hear at family gatherings,
but rather 'something from the *tasnif* (repertoire) of Ustad
ʿAli Dust Nami, from the time of ʿAbdullah Khan Uzbek'.[40]
Jahangir's well-known interest in miniature painting also
shows up, when he brings out portraits which his artists
have done of the Uzbek rulers ʿAbdullah Khan and ʿAbd
al-Muʾmin. He asks his Central Asian visitor to tell honestly
whether they are accurate likenesses; when Mutribi
comments that Abdullah was a bit thinner and had a

crooked chin, Jahangir calls out the painter on the spot and has him correct the portrait.[41]

What is absent throughout from Jahangir's line of questioning is anything concerning information which could be considered politically relevant or useful. In other words, the Emperor's interest in hearing about Central Asia was entirely sentimental. Thus, one of the most fascinating aspects of Mutribi's memoirs is what they unconsciously reveal about the persisting Mughal attitude toward the Central Asian homeland.

Mutribi would have us believe that the Emperor greatly admired his literary abilities. In one case, Jahangir recites a couplet and asks Mutribi to reply in matching rhyme and metre (*mujawaba*). When the author does so, a scoffing attendant asserts that the couplet isn't Mutribi's, upon which Mutribi spontaneously comes up with three more, silencing the sceptic.[42] But during a later session it is clear that Jahangir who, like most rulers, also considered himself a poet, has his own criteria for judging good and bad verse. When Mutribi, in accordance with the Emperor's request, recites a couplet by the late Uzbek ruler ʿAbdullah Khan, the ever-present scoffing attendant says, 'What a stupid couplet!' Jahangir silences him with the words, 'If ʿAbdullah Khan's couplet is stupid, then you're stupider', meaning presumably that one doesn't criticize the work of a king.[43]

While the first passage seems intended to convey that the author was particularly skilled as a poet, reading between the lines of the text suggests that the Emperor mainly enjoyed using Mutribi as an informant and a straight man and otherwise held him in no special esteem.

Mutribi's writing offers no indication that he experienced or had any interest in Indian life outside the confines of the royal court. All that his account offers to let the reader know he is in India is the overall sense of grandeur: everything there is bigger, better, more ostentatious. This is certainly the impression Jahangir was striving to instil in his guest, and if the Emperor's aim was to have his wealth and majesty reported and described 'back home', then he was certainly successful in this.

Mahmud's youthful adventurousness is quite a contrasting approach. Unlike Mutribi, he seems singularly dedicated to seeing what is most alien and astonishing to him, which equates to Hindu culture in general. He is the sort of traveller who focuses on what is different rather than on what is familiar. Although he does seek out the fellowship of Muslims and takes for granted Islamic charity toward travellers, these things are mentioned only in passing, as if inconsequential and unworthy of comment. Mahmud details Muslim life in India only when it strikes him as odd or anomalous. One of the first examples is his reaction to the violent Muharram activities he observes on arriving at Lahore. These Shiʿa rites surely appeared strange to his eyes, as Central Asia was overwhelmingly Sunni. On the occasion of Mahmud's visit, the processions resulted in over thirty sectarian murders.[44] Further into India, Mahmud often marvels at the number of Indian Muslims who participate in river bathing rituals together with Hindus. At Benares, he asks the Muslim bathers why they are participating in an infidel ritual; they respond by raising their hands toward the sky and then pointing to their foreheads—such is their destiny.[45]

Mahmud's pre-occupation with the exotic need not be taken as evidence that India lay outside the boundaries of the Islamic world as he perceived it, however; only that it was the diversity within that world that interested him. One imagines that had Mahmud's travels taken him to Ottoman lands, he would have written most extensively about churches, Easter, and Greek or Armenian women. His silence regarding the familiar and 'home-like' aspects of Mughal India is itself a type of subtle illustration that in his mind, he had not yet crossed beyond the geographical frontier of Islamic Asia, although he does eventually travel to lands that are truly foreign, further to the south.

After bathing ghats, Mahmud is perhaps most fascinated by Hindu temples and what goes on in them, amazed and often overwhelmed by the sheer numbers of thronging people. At Lale Bar Sang temple in Benares, where the author finds himself lost in a crowd of 30,000 chanting worshippers, he seems simultaneously thrilled and oppressed, concluding his account with the words, 'I almost passed out...so I left town and headed onward... .'[46] The crowds are omnipresent in secular as in religious pursuits, as at Patna where the author hears of 'an incomparably beautiful woman' who is known to bathe in the river at a certain hour of the day. Mahmud seeks out this spectacle and finds such a large audience assembled that he can only squeeze himself in on a rooftop. Upon the woman's appearance the crowd goes wild and Mahmud waxes lyrical describing her beauty, until finally he sobers up and, realizing she is out of his reach, he gets up and leaves.[47]

Mahmud recounts many instances of his 'going native' amongst the Hindus—a thing his readers in Bukhara province, a region known for orthodox Muslim piety, would surely have found distasteful, just as proper London society did regarding similarly adaptable Englishmen in colonial times.[48] Mahmud isn't too proud to accept the charity of Hindus, or to follow their examples. In Bengal, at the temple of Medinapur, where 50,000 pilgrims have gathered and 'women and men mix together, their bodies naked, chanting *Hari*', (a name of Vishnu) Mahmud takes off his turban and his shoes and chants *Hari* right along with them, displaying a religious flexibility worthy of the Victorian traveller Richard Burton.[49]

India seems to represent to Mahmud a whole spectrum of oddities, ranging from the merely curious to the horrific, which elicit a corresponding array of responses within him. While he finds the crowds and chants exotic, and other spectacles humorous—such as the grinning one-legged aborigine who hops three *dharᶜ* at a step and is amazed that other men walk on two feet[50]—other phenomena prove too much for him to handle.

One such instance occurs in Allahabad. Mahmud, aghast at the way the merchants and the wealthy are throwing rupees by the thousands into the river, remarks on the foolishness of the practice to a Hindu acquaintance, who replies 'with flames of anger bursting from his mouth' that it is eternity and not money that a Hindu values, and to prove his point goes up to an attendant priest whom he slices in two with a sword, as a sacrifice, before the astonished traveller's eyes.[51] The author cites other instances of grisly suicide, such as a Hindu woman warrior captured in battle who, being refused her request for death, rips out her own tongue and dies.[52]

On another occasion, while seeking shelter in the woods during a severe thunderstorm one night near the Bengal town of Davnapur, Mahmud is beckoned by a voice calling his name. Thinking someone is offering him a place to stay, he approaches and sees an inhumanly hairy figure standing in a pool, eating the raw liver of a man Mahmud recognizes as one of his travelling companions.[53] When he relates this episode in town the following day, the response is matter-of-fact: the cannibal somehow calls everyone by name. Mahmud has more to say about the sect of so-called 'liver-eaters' (*jigar-khwar*) of Bengal and Orissa later on, including one instance of a nine-year old girl who is turned in by her own parents to the Mughal governor for justice.[54] The methods described by Mahmud for determining a true *jigar-khwar* from an innocent are reminiscent of European witch tests: one can either rub pepper in the suspect's eyes to see if it irritates them, or dunk him by the legs into a body of water to see if he floats.[55]

The Central Asian traveller displays an equal amazement at India's natural world, from his descriptions of the destructive power of cyclones (for example, his shipwreck,[56] or when he describes an entire garden of tall trees being completely flattened[57]) to his impressions of the animal kingdom, which range from whimsical to terrifying. *Enroute* to Rajmahal, Mahmud visits a river port known informally as 'Monkeytown', where he estimates at five to six thousand the monkeys surrounding the boats to beg for food. The biggest ape watches from a distance, and settles disputes between his clamouring fellows by pointing a finger at them. The sailors all call him 'The Monkey King'.[58] At another point Mahmud describes two highly intelligent apes in an Orissa town who were used to find thieves. Names would be written on scraps of paper, from which the apes would determine the guilty party, although occasionally disagreeing between themselves on the verdict.[59] Baqir Khan, the Mughal governor of Orissa whom Mahmud served for three years, sent these apes as a gift to Jahangir, but Shah Jahan acceded to the throne in the meanwhile and sent the apes back as worthless. This was probably meant as a snub to Baqir Khan, who had supported Jahangir during Shah Jahan's rebellion.

Mahmud encounters herds of wild buffalo, which he also estimates at no less than five thousand—seemingly his figure of choice. He reports seeing a companion shoot one bull twenty-five times, but the indestructible beast simply runs off. Only the night before Mahmud has had the fright of his life sleeping near a Bengal swamp, where he was awakened by the rustling of a crocodile which snatched one of his companions and dragged him to a watery death. The locals say there have already been twenty-four such victims, but all attempts to catch the crocodile have been in vain.[60] On Ceylon, Mahmud makes a fantastic-sounding reference to a lion-like beast which shoots a stream of fatal 'urine' at its prey.[61]

Mahmud's vagabond mode of adventure-travel seems to have been no less common in the seventeenth century than the conservative, fortune-hunting style favoured by the likes of Mutribi. In a *khangah* (sufi lodge) at the port of Rajmahal, Mahmud mentions meeting an assortment of travellers like himself, who have come from all over—from his native Balkh, as well as from Bukhara, Khorasan, ʿIraq (Western Persia), Baghdad, Turkey, and Syria. Many of them are raving about southern India, particularly Ceylon, so that Mahmud decides to head in that direction next.[62] Indeed, one encounters a similar atmosphere in today's youth hostels, where young, shoestring-budget travellers from all over the world meet and swap stories about the 'best places' to go, often getting inspired to visit locations they hadn't thought of before. This passage is especially significant in that it shows Mahmud to be not a unique case but rather a *type* of traveller, by no means unusual at the time, which India attracted from every corner of the Muslim world.

After witnessing the beginning of the Jagannath festival, where he is awed by the immensity of the idol and its chariot and flabbergasted by the number of 'pious suicides' either jumping off the rolling statue or throwing themselves under the chariot's massive wheels,[63] Mahmud heads southwards beyond Mughal territory. He meets Europeans—probably French—at Conakry,[64] then visits the Deccani towns of Golconda and Bijapur[65] before continuing on to Ceylon, which he likens to the promised Paradise. (The local governor has temporarily forbidden pilgrimages to Adam's Peak, because of the skunk-lion mentioned above.)[66] He is particularly enthralled by an island of Ceylonese 'virgins', whose virginity, no matter how passionately one makes love to them, is miraculously restored after every encounter. Strangely, this miracle ceases to occur if the girls should leave their native island.[67]

Returning northward on a European ship Mahmud is shipwrecked,[68] and coming ashore in Orissa the passengers are arrested by Mughal officials. The Europeans explain to Mahmud that under such conditions the local governor is permitted to take possession of the ship and its valuables and enslave its passengers, but they are unable to flee. The attempts of one European passenger to save Mahmud from their captors by telling them he is a scholar and a poet

backfires, since the Mughals then assume Mahmud is a
European priest, and they whip and mistreat him all the
more harshly, making him walk barefoot through a thistle-
covered forest bed. The captives are taken to the seat of
the Mughal governor, Baqir Khan, at Cuttack. As it is three
days before the Persian New Year, Mahmud quickly
composes an elegy to springtime which he presents when
called before the governor. Noticing the Arabic in
Mahmud's preface, Baqir Khan calls the wayward Central
Asian into a private audience, after which he gives him
over to his brother Mirza Husayni with whom Mahmud
becomes fast friends. Mahmud is provided with a house
and servants, and asked to work translating Arabic into
Persian for the governor. He is assisted in this task by one
of his servants, an elderly man who turns out to be a scholar
fallen on hard times.[69] Eventually a local holy man by the
name of Shah Azmat makes it known to Baqir Khan that he
wishes to give his daughter in marriage to Mahmud, who
accepts the offer.[70]

Mahmud remains in Mughal service for three years,
during which he composes a 6000 couplet work titled
Akhlaq-i-Husayni. In 1628, shortly after Shah Jahan's
accession, he is invited with Baqir Khan to the imperial
court at Agra[71]—under greatly changed circumstances, it
may be remarked, from those of his first visit to that city.
After three years of marriage Mahmud's wife suddenly dies
at Agra, and he decides to return home to Balkh.

On his return trip to Central Asia Mahmud becomes
embroiled in a dispute between the then Safavid governor
of Qandahar, ᶜAli Mardan Khan, and a local Afghan
chieftain named Sher Khan, and is taken to Herat to testify
before the Persian authorities.[72] He finally makes his way
home to Balkh, however, and eventually becomes librarian
for Nazr Muhammad Khan.

Did Mutribi and Mahmud think of India as 'abroad'?
The question is not so simple. Ignorance of language and
custom plays a large part in making people feel 'foreign' in

a place they are visiting; Central Asian travellers to Mughal India in the seventeenth century would have felt to some degree at home in that Muslim-ruled land, an integral part of the *dar-al-islam* where, just as in Central Asia, the call to prayer was heard five times a day, Persian was everywhere understood, Hafez was recited and pilaf was served. Yet, in the timeless nature of provincials visiting the 'big city', they might also have been daunted by the diversity of the place, at times puzzled by what their co-religionaries found acceptable, often overwhelmed by the scale of things and occasionally shocked and appalled by what they saw.

Furthermore, people travel for different reasons and see things through different lenses. Some, like Mutribi, have specific material aims in mind and are more or less blind to everything else. Others, like Mahmud, shun what is familiar and seek out the exotic wherever they may be. What a comparison of the two types shows, is that for Central Asians in the seventeenth century, India loomed as the most obvious repository of potential experience and opportunity across the entire spectrum of desirable possibilities.

Mutribi and Mahmud both returned from India to their Central Asian home. Meanwhile, scores of their most illustrious compatriots—and hundreds or perhaps thousands of their more anonymous ones—came to India and stayed. The attraction India exerted on the minds of seventeenth century Central Asians is evident. It is equally evident that to go there posed a Central Asian no great difficulty, and that Mughal society was one in which a Central Asian could function effectively and live comfortably as a Muslim.

NOTES

1. See Igor de Rachewiltz, *Papal Envoys to the Great Khans*, London, 1971, pp. 16-29.
2. *Kitab ʿajaʾib al-Hind*, ed. P.A. van der Lith, French translation by L. Marcel Devic, Leiden, 1883-6, p. 2. See the discussion in André Miquel, *La géographie humaine du monde musulman jusqu'au milieu du 11e siècle*, Paris and The Hague, 1972, i, pp. 127-132.
3. Abu Rayhan Muhammad b. Ahmad al-Biruni, *Alberuni's India*, ed. and tr. E.C. Sachau, London, 1888; abridged version New York, 1971.
4. Ibid., pp. 17-20.
5. Vladimir Minorsky, tr., 'Gardizi on India', in *Iranica*, Tehran, 1964, p. 202.
6. *BN*, pp. 623-4.
7. Zain al-din, *Tabaqat-i-Baburi*, tr. H. Askari, Delhi, 1982, p. 180.
8. *Conversations With Emperor Jahangir*, tr. Richard Foltz, (Costa Mesa, CA: Mazda Publishers, 1998). The manuscript exists in a unique copy as a *khatima* to the *Nuskha-yi-ziba-yi-Jahangiri*, a work in the India Office Library, Ethé ii, no. 3023, therein and in Storey mistitled *Tarikh-i-Jahangiri*. The anthology portion of this work has been published in an edition by A.G. Mirzoev, Karachi, 1976. Mutribi's works are discussed briefly in Russian by B.A. Ahmedov in 'Tazkira Mutribi kak istochnik po istorii i kul'ture XVI-XVII vv.', *Istochnikovedenie i Tekstologiia srednevekogo Blizhnego i Srednego Vostoka*, Moscow, 1984, pp. 36-44; and Ahmedov, *Istoriko-geograficheskaya literatura*, pp. 165-173.
9. The travelogue attached to volume VI of Mahmud's work exists in two copies, one in the India Office Library, Ethé no. 575, and the other in Tashkent in the library of the Uzbek Academy of Sciences Oriental Institute. Sections of volume I also exist there; an edition of it has been published by the Pakistan Historical Society (Karachi, 1984).
10. *BA*, p. 2.
11. Ibid., pp. 17-18.
12. Gafurov, 'Bahr al-Asrar', p. 99.
13. IOSUAS MS 2253.
14. *KM*, p. 17.
15. Ibid., p. 32.
16. Ibid., p. 71.
17. Ibid., p. 36.
18. *BA*, p. 1.

19. '*khari ki ba man dar khalad andar safar-i-Hind/bih chun ba hadar dar kaf-i man dasta-yi sabuyi*' (cited in Gafurov, 'Bahr al-asrar', pp. 101-2).
20. *BN*, pp. 624-5.
21. Islam, 'Bahr al-asrar', p. 95.
22. Semёnov, 'Kul'turno-ploiticheskikh sviaziakh', p. 9; Dale, *Indian Merchants*, p. 45.
23. *BA*, p. 15.
24. Ibid.
25. Ibid., p. 22.
26. *KM*, p. 39.
27. Ibid., pp. 53-4.
28. In the *Tuzuk-i-Jahangiri*, the emperor describes in detail his daily intake of wine and opium, as well as his attempts to moderate his addictions (*TJ*, i, pp. 307-10; *JN*, pp. 174-5). In the end, it was probably this lifestyle that brought on his early death.
29. *KM*, p. 19; see Bernier, *Travels*, p. 119 regarding Aurangzeb's enquiries of the Uzbek ambassadors some six decades later.
30. Ibid., p. 69.
31. Ibid., p. 20.
32. Ibid., p. 23.
33. Ibid., p. 32.
34. Ibid., p. 33.
35. Ibid., p. 43.
36. Ibid., p. 28.
37. Ibid., pp. 30-1.
38. Ibid., pp. 33-4.
39. Ibid., p. 45.
40. Ibid., p. 50. Mutribi describes Ustad ʿAli's style as a blend of Timurid and 'Turk' influences.
41. Ibid., p. 61.
42. Ibid., p. 44.
43. Ibid., p. 62.
44. *BA*, pp. 9-10.
45. Ibid., pp. 21-3.
46. Ibid., p. 23.
47. Ibid., p. 25.
48. Mahmud does, however, mention at least one instance where he claims to have converted a Hindu friend to Islam (Ibid., pp. 81-2).
49. Ibid., pp. 33-4.
50. Ibid., p. 32. The aborigine had been captured from Zirbad and was being taken away as a gift for the Mughal Emperor. A *dharʿ* is equal to forty-one inches.
51. Ibid., p. 22.
52. Ibid., p. 80.

53. Ibid., p. 29. The scene recalls paintings representing Kali, the Hindu goddess of destruction, who is often portrayed surrounded by human bones and munching on body parts.
54. Ibid., p. 84.
55. Ibid., pp. 86-7.
56. Ibid., p. 63.
57. Ibid., pp. 78-9.
58. Ibid., p. 28. Rajmahal (Akbarnagar) is a port on the Ganges on the modern-day border between Bihar and Bengal.
59. Ibid., pp. 79-80.
60. Ibid., pp. 30-1.
61. Ibid., p. 56.
62. Ibid., p. 25.
63. Ibid., p. 37.
64. Ibid., p. 39.
65. Ibid., pp. 40-3.
66. Ibid., p. 54.
67. Ibid., p. 61.
68. Ibid., p. 63.
69. Ibid., pp. 65-8.
70. Ibid., p. 74.
71. Ch. Stori (Storey) and Yuri Bregel, *Persidskaya Literatura*, 3 vols., Moscow, 1972, ii, p. 1136. Ansar Khan points out that Baqir Khan, having supported Jahangir during Shah Jahan's rebellion, 'must have been anxious to ingratiate himself with the new emperor'. (Ansar Z. Khan, 'Mahmud b. Amir Vali's Description of Towns, Cities and Regions of South Asia in the Bahr al-Asrar', *Journal of the Pakistan Historical Society* (1990), p. 137.) It appears that the governor was ultimately successful in doing so.
72. *BA*, pp. 100-103.

CHAPTER 7

THOUGHTS AND ACTS OF THE MUGHAL EMPERORS REGARDING CENTRAL ASIA

The covetous mindset of the Mughal emperors towards their lost Central Asian 'homeland' had both sentimental and practical dimensions. At least during the reigns of the first Mughals, the official view was that Central Asia was simply a nicer place than India. Babur reminisces that 'there are few cities in the civilized world as pleasant as Samarqand'.[1] He also feels the pride of an owner who has been deprived of a prize possession: 'For nearly a hundred and forty years the capital Samarqand had been in our family. Then came the Uzbeks, the foreign foe from God-knows-where, and took over'.[2]

To add insult to injury, Babur finds India an inhospitable, uncivilized and heathen country, hardly an adequate consolation prize for the home he has lost. Maintaining this theme several decades later, Akbar's chronicler, Abu'l Fazl, implies that attachment to Central Asia is a basic quality of the Timurids, explaining that Timur himself didn't remain in India after his conquest because he was 'impelled by the love of his native land'.[3] This attachment manifested itself in the case of every Mughal emperor to some degree, be it through taste in fruit or respect for Bukhara-trained religious scholars.

The practical aspect of the Mughals' preoccupation with Central Asia, though somewhat less powerful, was not non-

existent. True, neither the basic wealth nor the stability of
the empire depended on the subjugation of Central Asia.
But the route connecting the subcontinent with the north-
west had always been an important gateway, and it was in
Mughal interests to keep it open and controllable. Babur
states that Kabul and Qandahar were the two trade marts
between Hindustan and Iranian Khorasan,[4] arguably India's
most crucial land connections throughout history.
According to Abu'l Fazl, 'the wise of ancient times
considered Kabul and Qandahar as the twin gates of
Hindustan, the one leading to Turkestan and the other to
Persia. The custody of these highways secured India from
foreign invaders, and they are likewise appropriate portals
to foreign travel'.[5]

It was probably for a combination of reasons, therefore,
that the Mughals, unable to re-conquer their former
Central Asian possessions, developed the fiction that the
Uzbeks were merely their vassals there. The Mughal
chronicles' usage of the word *wilayat* (province) when
referring to Balkh and Transoxiana may not be without
significance, given their preoccupation with their lost
Central Asian roots. One example is in the *Ma'athir-al-
'umara'*, where Khwaja Abdullah Ahrari of Samarqand is
said to have come from *wilayat*.[6] Other examples are found
in the *Ma'athir-i-ᶜAlamgiri*, a chronicle of Aurangzeb's reign,
which states that Mir Shihab al-din, a courtier of the Uzbek
ruler Subhan Quli Khan, 'came from the provinces to the
court of the World-Protector (Aurangzeb)'.[7] Likewise, the
same source says later that Subhan Quli's great-grandson
Khwaja Baha' al-din 'came from the provinces' (*az wilayat
rasida*); the passage also refers to Subhan Quli as the
'(provincial) governor' (*wali*) of Balkh.[8]

Earlier Mughal sources use the same term for the Uzbek
rulers. Jahangir, in his memoirs, calls Wali Muhammad the
wali-yi-Turan.[9] The *Padshah-nama*, an official chronicle of
Shah Jahan's reign, likewise refers to the Uzbek ruler of
the time, Imam Quli, as a 'governor' (again, *wali-yi-*

Turan).[10] The use of this subordinating terminology in reference to Central Asia and its rulers is one aspect of the evidence suggesting the official Mughal fiction that the Uzbek-held lands were vassal states under Mughal suzerainty.

The Thoughts of Individual Emperors

One of Babur's first acts following his conquest of Agra in 1526 was to send gifts to his relations in Central Asia, along with gifts to Iran and offerings to holy men in Samarqand, Khorasan, and the Hijaz.[11] According to the Russian academician A.A. Semēnov, the letters accompanying Babur's gifts to certain Central Asian figures demonstrate fully his goals and intentions concerning reconquest. Later, in a letter to his son Humayun, whom he had put in charge of the campaign to re-take the homeland, Babur stated his intention that every one of his subjects in India should assist in the task.[12] Encouraged by the fact that the Safavids had just managed to reconquer Khorasan from the Uzbeks, Babur sent orders for Humayun to march on Balkh, then proceed to Hisar, Samarqand, or Herat, or 'to whichever side favours fortune'. Humayun was to take Hisar as his governorship and give Balkh to his brother Kamran, and should they succeed in taking Samarqand, they should make it the Mughal capital.[13]

In 1528, after Humayun had left Badakhshan in command of 40,000 troops and set out towards Samarqand, Babur instructed him to wait since 'we shall visit our hereditary kingdoms' (*wilayat-i-mawruthi*) once the necessary 'Hindustan affairs are settled'.[14] In a 1529 letter to Khwaja Kalan Ahrari in Samarqand, he again expresses his desire to return home to Central Asia, once he has settled matters in Hindustan. 'How can one forget the pleasures of that country', he says; '...how can one forget a licit pleasure like melons and grapes?'[15] Within a year, however, Humayun was to fall gravely ill, and Babur's concern for his son's well-being exceeded his desire to recapture his homeland. Following an ancient Turko-Mongol practice, Babur sought to take Humayun's illness upon himself instead, and thus sacrificed his own life without achieving his dream.

Humayun, as it turned out, proved not only unable to retake Central Asia, but eventually lost even the Indian empire his father had founded. Had he sufficient military strength and success, it is not entirely clear whether he would have preferred returning to rule his hereditary Central Asian lands or his Indian ones. During his stay in Iran the talk, when not centred on hunting or religion, was all of re-taking India from the Suri Afghans. (In return for military support offered by Shah Tahmasp, the Mughals would return Qandahar to the Safavids.)[16] But on arriving in Kabul in 1549, with a Safavid army under his command and the mission seemingly well underway, Humayun abruptly decided to detour and 'resolved to go to Balkh'.[17] It appears that he would have directed his campaign thence toward Central Asia rather than India, but for his brother Kamran's lack of co-operation on which the failure of the mission is blamed.

Akbar, who came to the throne of northern India as a child just months after his father at last re-established Mughal rule there, was for the first years of his reign too pre-occupied with assuming power on his own behalf and consolidating his Indian kingdom to seriously consider an invasion of Central Asia. Such a project soon became unfeasible in any case, as the region was under the tight control of the very capable Uzbek ruler ʿAbdullah Khan.

Yet Abu'l Fazl intimates that Akbar's prevarication didn't mean he wasn't set on reconquest, just that 'the time of the appearance of designs was in the future'.[18] When the Badakhshani Timurids, Sulayman and his son Ibrahim, marched on Balkh, Abu'l Fazl called their attempt unreasonable, implying that this was really a job only for

Akbar.[19] The chronicler further states that on at least one occasion Akbar ignored ʿAbdullah Khan's ambassadors because he 'had thoughts of reconquering his ancestral territories'.[20] His plan, according to Abu'l Fazl, was similar to Babur's; that is, to first conquer all of India as a prelude to the triumphant march 'home' to Central Asia: 'Should the wide country of India be civilized by means of obedient vassals (Akbar) would proceed to Turan...In this way the various classes of mankind would experience the joys of concord'.[21]

References to Central Asia in Akbar's correspondence draw a sad picture of helplessness and frustration scarcely befitting such a powerful ruler. In a 1577 letter to ʿAbdullah Khan, responding to taunts by the Uzbek about having lost Qandahar to the Safavid 'wretches' (biganaha), Akbar pointedly remarks that the same can be said for nearly all the Timurid lands. (The Uzbeks had taken over far more Timurid territory than the Safavids had.)[22] In a 1587 despatch to the Mughal ambassador at Bukhara, Hakim Humam, Abu'l Fazl writes that at last 'His Majesty has turned his attention to the conquest of Turan', adding, however, that Akbar 'is prepared to change the course of his conquest towards the island of Farang (i.e., European ports in Gujarat) if a satisfactory treaty (with ʿAbdullah Khan, being negotiated by Hakim Humam) is forthcoming'.[23]

Jahangir, in his memoirs, confirms that his father never ceased to think of re-conquering Central Asia, and describes his own plans to return there and leave India to his son Parviz:

> My intention...was of two kinds; one, that inasmuch as the conquest of Transoxiana was always in the pure mind of my revered father, though every time he determined on it things occurred to prevent it, if this business [of getting Hindu rulers to submit] could be settled, and this danger dismissed from my mind, I would leave Parviz in Hindustan, and in reliance on Allah, myself start for my hereditary territories...[24]

A pleasure-loving emperor who was more talk than action, Jahangir perpetuated the theme of straightening things out in India, then re-conquering the homeland. In his typically pompous way, he states in his memoirs that:

> As I had made up my exalted mind to the conquest of Transoxiana, which was the hereditary kingdom of my ancestors, I desired to free the face of Hindustan from the rubbish of the factious and rebellious, and leaving one of my sons in that country, to go myself with a valiant army in due array, with elephants of mountainous dignity and of lightening speed, and taking ample treasure with me, to undertake the conquest of my ancestral dominions.[25]

Strangely, in Jahangir's memoirs the subject is never brought up again after this strongly-worded passage. Yet according to the Indian historian R.C. Verma, the reason Jahangir sent no goodwill messages to Central Asia until 1621 was because he 'was always contemplating conquering it'.[26] But this lapse in diplomacy was perhaps simply a tit-for-tat situation, since Imam Quli had broken off relations due to a perceived insult (see Chapter Two). Nur Jahan seems finally to have succeeded in getting relations re-established, although according to M. Athar Ali, it was Imam Quli's mother who first made overtures to Nur Jahan in 1621. He suggests that it was Safavid mobilizations that inspired Imam Quli and Jahangir alike to re-establish relations.[27]

An interesting aspect of Jahangir's sentimentality toward Central Asia seems to be his love of jade. While jade is found primarily in East Turkestan, it clearly reached India via the trade routes which passed through Transoxiana, as Hsüang-tsang's account attests as early as the seventh century CE. It is beginning with the Jahangir period, however, that jade carving starts to flourish in India. Jahangir himself acquired many jade vessels which had belonged to Ulugh Beg, and had his name inscribed upon them next to that of Timur's grandson.[28]

In his conversations with Mutribi Samarqandi, Jahangir showed himself, even at the end of his life, to be most interested in the state of things in Central Asia. Despite this, Riazul Islam believes that he had no real ambition to invade Turan and 'remained indifferent to his Central Asian neighbours beyond the Hindu Kush'.[29] The emperor was at least interested enough, however, to allow Nur Jahan to send Mir Baraka, a Bukharan in Mughal service, to patch things up with Imam Quli and pay Mughal respects to the Juybari shaykhs.[30] Mir Baraka seems to have remained in Central Asia until 1627, when he returned to India in the company of Imam Quli's ambassador ᶜAbd al-Rahim Khwaja, one of the Juybari shaykhs, in anticipation of whom Jahangir delayed his trip to Kashmir (see Chapter Three, note 15, and Chapter Six, note 35). As has been noted previously, Jahangir died soon after the time of ᶜAbd al-Rahim's arrival, but Shah Jahan ensured the continuing support of the Juybari family by sending Hakim Hazik (a son of Akbar's favoured envoy, Hakim Humam) to Bukhara, bearing 50,000 *tanga*s in gifts for the shaykhs there.[31]

Of all the Mughal emperors since· Babur, the one most genuinely preoccupied with regaining the homeland was Shah Jahan. The evidence is strong that his intentions were formulated very early in his mind. His official chronicles describe only friendly relations with the Uzbeks during the first ten years of his reign. Yet he cannot have easily forgiven Nazr Muhammad's foiled siege of Kabul during the Mughal succession struggles of 1629, and he was continually sending large sums of money to well-wishers in Central Asia in an effort to ensure a favourable party there.[32]

The earliest clear textual evidence of Shah Jahan's designs comes from a letter sent by Hasan Khan Shamlu, the Safavid governor of Herat, in 1640, responding to an earlier letter from the Mughals which seems to have outlined their intention to regain their 'hereditary dominions' (*mulk-i-mawruthi*) and the cemetery of the great ancestors (*gurkhana-yi-ajdad-i-ʿizam*). Hasan goes on to recapitulate that Shah Jahan has stated his intention to return that year to the 'pleasure-ground' (*nuzhat-abad*) of Kabul and that, before arriving, will send 'one of the pearls of the realm' (*yaki az laʿli-yi-muhit-i-saltanat*; i.e., one of his sons) to conquer the fortresses of Balkh and Badakhshan.

Hasan asks that if this be indeed the plan, then the Mughals should let him know, so that he may send the Safavid armies under his command in order to help the project. The Safavid governor, of course, wishes to be convinced that the Mughals' goal is in fact Central Asia and not Khurasan; as has been mentioned, the Uzbeks posed a more real and constant threat to the Safavids than they did to the Mughals.[33] In a subsequent, letter an increasingly nervous Hasan asks the Mughal general, Asaf Khan, for the precise date they plan to 'set out for Turkistan' in order to regain their 'hereditary cemetery' (*gurkhana-yi-mawruthi*), so that the Safavids and Mughals might join victorious armies together to 'destroy the foundations of Uzbek opposition' and that 'this accord should be cited over centuries'.[34] In the event, the invasion was to occur five years later and without Safavid help.

Describing Shah Jahan's Balkh campaign, the Mughal chronicles confirm that reconquest had been the Emperor's goal from the start, and also that Nazr Muhammad's bid for Kabul had been a key factor:

> From the time of the last Emperor Jahangir's death, when Nazr Muhammad Khan had vainly attempted to seize Kabul, the mighty soul of the world-subduing monarch had been bent upon the countries of Balkh and Badakhshan, which were properly his hereditary dominions.[35]

The same passage attributes the fifteen-year delay in implementing the plan to 'various impediments of state necessity'. One can interpret this to mean the perennial problem of 'putting India's affairs in order' which, by this time, meant the attempt to reduce the Shiᶜa sultanates of the Deccan, that seemingly interminable task which would later consume four decades of Aurangzeb's reign. In the view of A. Ansari, Shah Jahan also had first to regain Qandahar from the Safavids, both in order to stabilize the southern flank and to persuade the Ottomans and the Uzbeks that he was aiming for Iran rather than Central Asia: 'His (Shah Jahan's) plan after the conquest of Qandahar seemed to be to renew his friendly relations with Persia as a preparation for his intended attack on Balkh'.[36]

It is very possible that Shah Jahan was attempting to launch his invasion of Central Asia at least as early as 1639, but was put off by Uzbek defensive mobilizations. R.C. Verma states that while the standard view of Central Asian historians is that the Mughals were lured on by the apparent strife between Nazr Muhammad and his brother Imam Quli, which they turned out to have overestimated, he believes it unlikely that Shah Jahan intended to launch an invasion at that point, stating that tensions were still too high with the Safavids over the Mughals' re-taking of Qandahar.[37] Riazul Islam, meanwhile, points out how Hasan Khan had actually offered the Mughals his assistance in 1640, although this offer was dissipated upon the governor's death and the strengthening of Shah Safi's resolve to recover Qandahar for the Safavids.[38]

It is remarkable that the humiliation of having to withdraw from Balkh after an occupation of less than two years was not sufficient to put Mughal dreams of Central Asia to rest. Aurangzeb, having been field commander at Balkh throughout most of the occupation, was in a better position than anyone to understand the futility of overextending the empire in that direction. And indeed, on becoming Emperor himself he directed his attentions most energetically towards the Deccani sultanates and the Marathas to the south. But a letter to his son, the Crown Prince Muᶜazzam, offers undeniable evidence that he hadn't given up on Central Asia altogether.

If a father is unable to finish a work the son must carry it to completion...This mortal creature has a wish which is still unfulfilled. It was the desire of Shah Jahan that I should send a grandson of His Majesty's to those districts (i.e., Balkh) with a grand army and sufficient equipment.[39]

The Venetian Manucci, who was for a time at Aurangzeb's court, also attests to the Emperor's continued intentions toward Central Asia, stating that he 'still treasured in his mind the design of conquering that land'. He explains Aurangzeb's failure to act on this design by the pragmatic recognition that such a venture could be destabilizing when Aurangzeb had barely established his power in India, and adds that the Emperor knew from his own experience in 1646 how difficult was the terrain and how harsh the climate en route to Balkh.[40] Manucci later states that, on the departure of Subhan Quli's ambassadors in 1662, Aurangzeb gave them robes (*sarapa*) which, although the Uzbeks did not know it, were given only to subjects, and that in doing so, Aurangzeb declared the Uzbeks a subject population. The Raja of Udaipur, though willing to pay the Mughals an annual tribute, repeatedly refused to don such robes.[41]

Aurangzeb maintained patronage and correspondence with religious figures of Balkh, such as ᶜAbd al-Ghaffar Dihbidi, from the time of the Balkh campaign onwards.[42] Bernier states that on receiving Subhan Quli's embassy, Aurangzeb praised their gifts and the fertility of Central Asia, and 'asked two or three questions concerning the College (madrasa) at *Samarcande*'. This demonstrates that Central Asia continued to be in the Emperor's thoughts, if not in his immediate plans.[43]

The Balkh Campaigns

Despite nearly two centuries of rhetoric, only two Mughal emperors actually attempted to reconquer the Central

Asian homeland: Humayun in 1549 and Shah Jahan almost a century later in 1646. Acts by other Mughal emperors, however, demonstrated in different ways the Mughal mindset according to which Central Asia was 'theirs'. Most notable perhaps was the money sent by both Jahangir and Aurangzeb to Samarqand for the maintenance of Timur's mausoleum, the *Gur-i-Amir*. This assumption of responsibility highlights a very important psychological connection, suggesting that Mughal culture retained undercurrents of not only Islamic but perhaps pre-Islamic ancestor worship.

In 1549, the dethroned Humayun was ostensibly on his way to recapture his father's Indian conquests from the Suri Afghans. However, after dislodging his brother Kamran from Kabul he abruptly decided to make a detour towards Balkh, clearly signaling his intentions to proceed in the direction of Samarqand. According to his sister Gulbadan Begum, Humayun summoned his three brothers Kamran, Sulayman, and Askari to join him, although not surprisingly, Kamran failed to respond.[44] The Mughal army defeated the Uzbeks, led by Pir Muhammad, outside Balkh, and Pir Muhammad seems to have been prepared to capitulate, when the Mughal soldiers unexpectedly began deserting and heading back towards Kabul.

Akbar's historian, Abu'l Fazl, places the blame for the failure of the 1549 Balkh campaign squarely on Kamran and the Mughal officers.[45] Annette Beveridge, translator of the *Humayun-nama*, suggests that the Mughal deserters were probably intimidated by news of a huge Uzbek force coming from Bukhara, and may have feared that if Kamran should retake Kabul in their absence their families there would be in danger.[46] Either way, this must have been the crowning frustration in the exasperating military career of the hapless Humayun, whose final vindication of at last recapturing Delhi five years later was cut short by his accidental death from falling down a flight of stairs.

The Mughal stronghold of Kabul at the north-western edge of the empire was the natural staging point for any attempt on Balkh and Central Asia. It was also a favourite royal hunting ground, which enabled the Mughals to explain away any mobilization there as simply a recreational outing. In this way, Shah Jahan dismissed to the Uzbeks his presence in the area almost annually from 1639. The Mughal chronicles, however, reveal that the Emperor's true reason for setting up the royal camp at Kabul was to prepare for the invasion of Balkh and Badakhshan, 'which were once included in the kingdom of his imperial ancestors'.[47] Apprised of the Mughal mobilization in 1640, Nazr Muhammad ceased quarrelling with his brother, Imam Quli, who immediately set out from Bukhara with all his troops. According to the *Tazkira-yi-Muqim Khani*, Imam Quli was welcomed at Balkh by:

> Nazr Muhammad Khan, his nobles, and 100,000 men of all ages and ranks, and rode into town on a road covered with brocade and other valuables that the inhabitants had brought for his reception.[48]

It was at this point that Shah Jahan sent the Uzbeks word that he had only come on a hunting trip. The Mughal chronicles, however, admit the extent to which this setback upset the Emperor, who temporarily re-directed his frustrated energies towards improving the roads into Badakhshan.[49]

The strife between the ruling Uzbek brothers was resolved for good when Imam Quli, old and nearly blind, summoned his younger brother to Bukhara and abdicated in his favour, leaving the whole of the Bukhara and Balkh territories under the nominal rule of Nazr Muhammad. This new situation was not accepted by a number of influential Bukharans, however, and a rebel party led by Yalangtosh Biy browbeat Nazr Muhammad's son ᶜAbd al-ᶜAziz into open opposition. In early 1645, with Nazr

Muhammad pre-occupied by his son's rebellion, a Mughal force under Khalil Beg took the strategic fortress of Kahmard without a fight. The Mughals left an insuffcent garrison there, however, which was soon chased out again.[50]

The Central Asian sources of the early eighteenth century all agree that Nazr Muhammad did, in fact, solicit help from the Mughals in dealing with his internal political situation. The *Tazkira-yi-Muqim Khani* states that 'this old man, removed from power, betrayed by several of his own children and rejected by the Uzbek nobles, thought of recovering his authority by calling for the help of strangers' by writing a letter to Shah Jahan 'complaining of his son's and the army's treason, and begging for assistance'.[51] The author of the *Tarikh-i-Qipchaq Khani* corroborates this, and adds that Shah Jahan had been 'waiting all his life' for such an opportunity.[52] The *Silsilat al-salatin*, likewise, describes how Nazr Muhammad sent Nazr Biy with a letter to Shah Jahan asking for help so that he might 'with the assistance of the Indian army punish the Uzbek tribe and help the oppressed out of the tyranny of these malevolent people'.[53] While the Mughal sources are less explicit, the wording of Shah Jahan's letters to Nazr Muhammad strongly supports the interpretation that the Uzbek had indeed called for Mughal intervention.[54]

Another pretext Shah Jahan used to justify his Balkh adventure was concern for the well-being of the region's Muslim inhabitants. His chronicler states that as Nazr Muhammad, being 'involved in his own affairs', was unable to defend his Muslim subjects from being defamed by Uzbek and 'alman' raiders, Shah Jahan felt compelled to send his son Murad Bakhsh at the head of 60,000 troops in order 'to restore the rights of the injured and oppressed [and] coerce the infidel Uzbeks and Almans'.[55] The same excuse is given in letters to Hasan Khan and the Safavids, where Shah Jahan asserts that 'the important thing is for the impoverished to be taken care of'.[56] This explanation is also offered by Saᶜadullah Khan.[57]

This theme is conveniently consistent with the official fiction that the Uzbeks were simply brotherly vassals whom the Mughals were content to leave looking after their lands in Central Asia for them as long as things ran smoothly. In the 1640s, things had ceased to run smoothly, and 'innocent civilians' were suffering as a result, so the Mughals felt it incumbent upon them to step in and set things right again.

This way of looking at the situation also made it easier for the Mughals to later rationalize their withdrawing and reinstating Nazr Muhammad on the throne of Balkh. They had come and put things right again, restored order, and left, or so one is led to believe. The sad truth is that they hadn't put things right at all; the year-and-a-half Mughal occupation of Balkh and the determined resistance from the local countryside to their domination left the province utterly devastated, far worse off than before, and the cost in human suffering may never be measured.

Nazr Muhammad, for his part, was never taken in by Shah Jahan's friendly rhetoric, and his behaviour over the next two years was that of a thoroughly harried, paranoid, and desperate man. Despite a letter from Shah Jahan expressing sympathy for the Uzbek's internal political problems and assuring him that the approaching Mughal army would render him 'every kind of support',[58] as well as promises to let him retain the throne of Balkh and even re-take Transoxiana with Mughal help,[59] Nazr Muhammad clearly saw through the rhetoric and was making calculations of his own. To the Mughal ambassador present at his court he stated his intention to turn the city over to Murad Bakhsh as soon as the Mughal prince should arrive, and then to depart on the Hajj, via Kabul, so that he might pay his respects to Shah Jahan.[60] As the Mughal army drew near, he wrote to Murad Bakhsh repeating this intention, asking only for a few more days to prepare for his pilgrimage.[61]

In the end Nazr Muhammad fled Balkh and headed westwards toward Andkhuy just as the Mughal army arrived, apparently as soon as or just before Prince Murad Bakhsh's envoy, Rustam Khan, entered the city.[62] Shah Jahan reproaches him for this in a letter sent after him, saying he should rather have come to the Mughal court at Kabul, but at the same time he apologizes for his son Murad's rashness in entering Balkh which he acknowledges as inappropriate. The Mughal Emperor goes on to speak as if Nazr Muhammad's flight to the west actually represented an intended march on Samarqand, saying that if he wanted to invade Transoxiana he should have said so and Shah Jahan would have sent 'all the army and munitions of Badakhshan' to help. Concluding on a note of re-assurance, Shah Jahan tells the fleeing Uzbek that he will send him his three young sons who have been enjoying the protection of the Mughal court. (Actually Nazr Muhammad's sons refused to go, preferring to stay on with the Mughals.)[63] Unconvinced, Nazr Muhammad went to Iran and sought refuge at the court of Shah Safi's successor, ᶜAbbas II.

One cannot fault Nazr Muhammad with being overly cautious. In fact, on hearing the news that Murad Bakhsh had entered the city of Balkh, Shah Jahan threw a party at Kabul which lasted eight days.[64] This is hardly the behaviour of one who genuinely feels that his son has acted rashly! Furthermore, the Emperor sent a letter to Shah ᶜAbbas informing him of the Mughal conquests, and expressing confidence that Samarqand and Bukhara would soon follow; this letter may have arrived at the Safavid court while Nazr Muhammad was a guest there.[65] The *Tazkira-yi-Muqim Khani* claims that whereas the bulk of the Mughal army actually believed they were going for the purpose of aiding Nazr Muhammad, the Prince had secret orders to take the city which were known only to him and a few of the Mughal generals, one of whom alerted the Uzbek khan by letter.[66] According to the *Silsilat al-salatin*, Shah Jahan's plan all along had actually been to have Nazr Muhammad captured and sent to India, where he would subject him to the 'radiant light of royal judgement', perhaps for his 1629 Kabul incursion.[67]

With Nazr Muhammad on the run and the Mughal army installed within the Balkh city walls, a sort of uncomfortable status quo was established wherein the invading army tried vainly to acquire sufficient food and supplies and the local population, with a few exceptions such as the local *sayyids*, did their best to make them feel unwelcome. Shah Jahan left Kabul for Lahore and eventually sent Aurangzeb to replace Murad Bakhsh who had left his post without authorization. Murad Bakhsh had twice written to his father explaining the difficulties the Mughal army was experiencing and asking to be allowed to return to India. Shah Jahan's firm reply on both occasions was for the Prince to remain at his post. In his response to the first letter, Shah Jahan insists that Balkh province is 'the key to the conquest of Turan'. After Prince Murad's second letter, Shah Jahan sent Sacadullah Khan to Balkh to take control of the situation.[68]

cAbd al-cAziz, meanwhile, was making preparations to launch a campaign from Bukhara to retake Balkh for the Uzbeks. Hearing of this, Shah Jahan returned to Kabul from India with his entourage.[69] An Uzbek envoy, Mirak Shah, arrived at Balkh and told Aurangzeb that it was 'generally understood' that the Mughals intended to restore Balkh to Nazr Muhammad, but that it would be better for them to turn the province over to 'his most beloved son, Subhan Quli Khan'. A week-long battle between the Mughal and Uzbek armies followed, in which Aurangzeb soundly defeated the combined forces of Nazr Muhammad's sons cAbd al-cAziz and Subhan Quli. The Mughals are said to have lost a thousand men, and the Uzbeks five to six thousand. The Uzbeks appear to have been demoralized by the sight of Aurangzeb calmly dismounting to perform his ritual prayers in the midst of battle.[70]

Despite their success in defending Balkh city, however, the Mughal soldiers remained there with such reluctance and, with the onset of winter, in such increasingly dire circumstances that it is hardly conceivable they could have continued the campaign further into Central Asia; indeed it was all they could do to hang on where they were. The situation differed from that in India, where control of towns was the key to controlling the surrounding region. Although the Mughals enjoyed at least some support within the city of Balkh, particularly amongst the local *sayyids*, they were unable to deal with the hit-and-run guerrilla tactics of the Afghan mountain men, and were never able to establish adequate supply lines across the Hindu Kush to India.

The *'alman'* tribesmen seem to have been the occupying force's most persistent problem. The farmlands surrounding the city of Balkh were ravaged and had ceased to be productive, and although the *Shah Jahan-nama* states that the Mughals 'tried to console the peasantry' by providing seed and helping to till the fields, most of the grain was destroyed 'because of the inroads of the Almans'. A majority of the Mughal officers were disgusted and wanted to return to India, Aurangzeb included.[71] The *Tazkira-yi-Muqim Khani* describes the severity of the winter of 1646-7: 'Men burned themselves in fires they lit for warmth, and no one left their house for fear of being frozen'.[72] Such were scarcely victorious conditions for the Mughal army supposedly on the way to realizing the dynastic dream.

Nevertheless, a passage from the *Ma'athir al-'umara'*, a mid-eighteenth century Mughal source, indicates that precisely this outcome had been foreseen by more than one of Shah Jahan's advisors prior to the initiation of the Balkh campaign. It is worth quoting in full:

The author of the *Dhakhirat al-Khwanin* has stated that when the Emperor conceived the idea of conquering Balkh and

Badakhshan he asked Tarbiyat Khan for his opinion on the subject. That honest man, who had recently become acquainted with the countries, represented without any dissimulation that the Emperor should never contemplate carrying out any campaigns there. As horses and men there were more numerous than ants and locusts, and as Indians would not be able to withstand the snow and cold of the country, there would be no end to the affair. By chance the Emperor also asked Mulla Fadl Kabuli—who was one of the most learned men of the age—what he thought of extricating his ancestral properties from the hands of the Changezi princes (the Uzbeks). The Mulla replied that to make war on the people of that country—who were all Muslims—was contrary to the shariᶜa law, and would end in loss and destruction. The Emperor was greatly offended and said that if time-servers pronounced such judgements, and *bakhshis* frightened the soldiers about snow and cold, how could campaigns be carried out.[73]

In the end Shah Jahan was forced to accept the reality of the situation, and to focus on how to return the conquered territories to Nazr Muhammad. The official position was that 'this very design had been buried in the depths of His Majesty's comprehensive mind; namely, that once the kingdoms of Balkh and Badakhshan had been rid of the thorns of turbulence and anarchy, he should restore them safely to Nazr Muhammad Khan'.[74] Actually, this solution seems to have formulated itself when Nazr Muhammad, cautiously making his way back from Iran, heard of Aurangzeb's victory over ᶜAbd al-ᶜAziz's Uzbek forces and sent the Mughal prince a letter of submission which the latter forwarded to Shah Jahan. In response the Emperor made known his decision that if Nazr Muhammad would come and present himself before Aurangzeb, then Balkh would be returned to him and the Mughal army would go back to India.[75] Conducting the procedure in this way, of course would leave Nazr Muhammad appearing to be a willing Mughal vassal. Aurangzeb was unable to convince the erstwhile Balkh ruler, however, of the Mughals' good intentions and Nazr Muhammad refused to meet him personally, claiming illness and other excuses. After a frustrating cat-and-mouse interlude Aurangzeb gave up and after turning over Balkh to Nazr Muhammad's grandson Qasim Sultan in mid-October,[76] began the long journey back to India, which the Mughal chronicle, in a remarkable turnaround from the attitude expressed by Babur, calls 'the type of Paradise'.[77]

On the way home much of the Mughal army either fell victim to guerrilla-style attacks from tribal raiders or succumbed to the hardship of winter travel over difficult mountainous terrain. The retreat was a disaster, and the whole enterprise had been a great drain on the empire's resources. The campaign had cost the Mughal treasury some forty million rupees in all, and all they had to show for their trouble was a frontier some fifty kilometres further north from Kabul than it had been previously.[78]

The effects on the Balkh region of the brief Mughal presence were disastrous for production and trade, and only worsened an already bad political situation. Revenue from the province had been halved during the first year of the Mughal occupation, and halved again during the second year.[79] The resulting depreciation of the local currency, the *khani*, was very harmful for local commerce.[80]

Nazr Muhammad therefore regained the throne of a thoroughly destitute province, and was reduced to begging financial assistance from Shah Jahan the following year. (He also sought the return of his three young sons, who still preferred life at the Mughal court.)[81] The Mughal Emperor responded with a gift of 20,000 rupees for the Uzbek ambassador, Khwaja Khan, and a lakh (100,000) for Nazr Muhammad.[82] Six months later, Shah Jahan sent the Uzbek ruler's youngest son, ⁽Abd al-Rahman, back to Balkh with another lakh of rupees, although the two remaining sons, Khusrau and Bahram, refused to go 'on account of the indignation they still felt for their father'.[83] Two years later, in June 1651, 'the bounty-dispensing and poverty-dispelling' Shah Jahan sent another lakh of rupees to Nazr Muhammad, along with two lakhs' worth of jewels.[84] These gifts were scarcely enough to remedy the damage done, however, either to Nazr Muhammad or to the lands he ruled. Nor was Shah Jahan's generosity sufficient to camouflage the damage the Balkh failure had done to Mughal prestige, as Marathas and others to the south took heart and rose in rebellion. Finally, the experience seems to have taught a vital lesson to Prince Aurangzeb, who had served as a faithful instrument of his father's will but would soon overcome it with his own.

The lesson re-emerges in altered forms throughout Aurangzeb's reign. In a letter to his son Muʿazzam, he blames the failure of the Balkh campaign on the impetuousness of his brother Murad Bakhsh, on account of whom 'the kingdoms conquered and possessed were lost, and money was wasted on them. It is for this reason that it is said that "a daughter is better than an unworthy son."'[85] During the Bijapur siege of 1685, Aurangzeb's adviser Hasan ʿAli Khan makes a revisionist reference to the Balkh retreat, saying:

> In view of the good of the army and the happiness of the people at large, I think a retreat is advisable. When in the Balkh campaign Prince Murad Bakhsh owing to the rigour of the winter would not stay there, he had to give up sieges and battles by order of Shah Jahan and return to court.[86]

Other Mughal Acts

As descendants of Timur the Mughal emperors—certain of them, at least—assumed the responsibility for the upkeep of his mausoleum at Samarqand, clearly demonstrating that they thought of it as a 'family monument'. One such instance is cited in the *Tuzuk-i-Jahangiri,* on the occasion of the 1621 embassy to Bukhara led by Mir Baraka. As has been mentioned earlier, among the tasks assigned the Mughal envoy, whom Nur Jahan sent to patch up differences with Imam Quli Khan, was to take money to the caretakers of the *Gur-i-Amir*.

This act was repeated decades later by Jahangir's grandson, Aurangzeb. Despite his personal involvement in the Balkh failure and his much greater interest in subduing the Deccani sultans, Aurangzeb was greatly disturbed to hear from a Central Asian visitor, Sayyid Oghlan, of the state of disrepair into which Timur's monument had fallen. As a result, according to Maliha Samarqandi, he issued an order 'on behalf of the souls of our ancestors', to provide the sum of twelve rupees per day as upkeep.[87] Maliha goes on to describe at some length the failure of Aurangzeb's gesture, largely due to the abuses of Mulla Wali who was entrusted with the project. (Mulla Wali was a descendant of Mir Baraka.)[88]

Aurangzeb's respect for Central Asian religious scholarship is demonstrated by his appointment of Mulla ʿAuz to the powerful post of censor, mentioned previously. The compilation of Hanafi law, the *Fatawa al-ʿAlamgiriyya*, which Aurangzeb commissioned, is comprised mainly of Central Asian sources (as were most eastern Hanafi law books—a legacy of the Timurid period). The Emperor also commissioned a copy of Mahmud b. Amir Wali's *Bahr al-asrar* in 1675, demonstrating his interest in reading a Central Asian's view of history.[89]

NOTES

1. *BN*, p. 91.
2. *BN*, p. 171.
3. *AA*, iii, p. 387.
4. *BN*, p. 265.
5. *AA*, ii, pp. 408-9.
6. *MU*, i, p. 97.

7. '*az wilayat ba dargah-i-jahan-panah rasidand*' (*MA*, p. 56 (text p. 90)).
8. Ibid., p. 101 (text p. 163). Sarkar wrongly translates *wali* as 'king'.
9. *TJ*, i, p. 118; *JN*, p. 68. Rogers translates the word as 'ruler'.
10. *PN*, i, p. 193, and again on p. 194.
11. *BN*, pp. 630-1.
12. 'The propensity of the founder of the empire of the Great Mughals towards his native land is expressed in correspondence with his *pir*, Khwaja Ahmad-i-Kasani (otherwise known as Makhdum-i-ʿAzam), who was also from Ferghana' (Semĕnov, 'Kul'turno-politicheskikh sviaziakh', p. 8). Unfortunately, Semĕnov does not give references for these letters, other than that they belong to the Uzbekistan Academy of Sciences.
13. Islam, *Calendar*, i, p. 65; *BN*, p. 741.
14. *AN*, i, p. 270 (text p. 113).
15. *BN*, p. 761.
16. Iskandar Beg Munshi, ʿ*Alam ara-yi-ʿAbbasi*, tr. Roger Savory, Westview Press, Boulder, 1978, pp. 160-6. See also M.R. Karimi, 'Humayun in Iran', *Islamic Culture* 42/1 (1969), pp. 5-11.
17. *HN*, p. 188 (f.73a).
18. '*saʿadat dar nihad-i-shan bud*' (*AN*, ii, p. 527 (text p. 362)).
19. Ibid., p. 189 (text p. 123-4).
20. *AN*, iii, p. 296 (text p. 211).
21. Ibid., pp. 616-7 (text p. 415).
22. Islam, *Calendar*, ii, p. 207.
23. Ibid., p. 213.
24. *TJ*, i, p. 26; *JN*, p. 16.
25. *TJ*, i, p. 89; *JN*, p. 53.
26. R.C. Verma, *Foreign Policy of the Great Mughals*, Agra, 1967, p. 69.
27. Ali, 'Jahangir and the Uzbeks', p. 111.
28. M.L. Nigam, 'Central Asian Contributions to the Art of Jade Carving in India', in *[Proceedings of the] Indo-Soviet Seminar on Scientific and Technological Exchanges between India and Soviet Central Asia in the Medieval Period*, ed. B.V. Subbarayappa, New Delhi, 1985, pp. 192-202.
29. Islam, *Indo-Persian Relations*, p. 86.
30. Ibid., p. 90.
31. *MatT*, ff.132b-136b.
32. Islam, *Indo-Persian Relations*, p. 99.
33. *SL*, f.77b.
34. Ibid., ff.80b-81b.
35. *SJN*, p. 335; *PN*, ii, pp. 598-9. The Mughal official Saʿadullah Khan, in a letter to the Safavid governor of Khurasan, Hasan Lafabeli, gives Nazr Muhammad's action as the main pretext for the invasion (M. Athar Ali, 'The Objectives Behind the Mughal Expedition into

Balkh and Badakhshan 1646-7', *Proceedings of the 29th Indian History Congress* (1967), p. 165, citing *Jami' al-insha* ff.4b-5a).

36. Ansari, 'Northwestern Policy', p. 122.
37. Verma, 'Foreign Policy', pp. 78-9.
38. Islam, *Indo-Persian Relations*, p. 106.
39. *Ruq'at-i-'Alamgiri*, J.H. Bilimoria, tr., Delhi, 1972, letter 1, pp. 3-4. But as Mu'azzam has failed at this point even to re-take Qandahar from the Safavids, Aurangzeb goes on to say that he is less concerned with the taking of provinces than for the reputation of his son.
40. Manucci, *Storia*, ii, p. 32.
41. Ibid., p. 39.
42. Islam, *Calendar*, ii, p. 262.
43. Bernier, *Travels*, p. 119.
44. *HN*, p. 191 (f.74a).
45. *AN*, i, p. 549 (text p. 289).
46. *HN*, p. 192, footnote.
47. *SJN*, p. 325.
48. *TMK*, pp. 97-101. A slightly later and more detailed Central Asian version can be found in the *SS* (ff.225a-261b; see also Ziaev, 'Silsilat al-salatin', pp. 140-82), although its author, Mir Muhammad, seems to have relied heavily on the earlier Mughal chronicle by Kambuh, *'Amal-i-Salih* (in which the account of the Balkh invasion runs from ii, 354 to iii, 18). Kambuh expands his account in *Waqi'at-i-Muhammad Salih*, India Office Library MS Or.1683. A third Central Asian source from the early eighteenth century, the *Tarikh-i-Qipchaq Khani*, mentions the invasion only briefly (*TQK-T*, ff.113b-114b).
49. *SJN*, p. 330.
50. Ibid., p. 328.
51. Senkowski, *Supplément*, p. 44.
52. *TQK-T*, f.113b.
53. *SS*, f.223a.
54. *PN*, ii, pp. 573-6.
55. *SJN*, p. 335; *PN*, ii, p. 436.
56. *'ilat-i-'ali bar iftitah-i-anwab-i-murasilat-i-asmanishin fuqara' wa 'ibad-ullah tarafin ast'* (*SL*, f.78b).
57. Ali, 'Objectives', p. 166, citing *Jami' al-insha*, ff. 143b-148b.
58. *SS*, ff.223b-225a.
59. *AS*, ii, pp. 368-9.
60. *SS*, f.233b; *AS*, ii, p. 369.
61. *SS*, ff.233b-234a.
62. According to the *SS*, Nazr Muhammad left Balkh city on 29 Jumada I 1056/13 July 1646 (f.235b); the *AS* puts it at a day earlier (*AS*, ii, p. 372).
63. *PN*, ii, pp. 573-6.

64. *SJN*, p. 353.
65. *SS*, f.244b; Ziaev, 'Silsilat as-salatin', p. 178.
66. Senkowski, *Supplément*, p. 44.
67. *SS*, f.233b; Ziaev, 'Silsilat as-salatin', p. 153. Ziaev misdates Nazr Muhammad's Kabul attempt to 1639, instead of 1629.
68. *SS*, f.237b-238a.
69. *SJN*, p. 372.
70. Ibid., p. 391.
71. Ibid., p. 394.
72. Senkowski, *Supplément*, p. 46.
73. *MU*, ii, p. 932.
74. *SJN*, p. 393.
75. *AS*, iii, p. 5.
76. Ibid., p. 13.
77. *SJN*, p. 394.
78. Richards, *Mughal Empire*, p. 133. The *Shah Jahan-nama* puts the figure at two crore, or twenty million (*SJN*, p. 400).
79. *SJN*, p. 351.
80. Ibid., p. 358.
81. Ibid., p. 414.
82. Ibid., p. 416.
83. Ibid., p. 431.
84. Ibid., p. 449.
85. *RA*, p. 4.
86. *MA*, p. 264 (text p. 162).
87. *MuzA-T*, f.297b.
88. *MuzA-T*, ff.301a-302a.
89. Khan, 'Description', p. 130. The *Bahr al-asrar* manuscript in the India Office Library bears Mughal seals from 1675 and 1685.

CONCLUSIONS

Was the reconquest of Central Asia ever a practical policy for the Mughals, or just a pipe-dream that wouldn't die? Since in 1646 Shah Jahan came closest to accomplishing the Mughals' dynastic ambition of reconquering their ancestral lands in Central Asia, questions surrounding this issue should start there. The Indian historian, J.N. Sarkar's position is that:

> ...if Shah Jahan really hoped to conquer and rule Central Asia with a force from India, we must conclude that the prosperity of his reign and the flattery of his courtiers had turned his head and that he was dreaming the vainest of vain dreams. The Indian troops detested service in that far-off land of hill and desert, which could supply no rich booty, no fertile fiefs and no decent house to live in. The occupation of that poor, inhospitable and savage country meant only banishment from home and comfort and ceaseless fights and watching against a tireless and slippery enemy. The finest troops must be worn out and the richest treasury exhausted in the attempt to keep hold of such a country and no gain in glory or wealth was to be expected.[1]

Another Indian historian, R.C. Verma, disagrees with this assessment. He argues that imperialism was the 'predominant motive force' of the Mughal Empire, and that with most of the subcontinent subservient in Shah Jahan's time, the most feasible direction for expansion was towards the north-west. This option offered several convenient pretexts, including the Mughals' hereditary claim and the argument for defending 'the poor and the religious' from the ravages of civil war. With Shah Jahan's hand free in India and with Central Asia weakened by internecine strife, the moment for invasion seemed opportune.[2]

Riazul Islam attributes Shah Jahan's motivations to nothing more than what he calls simple *mulkgiri* (land-grabbing). He asserts that even in the context of the time, the Timurids' hereditary claim on Central Asia was not a particularly strong one, and that the 'humanitarian' propaganda about saving innocent Muslims was 'merely a specious description of the oft-occurring internecine warfare among the various sections and tribes of the people of Central Asia'. Islam believes that the complaint regarding Nazr Muhammad's attack on Kabul in 1629 had been quickly forgiven at the time and was merely 'resurrected only to provide a plausible excuse for the unwarranted Mughal invasion of Central Asia'. Finally, he attributes the Mughals' claim of protecting the Bukhara *sayyids* to an effort to gain the sympathies of the Safavids.[3]

Yet another interpretation has been proposed by M. Athar Ali, who states that while the bipartite Uzbek administration up to Imam Quli's abdication had posed little threat to the Mughals, the potential of first Nazr Muhammad, then of his son ʿAbd al-ʿAziz, wielding re-centralized power was perceived as a greater menace.[4] This argument is unconvincing, however, in light of the fact that Shah Jahan was clearly attempting to organize the invasion well prior to the threat that the Uzbek appanages would re-unite.

What exactly were Shah Jahan's intentions in sending his army to Balkh, and how far did he actually hope to take the campaign? It is true that the Mughal Empire was a military state which thrived on expansion, and that looking at the circumference of the Mughal borders in 1645, the north-western frontier seemed to be the most promising direction in which to move. Verma believes that Shah Jahan's wish was to annex Badakhshan and to have Nazr Muhammad rule Balkh and Bukhara as a Mughal vassal,[5] and a letter the Emperor sent to his son, Murad Bakhsh, instructing him to 'help' the Uzbek capture Bukhara would seem to support this view.[6] While Babur and Humayun, and perhaps even Jahangir, apparently would have relocated the Mughal capital to Samarqand if he had been able to, there is nothing to suggest Shah Jahan would have done so.

Yet it must be explained, if Shah Jahan's desire for Central Asia is to be understood in practical terms, why he would have been willing to spend forty million rupees trying to conquer a territory that only produced several million per year in revenue.[7] While the cost of the campaign may have greatly exceeded the Emperor's anticipations, he surely cannot have believed the conquest would be easy. There is no evidence that Nazr Muhammad would have been willing to rule as a Mughal vassal, even if such had been Shah Jahan's plan. In fact, he was most unco-operative in every respect, and clearly had no trust whatsoever in Mughal promises.

In assessing the motives behind the Mughals' Balkh invasion, it may be that economic and political factors are ultimately beside the point. Perhaps it simply must be conceded that practicality gives way to psychology in Shah Jahan's case. He had inherited the most powerful empire in the world, but along with it came a deeply-instilled hereditary obsession, a burning emotional factor which had to contend with the practicalities of running that empire. The moment may indeed have been most opportune in Shah Jahan's time to launch the long-contemplated attempt to regain the ancestral lands, but the desire to do so had never faded from the hearts and minds of his imperial predecessors. In the end it was their Central Asian roots that defined much of the psyche of the Mughal emperors, and they could not escape from the task to which it compelled them.

The Eastern Islamic World

John Richards is among those historians who treat the Mughals as simply an Indian Muslim dynasty. He states that:

> Although the first two Timurid emperors and many of their noblemen were recent immigrants to the subcontinent, the dynasty and the empire itself became indisputably Indian. The interests and futures of all concerned were in India, not in ancestral homelands in the Middle East or Central Asia.[8]

This is an overly Indo-centric view. The Mughals were Muslims before they were Indians, and Central Asian Muslims at that. The Mughals' military and administrative organization, their literary and artistic sensibilities, and religious outlook were all derived from Central Asia, and their own Central Asian origins continued to define the character of their empire in India in a variety of ways through the maintenance of a complex network of contacts.

In the minds of the Mughals, the Muslim societies of India and Central Asia were one world and not two. Simply put, seeing themselves as supreme monarchs, the Mughal emperors could not have contented themselves with ruling over an 'incomplete' entity. This psychological angle is one of the most important factors explaining the persistence of the Mughals' obsession with Central Asia, yet it is one which has been overlooked.

Unfortunately, our historical understanding of Muslim Asia has been hampered by the methods of inquiry which have been used. To a great extent, the writing of Indian history has evolved out of the British tradition, while that of Central Asia has been the domain of Russian and Soviet approaches. This has created a nearly impassable divide (symbolized on the map by the Wakhan corridor across the Pamirs) in the study of Eastern Islamic civilization, with the Mughals depicted simply as the most successful in a string of Indian Muslim dynasties on the one side, and endless ideologically-driven debates on the nature of Uzbek, Tajik, Kyrgyz, Qazaq, Turkmen, or Uighur identity on the other.

To attempt to understand the self-identity and world-view of a sixteenth or seventeenth century Asian Muslim according to 'nationality' theory, however, is inappropriate. A more useful approach would be to try to characterize the society, or cultural system, that such individuals lived in.[9] The available primary source evidence for the period demonstrates that in the sixteenth and seventeenth centuries, in many respects Muslims in India did indeed share a cultural system with the Muslims of Central Asia, often to a greater extent than with non-Muslims living within the same geographical area.

Studies on the history of India, of Central Asia, of Iran, or of relations between the three, may be adequate for political historians. For the cultural historian, however, the history of the eastern Islamic world as a field of study is still waiting to be established and defined. It is hoped that this book has been a step in that direction.

NOTES

1. Jadunath Sarkar, *History of Aurangzeb*, 4 vols., Bombay (reprint), 1972, i, p. 91.
2. Verma, *Foreign Policy*, pp. 82-3.
3. Islam, *Indo-Persian Relations*, p. 214. The Safavids claimed (falsely) to be *sayyids* themselves.
4. Ali, 'Objectives', p. 166.
5. Verma, *Foreign Policy*, p. 88.
6. *PN*, ii, pp. 528-35.
7. Richards, *Mughal Empire*, p. 133.
8. Ibid., p. 2.
9. See Clifford Geertz, 'Religion as a Cultural System', in *Anthropological Approaches to the Study of Religion*, ed. M. Banton, London, 1966, pp. 1-46.

APPENDIX
BIOGRAPHICAL REFERENCES FOR IMPORTANT CENTRAL ASIANS IN MUGHAL INDIA

I include here only individuals for whom there is strong evidence of Central Asian birth. I do not list many others whom I suspect to be Central Asians or who were born in India of Central Asian fathers or into families of Central Asian ancestry (such as the Bukhara *sayyids* of Delhi); nor do I include persons from the border region of Badakhshan.

ᶜAbd al-Baqi Turkestani (Murtaza Baqa). Administrator. (*AN*, ii, p. 174, iii, p. 351; *AA*, i, pp. 282, 596, 610).

ᶜAbd al-Karim b. Khwaja Kalan Juybari (ᶜAbdi/ᶜAbidin). Soldier. (*TJ*, i, p. 60, *MatT*, pp. 178-83).

ᶜAbd al-Karim Qazi. Poet. (Semēnov, *Traktat*, p. 68).

ᶜAbdullah Beg (Yakataz Khan). Administrator, diplomat. (*SJN*, p. 395; *MU*, i, pp. 509-11; ii, p. 961).

ᶜAbdullah Khan Firuz Jang Ahrari. Soldier. (*MU*, i, pp. 97-105).

ᶜAbdullah Khan Uzbek. Soldier. (*AA*, i, p. 321; *AN*, ii, p. 126; *MU*, i, pp. 82-84).

ᶜAbd al-Rahim Beg Uzbek. Soldier. (*MU*, i, pp. 48-9).

ᶜAbd al-Rahim b. Khwaja Kalan Juybari. Religious scholar, diplomat. (*PN*, i, pp. 193-5; *SJN*, p. 27; *MatT*, ff.208b-214a; Rahim, 'Mughal Relations', pp. 93-4; Ivanov, *Iz arkhivii*).

ᶜAbd al-Rahman. (*AN*, iii, p. 102).

ᶜAbd al-Rahman. Uzbek prince, son of Nazr Muhammad Khan. (*SJN*, p. 455; *MU*, i, pp. 68-70).

ᶜAbd al-Rahman Munᶜim. Poet. (*MuzA-T*, f.196b).

ᶜAbd al-Samad Ahrari (Saif al-daula/Dilar jang). Soldier. (*MU*, i, pp. 71-3).

ᶜAbd al-Shahid Ahrari. Religious scholar, administrator. (*AN*, ii, p. 195; *AA*, i, p. 539; *MT*, ii, p. 174; *TA*, ii, pp. 700-1; *MU*, ii, p. 895).

ᶜAbd al-Wahhab. Bukhara *sayyid*, administrator. (*TJ*, i, p. 75).

ᶜAbid Khan. (Qilich Khan). Administrator, judge. (*MU*, ii, pp. 409-10, 539-41).

Abu'l Biy (Abu'l Wali/Abu'l Baqa/Abu'l-Nabi/Bahadur Khan Uzbeg). Administrator. (*TJ*, i, pp. 27, 30, 61; *MU*, i, p. 351; *AN*, iii, pp. 820, 839; *KM*, pp. 30-1).

Abu'l Hasim. Religious teacher. (*MU*, i, p. 65).

Abu'l-Maᶜali. Soldier. (*MU*, i, pp. 132-6).

Abu'l-Maᶜali. Hanafi theologian. (*MT*, ii, p. 45).

Ahmad b. Mahmud. Diplomat. (Rahim, 'Mughal Relations', p. 194).

ᶜAli Quli Khan Shibani (Khan-i-Zaman). Soldier. (*AA*, i, pp. 319-20, 383; *AN*, ii, p. 104; *MU*, i, pp. 197-204; Welch, *India*, p. 151).

Alif Khan Aman Beg Barlas. Administrator. (*MU*, i, pp. 204-5).

Allah Quli b. Yalangtosh Beg Alman. Soldier. (*SJN*, p. 272; *MU*, i, pp. 208-10).

Aman Beg Chaghatai. Qipchak tribal elder. (*SJN*, p. 369).

Amir Sharaf Mahram Nasim Khwaja. Religious scholar. (*MuzA-T*, ff.234a-b).

Aqa Riza. Miniature painter. (*TJ*, ii, p. 20).

Arslan Biy (Shamshir Khan). Administrator. (*TJ*, i, p. 118; *MU*, ii, pp. 798-9).

Ashraf Khan Barkhurdar Ahrari. Soldier. (*MU*, i, pp. 97, 302-3).

Ata Muhammad. Sculptor. (Nizamutdinov, *Ocherki*, p. 14).

ᶜAwz Wajih. Religious scholar, administrator. (*MA*, p. 96; Richards, *Mughal Empire*, p. 175).

Babur, Zahiruddin Muhammad. Soldier, poet, founder of Timurid empire in India. (*BN*, *HN*, *AN*).

Bahram Sultan b. Nazr Muhammad Khan. Uzbek prince, courtier, administrator. (*MU*, i, pp. 355-65).

Baltun Beg. Soldier. (*MA*, p. 153).

Baqibillah. Naqshbandi teacher. (Algar, 'Naqshbandi', p. 142).

Bahram Bey. Soldier. (*TJ*, i, p. 202).

Dastur Nasafi. Poet, judge. (*MuzA-T*, f.67a-b).

Din-dar Khan Bukhari (Sayyid Bahwa). Soldier. (*MU*, i, p. 505).

Dughlat, Mirza Haydar. Historian. (*TR*).

Fahmi. Poet. (*MT*, iii, p. 405).

Fakhr al-din Ahmad Bakhshi (Tarbiyat Khan). Administrator, diplomat. (*MU*, ii, pp. 930-3).

Fazlullah Bukhari. Soldier, administrator, alchemist. (*MU*, i, pp. 556-8).

Ghurbati. Poet. (*TA*, ii, pp. 750-1)

Hafiz Tashkandi (Kumaki). Religious scholar. (*AA*, i, p. 540; *TA*, ii, p. 686).

Hajji Biy Kuschi. Teacher. (*SS*, f.199a)

Humayun. Second Mughal Emperor of India. (*BN*, *HN*, *AN*).

Husayn Biy. Soldier. (*TJ*, i, p. 202).

ᶜIbadullah Tashkandi Imtihan. Poet. (*MuzA-T*, f.37a).

Iskandar Khan Uzbeg. Soldier. (*MU*, i, pp. 691-2).

Ismaᶜil Beg Duldi. Soldier. (*MU*, i, p. 701).

ᶜIwad Beg Nayman. Poet. (McChesney, 'Muzakkir al-ashab', p. 75).

Jalal Kitabdar. Poet. (*MuzA-D*, p. 69; McChesney, 'Muzakkir al-ashab', p. 75).

Khawind Mahmud Ahrari. Naqshbandi sheikh. (*AN*, ii, pp. 301-2; *MU*, i, p. 87).

Khizr Khwaja Khan. Soldier. (*TA*, ii, p. 656; *TJ*, i, p. 67; *MU*, i, pp. 813-4).

Khusraw Biy. Soldier. (*TJ*, i, p. 206).

Khusraw Sultan b. Nazr Muhammad. Uzbek prince, courtier. (*SJN*, p. 341; *MU*, i, pp. 820-3).

Kuchak Khwaja. Courtier. (*AN*, i, p. 120 (text p. 281); *MU*, ii, p. 322)

Lamiᶜ Nasafi. Poet. (*MuzA-T*, f.282a).

Mahmud b. Amir Wali. Historian, traveller, religious scholar. (*BA*; Khan, 'Bahr al-Asrar'; Ahmedov, *Istoriko-geograficheskaia literatura*; Islam, 'Bahr-al-Asrar').

Maniᶜ Samarqandi. Poet. (*MuzA-T*, f.210b; McChesney 'Muzakkir al-ashab', p. 75).

Mansur Hajji. Diplomat, administrator. (*PN*, ii, p. 153; *TMK-L*, f.98; *MU*, i, p. 509; Rahim, 'Mughal Relations', p. 189).

Mirak-i-Sayyid Ghiyath. Landscape architect. (Subtelny, 'Mirak-i-Sayyid Ghiyas').

Mir Baraka. Diplomat. (*TJ*, ii, p. 196; *Ma'athir-i-Jahangiri*, f.143b; Rahim, 'Mughal Relations', pp. 92, 190).

Mir Jalal al-Din. Religious scholar. (*MA*, p. 167).

Mir Jumla Khan-i-Khanan. Religious scholar, judge, administrator.(*MU*, ii, pp. 74-6).

Mir Muhammad Amin. Soldier. (*MA*, p. 184).

Mir Musawwir. Miniature painter. (*NM*, ff. 60b-61a; Dickson and Welch, *Houghton Shahnameh*, p. 87).

Mir Sayyid ᶜAli b. Mir Musawwir. Miniature painter. (*GH*, p. 135; Dickson and Welch, *Houghton Shahnameh*, p. 178).

Mirza Baqi Anjumani. Soldier. (*KM*, p. 28).

Mirza Muflis. Religious scholar. (*AA*, i, p. 541; *TA*, ii, p. 686).

Mubariz Khan ᶜImad al-Mulk (Khwaja Muhammad). Administrator. (*MU*, ii, pp. 90-102).

Mufid Balkhi. Poet. (*MuzA-T*, f.194b).

Muhammad ᶜAli Turani. Wrestler. (*AA*, i, p. 253).

Muhammad Amin Khan Chin Bahadur (ᶜItimad al-daula). Soldier, administrator. (*MU*, ii, pp. 114-17, 412).

Muhammad Badiᶜ Sultan. Uzbek prince, courtier. (*MU*, ii, pp. 126-7).

Muhammad b. Mirak. Architect. (Subtelny, 'Mirak-i-Sayyid Ghiyas', p. 31).

Muhammad Muhsin. Diplomat, soldier. (*MU*, i, pp. 509-10).

Muhammad Murad. Portrait painter. (Semënov, 'sviaziakh', p. 8; Nizamutdinov, *Ocherki*, p. 32).

Muhammad Nadir Samarqandi. Miniature painter. (Gyuzal'ian, pp. 18-19).

Muhammad Sabir Hajji. Poet. (*MuzA-T*, f.314b).

Muhammad Sa'id Shibani (Bahadur Khan). Soldier, administrator. (*AN*, ii, pp. 150-1; *AA*, i, p. 328; *MU*, i, pp. 348-50).

Muhammad Salah Nasha. Poet. (*MuzA-T*, f.238a).

Muhammad Sharif. Draftsman. (Nizamutdinov, *Ocherki*, p. 14).

Muhammad Yar Arlat Balkhi. Profession unknown. (*MU*, i, p. 388).

Muhammad Yusuf b. Khwaja Baqa. Diplomat, historian. (*TMK*; Vambéry, *Bukhara*, p. 322).

Muhsin Khwaja. Religious scholar. (*TJ*, i, p. 390).

Mu'in b. Khwaja Khawind Dehbidi. Religious scholar. (*TA*, ii, p. 655).

Murad Turkestani. Wrestler. (*AA*, i, p. 253).

Musahib Beg. Soldier. (*MU*, ii, pp. 321-3).

Mushfiqi. Poet. (*MT*, iii, p. 328; *AA*, i, p. 583; *AN*, iii, p. 335; Semënov, 'sviaziakh', p. 9; Bečka, 'Tajik Literature', p. 503; Ahrari, *Mushfiqi*).

Mutribi al-Asamm Samarqandi. Musician, poet, scholar. (*NZJ*; *KM*; Foltz, *Conversations*; Ahmedov, *Istoriko-geograficheskaia literatura*).

Nadiri Samarqandi. Poet. (*AA*, i, p. 605; *MT*, i, p. 611).

Nasir Khwaja Naqshbandi. Soldier. (*MU*, ii, p. 605).

Nawruz Biy Darman. Soldier. (*TJ*, i, p. 202).

Nazr Biy. Soldier, administrator. (*MT*, ii, pp. 302-3; *AA*, i, p. 519).

Niyazi Samarqandi. Poet. (*TA*, ii, p. 737).

Niyaz Kashgari. Soldier. (*MuzA-T*, f.237a).

Pahlavan Baba. Soldier. (*TJ*, i, p. 202).

Qasim Arslan. Poet. (Semënov, *Traktat*, p. 63).

Qasim b. Dost Bukhari. Musician. (Spector, 'Musical Tradition', p. 439).

Qasim b. Qahi Samarqandi. Singer, poet. (*MT*, iii, p. 172 (text pp. 242-8); *MU*, i, p. 283; Semënov, *Traktat*, p. 63).

Qilich Khan Andijani. Administrator. (*AA*, i, pp. 35, 380; *MU*, ii, pp. 534-9).

Qilich Khan Turani. Soldier. (*MU*, ii, pp. 541-4).

Qipchak Khan Amin Beg Shaqawal. Administrator. (*MU*, ii, pp. 524-6).

Qubad Khan Mirza Akhor. Soldier, falconer. (*MU*, ii, pp. 531-4).

Quli Khan Bahadur b. Nazr Bey. Diplomat. (*MU*, i, pp. 825-6).

Razzaq-berdi Ataliq. Scholar. (*SS*, f.169a-b).

Sadiq. Religious scholar. (*AA*, i, p. 541).

Sadiq Bukhari. Wrestler (*AA*, i, p. 253).

Sahmi Bukhari. Poet. (*TA*, ii, p. 737).

Sami al-Sadat Khwaja. Religious scholar. (*MuzA-T*, f.86a-b).

Sa'id Turkestani. Religious scholar. (*AA*, i, p. 540; *TA*, ii, p. 685; *MT*, ii, p. 45).

Shafi'ullah (Tarbiyat Khan Barlas). Courtier. (*MU*, ii, pp. 926-30).

Shah Budaq Khan. Soldier. (*AA*, i, p. 402; *MU*, ii, pp. 745-7).

Sharaf al-Din Ahrari Samarqandi. Soldier. (*TA*, ii, p. 655; *MU*, ii, pp. 808-12).

Shihab al-din (Ghazi al-din Khan Bahadur Firuz Jang). Soldier. (*MA*, p. 91 (text p. 57); *MU*, i, pp. 587-92).

Tahir Sheikh. Soldier. (*MU*, ii, pp. 962-4).

Tardi Beg Turkestani. Soldier. (*AN*, i, pp. 14, 130, 182, 192-3 (text pp. 25, 316, 375-6, 393); *AA*, i, p. 318; *MU*, ii, pp. 940-4).

Tayyib Khwaja b. Taj al-din Juybari. Religious teacher. (*PN*, ii, pp. 611, 627, 678-9, 722; *AS*, iii, pp. 22, 153; *MU*, ii, pp. 964-5).

Wali Mulla. Shrine administrator. (*MuzA-T*, ff.301a-302a).

Waqqas Hajji (Shah Quli Khan). Diplomat, administrator. (*SJN*, pp. 84, 94, 191, 205; *MU*, ii, pp. 777-8).

Wasili-yi Marvi. Poet. (Semënov, *Traktat*, p. 64).

Yadgar Beg. Soldier. (*TJ*, i, p. 379).

Yadgar Khwaja Samarqandi (Sardar Khan). Administrator. (*TJ*, i, p. 164; *MU*, ii, pp. 712-3).

Yahya Ishtikhani. Poet. (*MuzA-T*, f.283a).

Yahya Khwaja Ahrari. Religious scholar. (*AN*, iii, p. 383).

Yusuf Mawdudi. Musician. (Semënov, *Traktat*, p. 63).

Yusuf Muhammad Khan Tashkandi. Courtier. (*MU*, ii, pp. 1009-1012).

Zakariyya Khwaja Ahrari. Soldier. (*TJ*, i, p. 31).

BIBLIOGRAPHY

Primary Sources

ᶜAbd al-Rahman Tali, *Tarikh-i-Abu'l Faydh Khan,* Institute of Oriental Studies, Uzbekistan Academy of Sciences MS 194; Russian translation A.A. Semenov, *Istoriia Abulfeizkhana,* Tashkent, 1959.

ᶜAbdullah Kabuli, *Tazkira al-tawarikh,* IOSUAS MS 2093.

Abu'l Fazl ᶜAllami, *Akbar-nama,* ed. ᶜAbd al-Rahim, 3 vols., Bibliotheca Indica, Calcutta, 1877-87; tr. Henry Beveridge, 3 vols., 1902-39, (reprint Low Price Publications, Delhi, 1993).
_____, *A'in-i-Akbari,* tr. Henry Blochmann (v. 1) and H.S. Jarrett (vols. 2 and 3), Bibliotheca Indica, Calcutta, 1877–96 (rev. Phillott and Sarkar, reprint Oriental Books Reprint Corporation, Delhi, 1977–8).

Abu'l Ghazi, *Shajarah-i-turk,* French tr. P.I. Desmaisons, *Histoire des Mongols et des Tatares,* St.Petersburg, 1874 (reprint Philo Press, Amsterdam, 1970).

Ala' al-dawla, *Nafa'is al-ma'athirat,* IOSUAS MS 848.

ᶜAqil Khan, *Waqiᶜat-i-ᶜAlamgiri,* tr. Zafar Hasan, Delhi, 1946.

Aurangzeb ᶜAlamgir, Muhammad Muhyi al-din, *Ruqᶜat-i-ᶜAlamgiri,* tr. J.H. Bilimoria, Delhi, 1972.

Babur, Zahiruddin Muhammad, *Baburnama* (Chaghatay Turkish transcription with ᶜAbd al-Rahim Khan-i-Khanan's

Persian translation and a new English translation), edited and translated by W.M. Thackston, Jr., Harvard University Dept. of Near Eastern Languages and Civilizations, Cambridge MA, 1993; English-only version Smithsonian, Washington, and Oxford University Press, New York and Oxford, 1996; Annette S. Beveridge, tr., *The Babur-nama in English*, London, 1921.

Bada'uni, ᶜAbd al-Qadir, *Muntakhab·al-tawarikh*, ed. W.N. Lees and Ahmad Ali, Bibliotheca Indica, Calcutta, 1865-8; tr. G.A. Ranking (v. 1), W.M. Lowe (v. 2), and W. Haig (v. 3), Calcutta, 1898-1927 (reprint Renaissance Publishing House, Delhi, 1986).

Bernier, François, *Travels in the Mogul Empire A.D. 1656-1668*, tr. Irving Brock, rev. Arthur Constable and Vincent Smith, 1934 (reprint Munshiram Manoharlal, New Delhi, 1992).

Biruni, Abu Rayhan Muhammad, *Alberuni's India*, ed. and tr. E.C. Sachau, London, 1888; abridged version edited by Ainslee Embree, Norton, New York, 1971.

Gardizi, 'Gardizi on India', tr. Vladimir Minorsky, in *Iranica*, Tehran, 1964.

Gulbadan Begum, *Humayun-nama*, copied and translated by A.S. Beveridge, Royal Asiatic Society, London, 1902 (reprint Sang-e-Meel, Lahore, 1987).

Haydar Dughlat, Mirza Muhammad, *Tarikh-i-rashidi*, tr. D. Ross, ed. N. Elias, London, 1895.

Inayat Khan, *Shah Jahan-nama*, tr. A.R. Fuller, ed. W.E. Begley and Z.A. Desai, Oxford University Press, Delhi, 1990.

Jahangir, Nuruddin Muhammad, *Jahangir-nama* (*Tuzuk-i-Jahangiri*), ed. Muhammad Hashim, Tehran, 1359 (1980); *Tuzuk-i Jahangiri*, tr. A. Rogers, ed. H. Beveridge, 2 vols., Bibliotheca Indica, Calcutta, 1909-14 (single volume reprint Munshiram Manoharlal, New Delhi, 1978); new translation by Wheeler Thackston forthcoming 1998.

Kambuh, Muhammad Salih, *ʿAmal-i-salih*, ed. G. Yazdani, 3 vols., Calcutta, 1923-9.

———, *Waqi-ʿat-i-Muhammad Salih*, British Museum (India Office Library) MS Or.1683.

Kashmiri, Badr al-din, *Rawzat al-rizwan fi hadikat al-ghilman*, IOSUAS MS 2094.

Khwafi Khan, Muhammad Hashim, *Muntakhab al-lubab*, tr. S. Moinul Haq, Karachi, 1975.

Kitab ʿaja'ib al-Hind, ed. P.A. van der Lith, French translation by L. Marcel Devic, Leiden, 1883-6.

Lahawri, ʿAbd al-Hamid, *Padshah-nama*, ed. Kabir al-din and ʿAbd al-Rahim, 2 vols., Bibliotheca Indica, Calcutta, 1923-46.

Mahmud b. Amir Wali, *Bahr al-asrar fi manaqib al-akhyar*, v. 6, part 4, India Office Library MS 575; v. 6 parts 2 and 3, IOSUAS MS 1375; v. 1 pt. 1, ed. H.M. Said, S.M. Haq, and A.Z. Khan, Karachi, 1984; *Safar-nama* (*khatima*), ed. Riazul Islam, Institute of Central and West Asian Studies, Karachi, 1980.

Manucci, Niccolao, *Storia do Mogor*, tr. William Erskine, 4 vols., Calcutta, 1907 (reprint Oriental Books Reprint Corporation, New Delhi, 1981).

Mir Muhammad Amin Bukhari, *ʿUbaydullah-nama*, Russian tr. A.A. Semënov, Tashkent, 1957.

Mir Muhammad Salim, *Silsilat al-salatin*, Bodleian MS Or.269.

Muhammad Amin, *Muhit al-tawarikh*, IOSUAS MS 835.

Muhammad Hadi Kamwarkhan, *Tazkira al-salatin-i-Chaghata*, ed. Muzaffar Alam, New Delhi, 1980.

Muhammad Hadi 'Maliha' Samarqandi, *Muzakkir-i-ashab*, IOSUAS MS 4270; Tajikistan Academy of Sciences MS Or.610.

Muhammad Hashim Kishmi Badakhshani, *Nisamat al-quds*, Sialkot, 1990.

Muhammad Salih, *Shibani-nama*, ed. P.M. Melioranskii, St.Petersburg, 1908.

Muhammad Talib b.Taj al-din Juybari, *Matlab al-talibin*, IOSUAS MSS 80, 3757, 10809; Preussische Staatsbibliothek MS Or. 1540.

Muhammad Yusuf b. Khwaja Baqa, *Tazkira-i-Muqim Khani*, Royal Asiatic Society MS 160, London; Russian tr. A.A. Semënov, *Mukimkhanskaya Istoriia*, Tashkent, 1956; abridged French tr., Joszef Senkowski, *Supplément à l'Histoire Générale des Huns, des Turks et des Mogols*, St.Petersburg, 1824.

Muʿtamad Khan, *Iqbal-nama-yi-Jahangiri*, Calcutta, 1895.

Mutribi al-Asamm-i Samarqandi, *Khatirat*, ed. A.G. Mirzoev, Karachi, 1977; tr. Richard Foltz, *Conversations With Emperor Jahangir*, Costa Mesa, CA: Mazda Publishers, 1998.

_____, *Nuskha-yi-ziba-yi-Jahangiri*, ed. A.G. Mirzoev, Institute of Central and West Asian Studies, Karachi, 1976.

_____, *Tazkira-i-shuʿara*, IOSUAS MS 2253.

Na'ini, *Zamzama-yi-wahdat*, IOSUAS MS 10226/II.

Nasafi, Mir Abid Saida, *Asarhoi muntakhab*, Dushanbe, 1977.

Nisari, Hasan, *Mudhakkir al-ahbab*, IOSUAS MS 56; Uzbek translation Tashkent, 1993.

Nizam al-din Ahmad, *Tabaqat-i-Akbari*, tr. B. De, 3 vols., Bibliotheca Indica, Calcutta, 1911-41.

Qipchaq Khan (a.k.a. Khwajam Quli Beg Balkhi b. Qipchaq Khan Qushbegi), *Tarikh-i-Qipchaq Khani*, Bodleian MS Or.117; IOSUAS MS 4468/II (the latter copy is mistitled *Tarikh-i-Shibani Khan*).

Saʿadullah Khan, *Maktubat*, Lahore, 1974.

Saqi Mustaʿid Khan, *Ma'athir-i-ʿAlamgiri*, ed. Maulawi Agha Ahmad ʿAli, Calcutta, 1870-1; tr. J.N. Sarkar, Bibliotheca Indica, Calcutta, 1947 (reprint Oriental Books Reprint Corp., New Delhi, 1986).

Shah Nawaz Khan and ʿAbd al-Hayy, *Ma'athir al-'umara'*, tr. Henry Beveridge, rev. Baini Prasad, 2 vols., Bibliotheca Indica, Calcutta, 1941-52.

Shamlu, Hasan Khan, *Khatirat*, ed. Riazul Islam, Institute of Central and West Asian Studies, Karachi, 1971.

Sharaf al-din, Akhund Mulla, *Tarikh-i-Mîr Saʿid Sharaf Rakim* (*Tarikh-i-rakimi*), Royal Asiatic Society MS 163, London.

Sidi ᶜAli Ra'is, *Mira'at al-mamalik*, Tehran, 1975; tr. Arminius Vambéry, *Travels of a Turkish Admiral*, London, 1899 (reprint Gautam Publishers, Lahore, 1994).

Tanish, Hafiz, *Sharaf-nama-yi-shahi* (*ᶜAbdullah-nama*), India Office Library MS 574, London; IOSUAS MS 2207; Russian tr. (with facsimile Persian text) M.A. Salakhetdinova, 2 vols., Moscow, 1983-9.

Zain al-Din, *Tabaqat-i-Baburi*, tr. H. Askari, Delhi, 1982.

Secondary Sources

Ahmedov, Buri A., *Istoriko-geograficheskaia literatura Srednei Azii XVI-XVIII vv.*, Fan, Tashkent, 1985.

_____, 'Tazkira Mutribi kak istochnik po istorii i kul'ture XVI-XVII vv.', *Istochnikovedenie i Tekstologiia srednevekogo Blizhnego i Srednego Vostoka*, Nauka, Moscow, 1984, pp. 36-44.

Ahrari, Z., *Mushfiqi, hayat va ijadiyat*, Donish, Dushanbe, 1978.

Aini, Sadruddin, *Mirzo Abdulkodiri Bedil*, Nashriëti Davlatii Tojikiston, Stalinabad, 1954.

Akimushkin, O.F. and A.A. Ivanov, 'O Maverannahrskoi shkole miniatiurnoi zhivopisi XVII v.', *Narody Azii i Afriki* (1966).

Alam, Muzaffar, 'Trade, State Policy and Regional Change: Aspects of Mughal-Uzbek Commercial Relations ca.1550-1750', *Journal of the Economic and Social History of the Orient* 37 (1994) pp. 202-27.

Algar, Hamid, 'The Naqshbandi Order: A Preliminary Survey of its History and Significance', *Studia Islamica* 44 (1976) pp. 123-52.

_____, 'Nakshband', *Encyclopaedia of Islam*, second edition, Brill, Leidèn.

Ali, M. Athar, *Apparatus of Empire: Awards of Ranks, Offices and Titles to the Mughal Nobility (1574-1658)*, Oxford University Press, Delhi, 1985.

_____, 'The Objectives Behind the Mughal Expedition to Balkh and Badakhshan 1646-47', *Proceedings of the 29th Indian History Congress*, (1967) pp. 162-7.

_____, 'Jahangir and the Uzbeks', *Proceedings of the 26th Indian History Congress*, (1964) pp. 108-19.

Allworth, Edward, *The Modern Uzbeks*, Hoover Union, Palo Alto CA, 1989.

Ansari, A., 'Shah Jahan's Northwestern Policy', *Journal of the Pakistan Historical Society* 5/2 (1957) pp. 113-23.

Ashrafi, M., 'K izucheniyu material'noi kultury po dannym miniatury Maverannahra XV-XVI vv.', in *Borbad and Cultural Traditions of Central Asiatic Peoples: the History and the Present*, Dushanbe, 1990, pp. 86-91.

_____, 'The School of Bukhara to ca.1550', in *Arts of the Book in Central Asia*, ed. Basil Gray, Serindia, London, and UNESCO, Paris, 1979, pp. 249-72.

Awan, M.T., *History of India and Pakistan, v.2, Great Mughals*, Ferozesons, Lahore, 1994.

Bahari, Ebadollah, *Bihzad, Master of Persian Painting*, I.B. Tauris, London, 1996.

Baikova, N.B., *Rol' Srednei Azii v Russko-Indiiskikh torgovykh sviaziakh: pervaia polovina XVI- vtoraia polovina XVIII v.*, Fan, Tashkent, 1964.

Bartol'd, V.V., 'Tserimonial pri dvore uzbetskikh khanov v XVII veke', *Sochineniia*, Izdatel'stvo vostochnoi literatury, Moscow, 1963, v. 2, pt. 2, pp. 388-99.

Bausani, Alessandro, 'Note su Mirza Bedil 1644-1721', *Annali Institute Università di Napoli*, nuova seria v. 6, 1954.

Beach, Milo C., *Early Mughal Painting*, Harvard University Press, Cambridge MA, 1987.

Beach, Milo C. and Ebba Koch, *King of the World: The Padshahnama, an Imperial Manuscript from the Royal Library, Windsor Castle*, Azimuth, London, 1997.

Bečka, Jiři, 'Tajik Literature from the 16th Century to the Present', in *History of Iranian Literature*, ed. Jan Rypka, D. Reidel, Dordecht, 1968.

Beisembiev, Timur, 'Chinghiz Khan's Law in Eurasia and its Impact on Sarmatism in the Commonwealth of Poland and Lithuania', *Labyrinth* 2/1 (1995).

_____, Idem., 'Ferghana's Contacts With India in the 18th and 19th Centuries', *Journal of Asian History* 28/2 (1994), pp. 124-35.

Bodrogligeti, A.J.E., 'Babur Shah's Chaghatay Version of the Risala-i Validiya: A Central Asian Turkic Treatise on How to Emulate the Prophet Muhammad', *Ural-Altaic Yearbook* 56 (1984), pp. 1-61.

Bongard-Levin, G.M., *Studies in Ancient India and Central Asia*, Calcutta, 1971.

Buckler, F.W., 'A New Interpretation of Akbar's Infallibility Decree of 1579', in *Legitimacy and Symbols*, ed. Michael Pearson, Centre for South and East Asian Studies, University of Michigan, Ann Arbor, 1985, pp. 131-48

Buehler, Arthur, 'The Naqshbandiyya in India', *Journal of Islamic Studies* 7/2 (1996) pp. 208-28.

Burton, J. Audrey, *The Bukharans*, Curzon, Richmond, 1996.

_____, 'Bukharan Trade, 1558-1718', Papers on Inner Asia, no. 23, Research Institute for Inner Asian Studies, Bloomington IN, 1993.

_____, 'Who Were the First Ashtarkhanid Rulers of Bukhara?' *Bulletin of the School of Oriental and African Studies* 51 (1988), pp. 482-8.

_____, 'Nazir Muhammad Khan Ruler of Bukhara (1641-5) and Balkh (1645-51)', *Central Asiatic Journal* 32/1-2 (1988), pp. 19-33.

Castman, A.C., 'Four Mughal Emperor Portraits in the City Art Museum of St. Louis', *Journal of Near Eastern Studies* 15/2 (1966).

Dale, Stephen, *Indian Merchants and Eurasian Trade, 1600-1750*, Cambridge University Press, Cambridge, 1994.

Dani, A.H., *New Light on Central Asia*, Sang-e-Meel, Lahore, 1994.

Davidovich, E.A., *Istoriia denezhnogo obrascheniia srednovekovoi Srednei Azii*, Moscow, 1983.

_____, 'Some Social and Economic Aspects of 16th Century Central Asia', *Central Asian Review* 12 (1964), pp. 265-70.

Dickson, Martin B., 'Uzbek Dynastic Theory in the Sixteenth Century', in *Trudy 25ogo mezhdunarodnogo kongressa vostokovedov*, Moscow, 1963, pp. 208-16.

_____, 'Shah Tahmasp and the Uzbeks', Ph.D. thesis, Princeton University, 1958.

Dickson, Martin B. and S. Cary Welch, Jr., *The Houghton Shahnameh*, Harvard University Press, Cambridge MA and London, 1981.

Doerfer, Gerhard, *Turkische und mongolische Elemente in Neupersischen*, 4 vols., Wiesbaden, 1963-75.

Dolinskaya, V.G., 'Khudozhnik-miniatiurist Mukhammed Murad Samarkandi', *Izvestiia Akademii Nauk UzSSR* 9, (1955).

Djumaev, A.B., 'Unikal'nyi istochnik po istorii Sredniaziatsko-indiskikh muzikal'nykh sviaziei (*Zamzame-yi Vahdat* Naini) XVII v.', in *Iz istorii kulturnykh sviazei narodov Srednei Azii i Indii*, Fan, Tashkent, 1986, pp. 115-24.

Ethé, Hermann. *Catalogue of Oriental Manuscripts in the India Office Library*, 2 vols., Oxford, 1903-37.

Farooqi, N.R., 'Six Ottoman Documents on Mughal-Ottoman Relations During the Reign of Akbar', *Journal of Islamic Studies* 7/1 (1996), pp. 32-48.

Foltz, Richard, *Conversations With Emperor Jahangir*, Costa Mesa, CA: Mazda Publishers, 1998.

_____, 'Cultural Contacts Between Central Asia and Mughal India', *Central Asiatic Journal* 42/1 (1998).

_____, 'Central Asians in the Administrations of Mughal India', *Journal of Asian History* 32/1 (1998).

_____, 'Central Asia in the Minds of the Mughals', in *Post-Soviet Central Asia*, ed. Touraj Atabaki, I.B. Tauris, London, 1997.

_____, 'Two Seventeenth Century Central Asian Travelers to Mughal India', *Journal of the Royal Asiatic Society*, ser. 3, 6/3 (1996), pp. 367-77.

_____, 'The Central Asian Naqshbandi Connections of the Mughal Emperors', *Journal of Islamic Studies* 7/2 (1996), pp. 229-39.

_____, 'The Mughal Occupation of Balkh: 1646-1647', *Journal of Islamic Studies* 7/1 (1996), pp. 49-61.

Gafurov, B.G., 'The Bahr al-Asrar II', *Journal of the Pakistan Historical Society* 14/2 (1966), pp. 98-103.

Golombek, Lisa, 'From Tamerlane to Taj Mahal', in *Essays in Islamic Art and Architecture*, ed. Abbas Daneshvari, Undena, Malibu CA, 1981, pp. 43-50.

Gommans, Jos J.L., *The Rise of the Indo-Afghan Empire*, Brill, Leiden, 1994.

Gopal, S., 'Indians in Central Asia in the 16th and 17th Centuries', *Proceedings of the 52nd Indian History Congress*, New Delhi, 1992.

Grek, T.V., 'Indiiskie miniatiury XVI-XVIII vv.', in *Al'bom indiiskikh i persidskikh miniatiurii XVI-XVIII vv.*, ed. L.T. Gyuzal'ian, Moscow, 1962.

Gross, Jo Ann, Khoja Ahrar: 'A Study of the Perceptions of Religious Power and Prestige in the Late Timurid Period', Ph.D. thesis, New York University, 1982.

Gulchin-Maʿani, Ahmad, *Karvan-i-Hind*, 2 vols., Astan-i-quds-i-razavi, Mashhad, 1369 (1990-1).

Guha, A., ed., *Central Asia: Movement of Peoples and Ideas from Times Prehistoric to Modern*, Indian Council for Cultural Relations, Delhi, 1970.

Gupta, S.P., *Archaelology of Soviet Central Asia and the Indian Borderlands*, 2 vols., Delhi, 1979.

Habib, Irfan, *An Atlas of the Mughal Empire*, Oxford University Press, Oxford University Press, Delhi and New York, 1982.

Haidar, Mansura, 'The Yasi Chinghizi (Tura) in the Medieval Indian Sources', in R.C. Verma et al., eds., *Mongolia: Culture, Economy and Politics*, Khama Publishers, New Delhi, 1992, pp. 53-66.

Hameed, H. Abdul, *Exchanges Between India and Central Asia in the Field of Medicine*, New Delhi, 1986.

Hoag, John D., 'The Tomb of Ulugh Beg and Abdu Razzaq at Ghazni, a Model for the Taj Mahal', *Journal for the Society of Architectural Historians* 27/4 (1968), pp. 234-48.

Imomkhojaev, R., *Tiurko-persidskoe dvuiazychie v literaturnoi zhizni Indii XVI v.*, Fan, Tashkent, 1993.

Inventarnaia kniga rukopisnykh dokumentov feodal'nogo-kolonial'nogo perioda Uzbekskogo Gosudarstvennogo Istoricheskogo Muzeiia goroda Samarkanda, State Historical Museum, Samarqand, n.d.

Istoriia Uzbekistana, v.3 (XVI- pervaia polovina XIX v.), Fan, Tashkent, 1993.

Ivanov, P.P., *Khoziaistvo Dzhuibarskikh sheikhov: k istorii feodal'nogo zemlevladeniia v Srednei Azii v XVI-XVII vv.*, Moscow and Leningrad, 1954.

Islam, Riazul, 'A History of Central Asia (The Tawarikh-i-Badiᶜa: An Introductory Paper)', *Journal of Central Asia* 13/2 (1990), pp. 5-45.

———, *A Calendar of Documents on Indo-Persian Relations (1500-1750)*, 2 vols., Iranian Culture Foundation, Tehran, and Institute of Central and West Asian Studies, Karachi, 1979-82.

———, ed., *Bahr al-asrar (travelogue portion)*, Institute of Central and West Asian Studies, Karachi, 1980.

———, ed., *The Shamlu Letters*, Karachi, 1971.

———, *Indo-Persian Relations*, Tehran, 1970.

———, 'The Bahr al-Asrar I', *Journal of the Pakistan Historical Society* 14/2 (1966), pp. 93-7.

Khan, Ansar Zahid, 'Mahmud b. Amir Wali's Description of Towns, Cities, and Regions of South Asia in the Bahr al-Asrar fi Ma'rifat il-Akhyar', *Journal of the Pakistan Historical Society*, 38/2 (1990), pp. 127-41; 39/1 (1991), pp. 5-21; 40/4 (1992), pp. 337-59; 41/1 (1993), pp. 13-30; 41/3 (1993), pp. 235-54.

Lentz, Thomas W. and Glenn Lowry, *Timur and the Princely Vision: Persian Art and Culture in the 15th Century,* Los Angeles County Museum of Art, Los Angeles, 1989.

Litvinskii, B.A., 'Archaeological Discoveries on the Eastern Pamirs and the Problem of Contacts Between Central Asia, China and India in Antiquity', in *International Congress of Orientalists* XXV, Moscow, 1960.

Lowick, N.M., 'Shaybanid Silver Coins', *The Numismatic Chronicle,* 7th ser., VI (1966), pp. 251-339.

Marefat, Roya, 'Beyond the Architecture of Death; the Shrine of the Shah-i-Zinda in Samarkand', Ph.D. thesis, Harvard University, 1991.

McChesney, R.D., *Waqf in Central Asia,* Princeton University Press, Princeton NJ, 1991.

_____, Central Asia in the 16th-18th Centuries', *Encyclopædia Iranica,* v. 5, fasc. 2, (1991), pp. 176-93.

_____, 'The Anthology of Poets: Muzakkir al-Ashab as a source for the history of 17th century Central Asia', in *Intellectual Studies on Islam,* eds. M. Mazzaoui and Moreen, 1990, pp. 57-84.

_____, 'The Amirs of Muslim Central Asia in the 17th Century', *Journal of Economic and Social History of the Orient* 26/1 (1980), pp. 33-70.

_____, 'The "Reforms" of Baqi Muhammad Khan', *Central Asiatic Journal* 24/1 (1980), pp. 69-84.

Miquel, André, *La géographie humaine du monde musulman jusqu'au milieu du 11e siècle,* 4 vols., Mouton, Paris and The Hague, 1967-88.

Mirzoev, Abdul-Ghani, ed., *Khatirat-i-Mutribi Samarqandi*, Karachi, 1977.

_____, 'Az torikhi ravobiti adabiyi Moveronnahr va Hind', *Sadoyi sharq* 5 (1964), pp. 35-9.

_____, 'Iz istorii literaturnykh sviaziei Maverannahr i Indii', *Trudy XXVIogo Mezhdunarodny kongress vostokovedov*, Moscow, 1963.

_____, *Saido Nasafi i ego mesto v istorii tadzhikskoi literatury*, Nashriëti davlatii Tojikiston, Stalinabad, 1954.

Moreland, William H., *The Agrarian System of Moslem India*, Cambridge, 1929.

Nizami, K.A., 'Naqshbandi Influence on Mughal Rulers and Politics', *Islamic Culture* 39 (1965), pp. 41-52.

Nizamutdinov, Ilyas G., *Ocherki istorii kul'turnykh sviazei Srednei Azii i Indii v XVI- nachalie XX vv.*, Fan, Tashkent, 1981.

_____, *Iz istorii Sredneaziatsko-Indiiskikh otnoshenii*, Izdatel'stvo Uzbekistan, Tashkent, 1969.

Nurutdinov, Sh., *Tazkira al-tawarikh*, Kabul, 1365 (1986).

Nyamdavaa, O., 'Who are the Mughuls?', in *Mongolia: Culture, Economy and Politics*, eds. R.C. Verma et al., New Delhi, 1992, pp. 85-8.

Pingree, David, 'Indian Reception of Muslim Versions of Ptolemaic Astronomy', in *Tradition, Transmission, Transformation*, eds. F. Jamil Ragep and Sally P. Ragep, E.J. Brill, Leiden, 1996, pp. 471-85.

_____, 'Islamic Astronomy in Sanskrit', *Journal for the History of Arabic Science* 2/2 (1978), pp. 315-30.

Prabodha-Chandra, B., *India and Central Asia*, Calcutta, 1955.

Rahim, Abdur, 'Mughal Relations with Central Asia', *Islamic Culture* 9 (1937), pp. 81-94, 188-99.

Richards, John F., *The Mughal Empire*, The New Cambridge History of India, Cambridge University Press, Cambridge, 1993.

_____, ed., *The Imperial Monetary System of Mughal India*, Oxford University Press, Delhi, 1987.

Rieu, Charles, *Catalogue of the Persian Manuscripts in the British Museum*, 3 vols., London, 1879-83.

Rossabi, Morris, 'The "Decline" of Central Asian Caravan Trade', in *The Rise of the Merchant Empires*, ed. J.D. Tracy, Cambridge University Press, Cambridge, 1990.

Sarkar, Jadunath, *History of Aurangzeb*, 5 vols. in 4, Orient Longman, Bombay (reprint), 1972-4.

Sbornik dokumentov, Russko-indiiskie otnosheniia v XVII v., Moscow, 1958.

Schimmel, Annemarie, 'Some Notes on the Cultural Activity of the First Uzbek Rulers', *Journal of the Pakistan Historical Society* 8/3 (1960), pp. 149-66.

Semĕnov, A.A., 'K voprosu o kul'turno-politicheskikh sviaziakh Bukhary i "Velikomogol'skoi" Indii v XVII v.', in *Materialy 2ogo soveschaniia arkheologov i etnografov Sredniei Azii*,

Izdatel'stvo Akademii Nauk USSR, Moscow, 1959, pp. 1-10.

_____, *Sredniaziatskii traktat po muzyke Dervisha Ali (XVII v.)*, Tashkent, 1946.

Sobranie vostochnykh rukopisei Akademii Nauk Uzbekskoi SSR, 11 vols. to date, Sharqshunoslik Instituti, Tashkent, 1952-85.

Spector, Joanna, 'Musical Tradition and Innovation', in *Central Asia: 130 Years of Russian Domination*, ed. Edward Allworth, 3rd edition, Duke University Press, Durham NC, 1994, pp. 434-84.

Spisok vostochnykh rukopisei fundamental'noi biblioteki Samarkandskogo Gosudarstvennogo Universiteta, Samarqand, 1977.

Storey, C. and Yuri Bregel, *Persidskaya Literatura*, 3 vols., Moscow, 1972.

Subbarayappa, B.V., ed., *[Proceedings of the] Indo-Soviet Seminar on Scientific and Technological Exchanges between India and Soviet Central Asia in the Medieval Period*, New Delhi, 1985.

Subtelny, M.E., 'Mirak-i Sayyid Ghiyas and the Timurid Tradition of Landscape Architecture', *Studia Iranica* 24 (1995), pp. 19-60.

_____, 'Babur's Rival Relations: A Study of Kinship and Conflict in 15th-16th Century Central Asia', *Der Islam* 66/1 (1989), pp. 102-18.

_____, 'Art and Politics in Early 16th Century Central Asia', *Central Asiatic Journal* 27 (1983), pp. 121-48.

Vambéry, Arminius, *History of Bukhara*, Arno Press, New York, 1973 (reprint).

Verma, R.C., *Foreign Policy of the Great Mughals*, Agra, 1967.

Welch, S.C., Jr., *India, Art and Culture 1300-1900*, Metropolitan Museum and Holt, Rinehart and Winston, New York, 1985.

Wolpert, Stanley, *A New History of India*, 5th edition, Oxford University Press, New York and Oxford, 1997.

Ziaev, Azamat H., 'Perepiska praviteliei Sheibanidov i Ashtarkhanidov s Iranom i Indiei', *Issledovaniia po istorii, istorii nauki i kul'tury narodov Srednei Azii*, Fan, Tashkent, 1993, pp. 99-109.

_____, 'Silsilat as-salatin kak istoricheskii istochnik', kandidat thesis, Uzbekistan Academy of Sciences, 1990.

INDEX

Q

Qandahar, xxviii, 6, 7, 8, 55, 60, 100, 122, 128, 130, 131, 135
Qumi, Qazi Ahmad, 69

R

Rasala-yi-walidiyya, 93
Richards, John, 3, 154
Risala dar hay'at, 84
Risala dar ʿilm-i-musiqi, 85
Roy, M.N., xxvii
Rumi, Mawlana, 4
Russia, 3, 12, 62, 64

S

Saʿdi, 1, 9, 80; *Bustan*, 80
Safavids, xxiii, xxiv, xxvi, 2, 4, 5, 6, 7, 12, 15, 18, 19, 23, 29, 34, 54, 78, 87, 100, 129, 130, 131, 134, 135, 139, 152
Salim, Mir Muhammad, 76
Sarkar, J.N., 151
Samarqand, xxv, xxiv, 3, 14, 15, 17, 19, 22, 25, 27, 37, 45, 62, 68, 73, 77, 79, 81, 84, 86, 88, 93, 95, 96, 97, 98, 107, 109, 110, 111, 113, 114, 127, 128, 129, 137, 141, 146, 153
Samarqandi, Muhammad Hadi 'Maliha', 70, 74, 147
Samarqandi, Mutribi al-Assamm, 31, 69, 70, 75, 97, 101, 107, 109-111, 113-17, 120, 122, 123, 133
Schimmel, Annemarie, 94
Semënov, A.A., xvii, 4, 129
Senkowski, Joszef, 30
Shah, Salim, 54
Shah Jahan, 13, 16, 17, 20, 22, 23, 24, 28, 30, 33, 34, 35, 36, 52, 54, 55, 58, 59, 61, 63, 76, 81, 83, 84, 86, 102, 120, 122, 128,

133, 134, 135, 136, 137, 138, 139, 140, 141, 142, 143, 144, 145, 146, 151, 152, 153
Shah Jahan-nama, 33, 143
Shah-nama, 81
Shajarah-i-türk, 5, 27, 37
Shamlu, Hasan Khan, 34, 133, 134, 135, 139
Shaykh-zada, 78, 80
Shibani, Bahadur Khan, 53
Shibani-nama, 38
Sindh, xxiii, 15, 58, 74
Silsilat al-Salatin, xviii, 33, 41, 52, 59, 76, 139, 141
Sistan, 8, 19
South Asia, xx, xviii, xix, xx, xxiv, xxvii, xxix
Suri, Sher Shah, 14, 41
Syria, xxix, 121

T

Tabaqat-i-Akbari, 7, 32, 73, 96
Tahsil-zij-i-Ulugh Beg, 84
Tali, ʿAbd al-Rahman, 13
Tajiks, 4, 41
Tajikistan, xxvii
Tajik SSR Communist Party, xvii
Tarikh-i-Qipchaq Khan, 76, 139
Tarikh-i-Rashidi, 13, 35
Tashkent, xxvii, 19, 73, 96
Tawarikh-i-ibadiʿa, xviii, 52, *also see, Silsilat al-Salatin*
Tazkira al-shuʿara, 71
Tazkirat al-salatin-i-Chaghata, 14
Tazkira-yi-Muqim Khani, 29, 30, 33, 34, 38, 39, 41, 72, 76, 138, 139, 141, 143
Thoughts and acts of the Mughal emperors, 127-50; thoughts of individual emperors, 129-36; Babar, 129, 130; Humayun, 129, 130; Akbar, 130, 131; Jahangir, 131, 132, 133; Shah Jahan, 133,